The
Job Hunting Online

Get Wired, You're Hired

Mark Swartz

Prentice Hall Canada Inc.
Scarborough, Ontario

To my wife Marianne, our daughter Stacia and son Jonah

Canadian Cataloguing in Publication Data

Swartz, Mark, 1960-
Get wired, you're hired : the Canadian guide to job hunting online

ISBN 0-13-851262-0

1. Job hunting - Canada - Computer network resources.
I. Title.

HF5382.75.C3S93 1997   650.14'0285'4678   C97-930359-1

Prentice-Hall Canada Inc., Scarborough, Ontario
A Division of Simon & Schuster / A Viacom Company

Prentice-Hall, Inc., Upper Saddle River, New Jersey
Prentice-Hall International (UK) Limited, London
Prentice-Hall of Australia, Pty. Limited, Sydney
Prentice-Hall Hispanoamericana, S.A., Mexico City
Prentice-Hall of India Private Limited, New Delhi
Prentice-Hall of Japan, Inc., Tokyo
Simon & Schuster Southeast Asia Private Limited, Singapore
Editora Prentice-Hall do Brasil, Ltda., Rio de Janeiro

ISBN 0-13-851262-0

Managing Editor: Robert Harris
Acquisitions Editor: Sara Borins
Substantive Editing: Greg Ioannou / Colborne Communications Centre
Copy Editor: Amber Wallace
Editorial Assistant: Susanne Frame
Production Coordinator: Julie Preston
Art Director: Mary Opper
Cover Design: Julia Hall
Cover Image: Kevin Ghiglione
Page Layout: Gail Ferreira Ng-A-Kien

2 3 4 5   W   01 00 99 98 97

Printed and bound in Canada.

TABLE OF CONTENTS

FOREWORD

Canadians are facing the greatest change that the world has seen since the Industrial Revolution. Hundreds of thousands of hardworking men and women have lost their jobs through no fault of their own, being downsized into the ranks of the unemployed or underemployed. At the same time, many more have found jobs with a future in industries that barely existed a decade ago, performing work that most of us would have had a hard time figuring out how to spell just a few years back.

One of the biggest challenges Canadians of all age groups face is adapting to change. Faced with the reality and the magnitude of change in The New Economy®, we need all the help we can get.

Get Wired, You're Hired will assist many Canadians as they seek to find their place in a world where so many of the old rules no longer apply. My sincere best wishes to Mark Swartz for writing a highly readable and very practical guide to job hunting in The New Economy.

Nuala Beck

® The New Economy is the Registered Trademark of Nuala Beck & Associates Inc.

ACKNOWLEDGMENTS

You'd think with all the technology around that a book could pretty well write itself. In fact, nothing could be further from the truth. It takes a team of dedicated people to pull something like this project off. That's why I'd like to express my gratitude to the following individuals.

People Who Helped Me Get Started

The folks at Drake Beam Morin: Especially Aug Bolte, Louise Limoges and Judith Gelber, who helped me through my first career transitions. And to Drew Davis and David Park for their continued support and flexibility.

Jim Carroll: Took time out of his incredibly busy life to read his e-mail and lend me a hand at a critical stage.

Frances Quittel: My very own "career babe." Gave me my first shot in the career spotlight.

Professors Ava Cross and Susan Cody at Ryerson Polytechnic University: My erstwhile confidantes, co-conspirators and advisors.

Sara Borins: Book person extraordinaire. Believed in my ideas and escorted me into authordom.

Lee Hasner: Long-time friend and spritual cohort. Keep on your path.

People Who Assisted Me Along The Way

Greg Ioannou: Editor-at-large and my primary advisor as I whacked away at the keyboard. Taught me lots of good stuff. By the way Greg—get a haircut and get a real job!

Sandra Kendall: The not-your-typical-research librarian at the Metro Toronto Research Library. She provided expert and timely guidance on using technology to find information.

People Who Added Their Professional Expertise To This Book

Nuala Beck: The new breed of economist, who has been generous with her time and counsel (also her trusted assistant Melanie Patterson for putting up with my constant calls).

Graham Donald: Executive director of the Canadian Association Of Career Educators and Employers.

Frank Feather: Futurist, career consultant and author.

James Fehrenbach: Manager of recruitment at Canadian Tire Corporation.

Janis Foord-Kirk: Career advisor, author and columnist—and source of inspiration.

Stephen Gibson: Publisher of *Online Resources For Human Resources.*

Bob Gordon: Director of the CanWorkNet project.

Kevin Hood: Small-business authority and great proofreader.

Jeffery Lawrence: Creator of the *Canadian Job Source* and a true Canadian renaissance man.

Kerry Mahoney: Supervisor of the Career Resource Centre at the University Of Waterloo.

Debbie McGrath: Vice president of The CEO Group. Definitely leading edge!

Marlise Nishikihama: Business project manager at Sympatico.

Margaret Riley: A pioneer in her own right, and now a colleague and friend. Led the way for the rest of us online career advisors.

Alan Schweyer: Manager of the National Graduate Register.

Shelley Suter: Is she *Globe and Mail* or Hi-Tech Careers? Either way, she's very obliging.

Thomas Vegh: Executive director of the Parachute Community Employment Centre. Bringing the wired world to those who need it most but can afford it least.

Gary Will: Creator of the Archeus career information Web site.

People At My Publishing Company

Thanks to everyone behind the scenes at Prentice Hall for bringing this all together. And to those I worked with personally, Susanne Frame, Robert Harris, Amber Wallace and David Jolliffe, a special note of appreciation.

People Who Make My Life Worth Living

Stacia and Jonah: My incredibly precious children. They've been so patient and joyful, even while asking in exasperation, "Is Daddy at the computer again?!"

Marianne: My wife, companion and best friend. None of this would have been possible without your support and love. All I can say is, "Grow old with me...the best is yet to come."

Helen and Sydney: The parents who have always stood behind me 100 percent. They showed me the way, and I am forever grateful.

My friends, family and colleagues: Let's do it!

INTRODUCTION

THE WIRED AGE IS HERE!

Want a new way to hunt for work, impress employers and upgrade your skills all at the same time? Here it is—get wired!

I'm not trying to overstate things when I say that the electronic revolution has forever changed the way that we look for work. Never before have so many people had so much access to useful and affordable technology. Remember how tedious and difficult writing up your résumé used to be? Now you can get one done, first-class, using inexpensive and customizable software. How about going for those lovely, relaxing interviews? Today you can prepare with an online coach, to reduce your anxiety and increase your odds of getting an offer.

You might even be thinking about a new career. If so, the Internet lets you look inwards, as well as to the outside world, in ways that weren't even conceivable just a few years ago. In fact, just about anything career-related can now be accomplished more quickly, and more efficiently, online.

What Does Getting Wired Really Mean?

Home PCs, the Internet, e-mail, fax machines, software, CD-ROMs, voice-mail—they've all burst onto the scene in recent years. When they first came out, they were hard to get and even harder to use. Not so anymore. Today they're user-friendly and widely available. Best of all, they've evolved to the point where they can truly help you reach your career goals.

Getting *wired* means, quite simply, learning how to use technology as part of your overall work-search. This refers to the Internet, with its components like the World Wide Web, e-mail, Chat and Newsgroups. It also includes the ever-expanding array of office equipment, computer technology and business systems that are changing the way we communicate.

It's Easier Than You Think As a career consultant, I've seen the power of these new technologies. They cover a broader range of possibilities than you may realize. Here are just a few impressive examples:

> Sanjay was an out-of-work computer programmer from British Columbia. He'd been trying unsuccessfully for months to find a job the traditional way. Then a friend told him that he could post his résumé on one of the growing number of Internet job banks. Some of these would actually match him automatically to vacancies on their database. All he had to do was send in a copy of his résumé. Because many hi-tech jobs are being posted on the Internet, he was able to secure two firm offers within five weeks.

> Michèle had just graduated from college in Quebec and was looking for her first full-time job. Like thousands of other recent graduates, she mailed out hundreds of résumés to employers across the province—with no success. Then she registered electronically on the National Graduate Register, and targeted specific employers using data from CD-ROMs at the local library. Two months later, she had been called for six interviews.

Stories like these are increasingly common. People from all walks of life are successfully using technology as part of their career search process. The potential of these new tools is virtually unlimited.

When Is a Job No Longer a Job?

You may have noticed that the subtitle of this book is *The Canadian Guide To Job Hunting Online*. Yet I often use the term *work-search* in place of *job hunting*.

To understand why, think back to all the changes in our economy in the early 90s. The job market was in turmoil, with mergers and layoffs dotting the landscape. Shrieks of anguish could be heard everywhere. Then one day, people began singing the praises of a wondrous new tool called the Internet. Their initial reactions were somewhat optimistic. "My job problems are over forever," they cried ecstatically. "Now I can find a job anytime I want. Look—they're all right here on the Net!"

Then reality set in. Traditional jobs became increasingly scarce. More and more people were forced to look at other work options, such as contracts or self-employment. The number of Canadians in business for themselves—consultants, franchisees and small business owners—shot up over the two million mark. The concept of "security" faded into oblivion as downsizing became the norm.

As for all those wonderful "jobs" that were on the Internet? Turns out they were almost exclusively for techno-dweebs (no offence intended).

Adapting to the Changes I use the word *work* throughout the book to describe employment because the word *job* no longer encompasses all the opportunities that are out there.

Sure, there are thousands of vacancies posted on the Internet, many of which are traditional positions, such as sales and marketing, finance, or production. But don't get too complacent. The fact is that you'll find most of these same postings in your newspaper's employment section. It's not like there's a hidden treasure chest of openings that no one else has ever seen (unless you're a hi-tech worker, in which case you'd better be surfing the Net for some exclusively-posted work opportunities).

What I'm trying to say is that there's a whole new way of using technology to manage your career and find the work you really want. Notice that I again substituted *work* in place of *job*. That's because I recognize that while you may be seeking a traditional job close to home, you're just as likely to be looking for a contract overseas, or considering starting the business you've always dreamed of. I only use the word *job* in this book to describe an employment arrangement where you work primarily for a single company or organization. This could be full-time, part-time, permanent or for a specified period only (contract-based).

A Little Skepticism Never Hurt Some of you may still have doubts about what these new tools can do for you. Or maybe you're thinking "Yeah, those techniques may work for other people, but they can't help me in my situation." If that's what's on your mind, read the following example to see what can really happen.

> Mark had a strong background in his field and wanted to get his book published. He had tried once before, years ago, but fell short of getting a firm contract. This time he resolved to get some assistance. The first thing he did was to go online and network. Mark sent an e-mail, which he had only learned to use a few months before, to a prominent author whom he had never met. The e-mail message outlined Mark's idea and asked for some friendly advice. Unbeknownst to him, that author forwarded the e-mail to his own publisher, who loved the idea for this new book. Mark was awarded a contract and is now a published author.

Um, wait a minute...that's *my* true story! By the way, many thanks to Jim Carroll, co-author of *The Canadian Internet Handbook*, for helping my dream become a reality.

Anyone Can Do It!

By showing you these examples, I'm hoping that one thing will stand out: it's not just computer geniuses and techno-wizards who are benefitting. Literally anyone can go online to increase their chances of finding work—no matter what that work is! Whether you're a graduating student or mid-life career changer, senior executive or administrative assistant, blue-collar worker or budding entrepreneur, there's something worthwhile for you here.

So What's in the Book?

I've tried to write this guide so that it satisfies your career needs no matter what level you're at. My intention is not to overwhelm you with jargon and sophisticated instructions.

Job seekers will find descriptions of all sorts of Internet Web sites and Newsgroups, software and CD-ROM programs, electronic résumé formats. You'll find instructions on things like posting your résumé online, identifying the career that fits your true personality, and networking with other job seekers and potential employers on the Net.

Self-employment resources are also covered extensively, ranging from Web links that show you where to obtain start-up financing to software that lets you grow and run your business with greater efficiency.

Here's a partial preview of how you can manage your career online, as shown in this guide:

- **Self-Evaluation:** Rediscover who you are, and what you really want from life.
- **Choosing a Career:** Explore new possibilities and select one that's right for you.
- **Creating Electronic Résumés:** Format and send your résumé online—the proper way.
- **Tapping the Hidden Job Market:** Target your prospects and network online to get ahead.
- **Starting a Small Business:** Use self-employment tools and tips to get up and running.

The bottom line is that searching for work the wired way gives you a distinct competitive edge. But if you stop to think about it, soon everyone will be doing it. That's the way our marketplace works. The harsh truth is that if you don't keep up, you'll get left behind in a cloud of cyber-dust!

A Made-in-Canada Solution

The solution to this problem is actually all around us. Up until now, though, it's been widely-scattered in bits and pieces. You can easily find dozens of books on technology and office equipment. And there's no shortage of "how to" literature on using the Internet. What's been missing is a simple, step-by-step approach on how to use these tools as part of your search for a job or self-employment. That's where this guide enters the picture.

Supply Must Equal Demand You might be wondering what drove me to assemble these disparate resources into one, well-organized guide. I wish I could give you some noble, altruistic answer, but it really comes down to a simple fact: my clients need this resource, and it is nowhere else to be found.

It wasn't that long ago that my clients started asking me questions that I couldn't answer. One day it was, "How do I format my résumé for e-mail?" The next day someone asked, "Where do I go to get up-to-the-minute news about the company I'm interviewing with tomorrow morning?"

I didn't need a psychic to reveal my future. I had two choices: either learn how to advise my clients about the new way of doing things, or watch them go out and find another consultant who could. That second option didn't much appeal to me (or my family, who like to eat regularly), so I chose the first.

Looking for Ready-Made Solutions That's when I ran to the bookstore to find out more. Sure enough, there were four or five brand new books on using the Internet for job hunting. I bought two of them and raced back to my office to crack them open. Guess what? They were practically useless to me as a Canadian. Not that they were technically inaccurate or lacking information. On the contrary, they were filled with advice and brimming with examples. Unfortunately, almost everything that they talked about applied only to Americans. Looking for a job in Nebraska? I learned how to do so by browsing the U.S.-based Online Career Center on the World Wide Web. Thinking of sending in your résumé by e-mail? These books tell you not to bother unless it's key-word formatted for scanning and tracking (whatever that means).

What About Us Canadians, Eh? "Hold on a second," I thought to myself. "There's something dreadfully wrong with this picture." I still had no idea how to find potential employers in Calgary or St. John's. And what about places to post your résumé online in B.C.? They must exist somewhere. Furthermore, are any Canadian companies really insisting on key-word résumés (whatever those are)?

Since then, I've spent countless hours mapping out the Internet, scouring software, tinkering with fax machines and reviewing CD-ROMs. I've also been in contact with career experts, people seeking work and employers who hire electronically. The result is a comprehensive guide of online career resources for Canadians.

My Personal Commitment to You

I don't like to over-promise. So before you go off hoping that this book will single-handedly turn your life around let's come back to earth. It's time to go over what you can realistically expect from using this guide.

What You Will Find Throughout each chapter, there are elements that bring ideas and hints into focus for you. In particular, watch for:

- **Cyber-Tips**: Clear, concise instructions on how to locate information and use the electronic tools that are critical to every stage of your career planning process.
- **Real-Life**: Short pieces of advice on how to get to where you really want to be by following tried and true practices.
- **Wired Wrap-Ups**: Summaries at the end of each chapter tie the information together and reinforce what this means in terms of finding and securing work.

Chapter 1 is designed to help you get the most from this book. I suggest that you read it before tackling the rest of the guide. It could save you some time and effort.

What You Won't Find I might as well be upfront with you. This book doesn't even come close to answering every single career-related question posed by humankind throughout the millennium. However, it will point you to resources that can be of assistance. But don't count on it to do the following:

- Providing quick and easy solutions to difficult situations (you're going to have to do all the legwork yourself, I'm afraid).
- Guaranteeing you a fantastic new job (it's up to you to decide for yourself what you really want, and how to best use the tools that I describe to help get you there).
- Turning you into a technological genius. (I do provide basic instructions on using technology to advance your career, but you'll have to practise and experiment *a lot* if you're thinking of becoming a pro.)

I've Been There Too

Just so you know, I've found myself—more than once—on the wrong side of a "rightsizing." (Translation: I've experienced the gut-wrenching trauma of losing my job when I worked in the corporate world.) I know how unsettling and harrowing being out of work can be. Searching for employment is a hard, grim fact in today's marketplace. Well over one million unemployed Canadians will attest to that.

There Are No Easy Answers As I struggled to rebuild my career, I read many books and articles to provide direction. Some of these promised an "easy" solution. That only made me angry and increasingly frustrated. In my opinion, these "simple" solutions trivialized the whole concept of finding work. It's true that anyone can get a job if they try hard enough and long enough. The tough part is securing the type of work that's right for you.

I'd be misleading you if I said you'll get high-paying, glamorous work by next Tuesday just by getting wired. It can be very difficult and time consuming to find work that is meaningful and satisfying. Period.

Why Not Give the New Techniques a Shot? The bright side is that the newest tools can make your search more efficient. In doing so, you may very well find work more quickly than otherwise. My real hope is that you use this book to help you uncover—and secure—the type of employment that you genuinely want!

Please don't look for a magic formula buried in these pages. All my suggestions are based on proven methods for planning your career and searching for work. What I've really done is to superimpose user-friendly technology over this broad framework. You get to decide which of these new techniques apply to your unique circumstances.

The Hidden Benefits There's one other thing I want to mention. Searching for work online really does have some built-in bonuses:

- It shows employers that you have the skills they're looking for today.
- You can now search for work or promote your business worldwide.
- These tools operate 24 hours a day, 7 days a week, giving you flexibility and exposure.
- The power of research is available to you like never before.
- Networking into the hidden job market is possible—right from your own home.

Wrapping It Up

In closing, this book is meant for anyone who wants to better their chances of finding, and securing, the work that they really want. It is written in plain language, with step-by-step advice on using the newest technologies effectively.

Regretfully, this guide will not transform you into a super-achieving career maven. Only you can make that happen—if that's truly your goal. Using the methods described here *will* give you a leg up on the people who are only using the old techniques to find work. This could very well be the edge that you've been looking for!

p.s. We all know that technology is changing rapidly, and this book is designed with that in mind. Once you're hooked up to the Internet, surf over to **http://wiredhired.com** for regular updates on new career-related sites and software. You'll also find a bonus chapter that describes people from a variety of backgrounds using the latest work-search tools.

PART 1

GETTING WIRED AND GETTING STARTED

CHAPTER 1

The Changing World of Work

Virtual Definition: **transition** (tran zish'ən) *noun*

Movement from one position or way of being to another. Characterized by the ending of a pre-existing state and the beginning of something new. Can be painful initially. Often holds out great promise as well.

I. THE WINDS OF ECONOMIC CHANGE

Remember the movie *The Wizard of Oz*? There's one scene that has always stuck with me. It's near the beginning of the film, where Dorothy is ripped from her home by a vicious tornado. She finds herself thrust into a completely unfamiliar world. Frightened, alone, and disoriented, with only her dog to talk to, she utters the classic line: "Toto, I don't think we're in Kansas anymore."

To me, this pretty well describes our economy in the 90s.

The New Realities

Swept away by the cyclone of change, the workscape that we once knew is no more; left instead is a confusing hodgepodge. Many of the older, established companies that ruled in the 70s and 80s have crashed into oblivion (remember Confederation Life, or Simpson's for that matter?). In their wake is a trail of layoffs and disgruntled ex-employees. Meanwhile, new firms and industries are springing up everywhere. They bring with them a fresh new energy and the promise of renewed growth. But do they offer the kind of jobs that we've been used to? The answer is, not really.

It's a Whole New Ball Game The enormity of this transition can be overwhelming. It was captured rather nicely in a recent discussion paper from the Canadian Ministry of Labour entitled "The Changing Workplace: Challenges and Issues." The introduction says it all: "How, when and where work is performed is undergoing significant transformation—a transformation driven by global economic change and the information society."

As a career consultant, I see the impact of this transformation in many ways. Many of my clients are experiencing profound shifts in their concept of employment. They no longer just talk about jobs; instead, they've started referring to "work opportunities." This catch-all phrase includes full-time jobs, part-time contracts, the fast growing realm of self-employment, and everything in between.

The language they use reflects these new realities. It now includes words like *downsizing* and *outsourcing*. Other times I hear them talk about "scaling back" their expectations. There are some people, however, who use a very different vocabulary. They talk to me about things like "freedom to explore" and "expressing their creativity through work." Like anything else, a big part of reacting to change is how you look at it; however, this doesn't necessarily make it any easier.

Adapting to the Shifts There's one impact that's the same regardless of your perspective: the way that people look for work has changed. If you're searching for a job today, the path is murky. Doing the exact same things that may have worked for you even two or three years ago may not get you far. You have to keep up with the latest recruitment techniques. On the other hand, hiring decisions are still made by humans (for now, at least); therefore, you can't rely totally on technology. A balanced, forward-thinking approach is your best bet.

As for self-employment, the tools of the trade—and the needs of your potential customers—are also in flux. Technology can definitely help you to find and attract new clients. Understanding how is a big part of the battle. That's where this book can be of assistance.

CYBER TIP In compiling research for this book, I often used Internet search engines and directories to help me find specific information. Some of it was even interactive, like the Ministry of Labour article I mentioned earlier. You can actually respond to the Ministry online. Their Collective Reflections site is on the World Wide Web at **http://207.81.16.12/disp_e.html**. And don't worry if you're not sure how to read or locate this Internet address; Chapter 2 contains some easy-to-understand instructions.

The Evidence Is Everywhere To emphasize how dramatic the shifts in the work world have been, try a simple exercise. Take out your business card (or somebody else's, if you happen to be between work assignments like more than one million other Canadians right now). What's on the card? If this were 10 years ago, you'd probably see the name and address of the company you worked for. Likely it was a large, well-established corporation. Your name, title and phone number would also be there. That's it.

Compare this with today. Let's start with the company name. Odds are that the organization you work for is smaller and newer than the one you were with 10 years ago. In fact, there's a good chance that you're now self-employed. As for phone numbers, give me a break! There's the business phone, car phone, pager and maybe even your home number (a result of the 24 hour service economy). And don't forget the beloved fax number. Which reminds me, do you remember when it was hip to have your own fax number? Nowadays, it gets lost in the clutter between your e-mail address and the URL of your Internet homepage!

II. WHAT DOES *WORK* MEAN TODAY?

There's no doubt that we're living through a period of colossal upheaval. Every time you pick up the paper (or scan the headlines on your Web browser's news agent), you hear about it. Jobs being slashed here, new skills called for there. It's not easy to adapt to these new transformations—especially when they're still changing! It helps, however, to understand what some of the major trends are. The truth is, they're shaping your prospects for work even as you read this.

The Pendulum Has Swung

I don't claim to be an economics expert. (My professors from York University, where I did my MBA program, would happily back me up on that one!) I do know that there are significant forces affecting the average Canadian. A few of the biggies? Cost cutting by corporations and deficit fighting by our governments have resulted in unparalleled restructuring. Add to this the effects of the North American Free Trade Agreement (NAFTA) along with ever-increasing global competition, throw in a healthy dose of demographics (that's right, blame those damned baby boomers again) and you've got yourself a potent mixture of dislocation and uncertainty.

The Quick and the Dead As with any period of change, we are seeing the victors and the vanquished. Nuala Beck, prominent Canadian economist and author, chronicles this well in her latest book, *Excelerate*. She points out that the New Economy® has created vast new industries that were only dreamed of 20 short years ago. Many knowledge-based companies are thriving. The computer has single-handedly transformed the work-scape. If you need proof, check out the job advertisements in your local paper. Over 50 percent of published positions are computer related on any given day.

Labour-intensive industries have not fared nearly as well. Employment rates with automotive manufacturers, construction companies and others like them have been hit particularly hard. The causes vary. Some say it's increased automation, others cite falling demand and rising costs. Whatever's behind it, the results are inarguable: Canadians are wondering where all the traditional jobs have gone.

Is the *Job* a Thing of the Past?

This brings us to a rather burning issue: what does the word *job* really mean today? I can recall what it *used* to mean. Before the great recessions of the 80s and 90s, a job offered steady employment (you heard me right) with the same company, over an extended period of time. Your salary and benefits would rise each year in a predictable fashion and there was room for upward mobility. And if you worked hard and produced consistent results, the company was loyal to you, giving you a sense of security.

Looking Back in Envy Don't laugh—that's really how it used to be for many of us. Now it seems like a description from the ancient past, distorted by age. Which reminds me of a little analogy: dinosaurs, the dodo bird and a job-for-life—what do these three things have in common? If you answered they're all extinct, you're correct!

In the 1990s, security and stability have evaporated. Even the best performers and most dedicated employees have become vulnerable. The whims of the marketplace are sovereign. With mergers, acquisitions, cutbacks, and restructuring, no one is "safe" anymore. Except for those who are moving with the times.

How Do You Work If You Don't Have a Job? So how do you manage your career with all these changes going on? By understanding, first and foremost, the new rules of the game. Perhaps the hardest thing to get used to is the trend towards *de-jobbing*. This is a not a pretty word. It describes the movement from full-time, steady jobs to contingent, contract-based work. The whole notion of long-term, stable positions may be a distant memory for many of us. Take heart, though, there is good news on the horizon. In our revamped economy, there is a great deal of work to be done!

"So what," you say? The era of the permanent job may well be in its twilight, but the dawn of the flexible work arrangement is upon us. Witness the recent rise in outsourcing, contract-based and part-time employment. This is evident in the number of jobs advertised in your paper (or on the Internet) that are actually contracts. They offer you work for a specified period of time, say for example 12 months. Sometimes they even throw in benefits, though your more likely to be on your own for things like pensions, medical insurance, dental care and vacation time.

My Days as a Pioneer My own career history illustrates the huge transformations that are taking place in the work world. I haven't always been a self-employed career consultant. If we go back to 1989, when I was searching for work, the vacancies advertised in the newspaper were for solid, permanent jobs. I, however, didn't want one of *those* anymore. What I needed was some short-term work that would carry me through the first of several career changes. Keep in mind that this was before the era of temporary positions, and that I was unemployed at the time. Oh, did I mention that our first child was just about to be born? You can probably guess how pleased my wife was when I told her I was looking for contract work, not a job.

Remarkably, I stumbled upon a type of ad that I had never seen before. It was for a five-month contract as a Temporary Marketing Manager. I felt as if my prayers had been answered. I put all my energy into applying for the position. I'm happy to report that I was offered the job on the very day that my wife gave birth to our daughter. I, of course, was delighted by this turn of events. My wife was...well, let's just say she was underwhelmed. She'd been hoping that I would have job security now that we had a child to take care of.

I tried to explain how wonderful it was to *not* be tied down to one particular company forever. But as my wife screamed expletives at me (she was in labour at the time, so I didn't take it too personally), I comforted myself with the knowledge that I was ahead of my time. Today you see flexible work arrangements like this in many areas, such as business, healthcare, governments and universities.

Self-Employment Comes of Age

This leads us to the other great shift in work-styles—the growing number of Canadians who are turning to self-employment. This number rose to almost 2.5 million people by the end of 1996. In fact, self-employment accounted for over 75 percent of the net gain in employment between 1990 and 1995, according to the Canadian Labour Congress.

People are going the entrepreneurial route for a variety of reasons. Some are choosing self-employment because it offers new opportunities. Many, however, are doing so because it's their only remaining alternative. As the supply of steady, traditional jobs has declined, we're seeing a substantial increase in:

- consultants,
- contract workers,
- franchise owners and agents, and
- small business people.

Career Self-Management for the Nineties

It's not just the self-employed who are thinking in new ways. Kevin Hood, a Canadian self-employment expert, says that "everybody must begin to understand that they are in business for themselves." This means that even if you have a traditional job, or are searching for one, responsibility for your career has fallen squarely on your own shoulders.

The Newest Form of Business: "Me Inc." The fact is that no company or organization is obliged to look after you. This point was driven home in a recent article in *Fortune* magazine. Entitled "Me Inc.," it described how we're shifting away from corporate paternalism. The old, unwritten contract between employer and employee has been broken forever. There's a new ethos for workers: "Do your best and create value-added, but be prepared to leave tomorrow."

A term being used to characterize this switch is *career resilience*. It's about doing what's necessary to stay competitive. Mainly, that means understanding the needs of the marketplace, upgrading your training as required, and doing work where and when it needs to be done. It implies a self-directed, flexible approach. Fortunately, the Internet and other online tools (discussed in Chapter 2) can help you in this regard.

Hold on to What You Believe In Does this mean that you must abandon your dreams of a meaningful, fulfilling career? Not on your life! I'm not suggesting for a moment that you give up your dreams. If anything, I'm encouraging you to pursue them whole-heartedly. It's just that you may have to adapt your route to take into account our altered work world.

How Work Itself Is Changing

If you've been out there earning a living for a few years (or trying to, anyway), you've probably witnessed some significant transformations. Here's a quick quiz. Do all your colleagues still work in the same building as you? Or are some people actually located in their homes now? How many administrative assistants does your firm still employ? Do they type correspondence for their supervisors? Or does each supervisor use a word processing program to write their own memos and letters? Last question now: Does your company have an Intranet yet?

My point here is that we're seeing fundamental shifts in the very nature of work. It's not just *what* we're doing that's different, it's also:

- **Where** we work: It now includes telecommuting, plus home-based and car-based offices.
- **Who** we work for: Tends to be smaller companies or some form of self-employment.
- **What** we work with: Personal computers (PCs), modems, faxes, voice-mail, Internets and Intranets.

- **When** we work: Some new flexibility here, but we're putting in longer hours on average.
- **How** we work: Increasingly with our minds (ideas and knowledge) rather than manually.

The Net Result

Change always brings with it a certain amount of anxiety and confusion, especially when it hits us where we make our living. This has left many people with a sense of diminished expectations. I will never underplay the trauma of this dislocation. Having experienced it myself, I'm only too aware of how disruptive it can be. But the prognosis for the future is not grim. Far from it, in fact. What we must come to terms with is this: there are plenty of opportunities in the workplace; they are just different from what we've been led to expect.

III. THE PROCESS OF FINDING WORK

The ways that we go about searching for work have also changed. Let's focus for a moment on those of you who are looking for some sort of job, as opposed to an entrepreneurial opportunity. It used to be that you could call a few recruiters, send out some résumés, and look for employment ads in your Saturday newspaper. Now we've been barraged with new technologies. The Internet, fax machines, home computers and CD-ROMs have given us new ways to proactively find work. Sooner or later, *someone* had to start using these to get an edge—now we all have to!

Canadian Recruiting Is Changing Too

Don't kid yourselves, though. We're not the only ones with updated tools and techniques. Companies and organizations are also upgrading their arsenals. Today's human resources or hiring department is leaner (and in many cases, meaner) than in the 80s. With fewer people doing less hiring, but with an ever-increasing pile of applications, something had to give.

What You Don't Know Can Hurt You It's futile to pretend that it is business as usual when it comes to finding work. It's not. There are certain things you can't afford to ignore. If you do, it may increase the time it takes you to secure employment. Here are some of the critical things to know:

- Companies are relying increasingly on technology to screen applicants. Today most companies ask you to fax in your résumé. Many more are now requesting an e-mailed version. This trend will accelerate as résumé scanning and applicant tracking become widely used.
- You're expected to do your homework. Look at the employment ads in today's newspaper. Did you notice that many companies have included their corporate World Wide Web address? They want you to look at their Web site *before* your interview!
- Hi-tech companies want hi-tech employees. If you plan to work in the computer, engineering or similar field, you'll find many positions posted on the Internet. In fact, a number of technology companies *only* advertise for workers there. The message is "If you can't find us, we don't want you!"
- Computer literacy is a requirement. Even low-tech companies and junior positions demand basic computer skills. More senior people pretty well have to know how to use a word processing program and create a spreadsheet. Being computer literate is no longer an advantage—it's an absolute must!

Marketing Yourself Effectively

While the methods of hiring are undergoing an evolution, the basic principles are not. Employers are still looking for keen individuals who bring with them the experience, needed skills and ability to contribute concretely.

Proactiveness is the Key Experience and skill, however, are no longer enough to get you hired. Fact is, they won't even get your foot in the door unless you know how to sell yourself properly. That's where thinking like a marketer comes in handy. You must begin to view yourself as a "product," which you are trying to sell in the "marketplace." Your "buyer" is someone who does the hiring at a company or organization and can offer you a position. Your goal is to satisfy the needs of this buyer better than any of your "competitors" (other applicants).

With this in mind, there's one thing that can help you find better employment sooner (O.K., two things, if you include that relative of yours who owns a big chunk of Microsoft): *targeting the hidden job market*. This is the process of identifying companies that hire people with your skills and background, then actively networking with the decision makers *before* a vacancy becomes available. (Chapters 6 and 7 discuss this in more detail.)

The Virtual Difference You might be saying to yourself, "Yeah, yeah, I've heard this all before. That's what everyone keeps telling me." I know. I'm the first to acknowledge that almost all career consultants say the same thing: networking is the way to access the 80 percent of work opportunities that may not be advertised. And practically every job-hunting guide teaches the same basic process. But how many teach you to do it *virtually*?

IV. HOW TO GET THE MOST FROM THIS BOOK

There's no techno-magic involved in this guide. I've already told you that it follows established principles promoted by career experts throughout North America. The bonus is in the technology. This is the first book that shows you *which* new tools to use at every stage in your work search. And it shows you *how* to use them—to give you a competitive edge!

The Career Planning Process

One thing I won't do is tell you to "dive right in." Your career is too precious to treat casually. There's nothing wrong with taking some time for reflection before getting started. With that in mind, I have a suggestion to make. This book will work best for you if you know where you've been, and where you really want to be going, career-wise. The best place to begin is with a clear idea of where you are, right now, in the career process.

Maybe you are out of a job. Or it could be that you're working, but would really like to switch careers. Some of you may even be thinking of starting your own business. What has become apparent is that the stage you find yourself in is no longer just a factor of your age. A 25-year-old college graduate could be looking to start her own consulting practice. A 42-year-old businessman could be thinking of becoming an actor. And a 63-year-old could very well decide to go back to school full time.

Knowing Where You Stand The important thing is to pinpoint where *you* are in terms of your search for work, then you can choose which chapters to concentrate on.

It might be helpful to view the career planning process as having three distinct stages:

1. Choosing the Right Career Direction
2. Preparing to Market Yourself
3. Securing Work

This model applies whether you're seeking to be employed by someone else, or are thinking of running your own business. Each of the three stages is associated with various activities and goals. This book is set up to take you through these activities in an organized manner, with tips on using technology every step of the way.

REAL LIFE *It's critical for you to honestly assess the stage you're at in your career; otherwise, you won't maximize your chances for success. This assessment should be based on where you really stand, not where you think you're supposed to be. Don't let your age, gender, schooling, past experiences or the expectations of others influence you. You are who you are—that's the true starting point!*

Stage One: Choosing the Right Career Direction

I didn't like having to choose a career when I was still in my teens. There was so much pressure to fit myself into an acceptable, pre-defined role, yet I had very little idea of what my options truly were. Unfortunately, that's how most of us tend to make the most important decisions of our lives.

Nowadays, I advise people to pursue a career that is right for them. I can't emphasize this point enough. Think about it—the average Canadian will work for a period that spans approximately 10,000 days. That's one long stretch of time. Your typical lifetime earnings will amount to somewhere between one and three million dollars.

It's Not Just About Money Finances aside, I strongly believe that we owe it to ourselves to do what we were meant to do. That means spending our lives working at something we enjoy, and that (hopefully) we're good at. An idealistic thought, I agree; nonetheless, it is possible.

If you're one of those people who is still wondering what to do with the rest of your life, don't fret. There are two actions you can undertake immediately. One is to begin a thorough self-evaluation; the other is to go out and truly explore your options. Fortunately, you can do these at any time in your life; whether you're still in school, or if you've got 2.4 kids, a mortgage, a spouse, and a job to contend with!

Self-Evaluation Most career advisors will tell you that everything starts by looking inwards. To do this, you'll want to examine things like your strengths and weaknesses, likes and dislikes, key accomplishments, plus your interests and values. What you're trying to do is determine which careers and work environments *you're best suited for*. As it turns out, there's a variety of online tests and inventories that help you to do just that. If this is the stage you're at, you'll want to start with the first half of Chapter 3.

Career Exploration Once you have an understanding of what's inside you, it's time to turn to the outside world. Your mission here is to determine which career is truly best for you. You can do this by investigating the career choices that came from the results of your self-evaluation (or from any of your other experiences). The goal is to get accurate information about the career and work environments that appeal to you. Some questions you should ask yourself include:

- What are my ideal career and work environments really like?
- Do they require special skills or education? Do I need to do any upgrading?
- Are the long-term prospects in this field positive? Or are they in decline?
- What compensation and potential for advancement can I realistically expect?

The second part of Chapter 3, Self-Evaluation: The Critical First Step, can help you find many of the answers you require.

Stage Two: Preparing to Market Yourself

Now it's time to decide where to go from here. There are two basic approaches when you come down to it. Regardless of the field you choose, or the type of work you decide on, you can either work for someone else, or become self-employed. (Yes, you can also retire, but then you probably wouldn't be reading this book.) In either case, there are steps you will have to take to get you from where you are today, to where you really want to be. The preparation stage consists of the things you need to do before you go out and start pounding the pavement.

Preparing for Employment by Others If you've decided to look for a job or a contract position, you'll need to market yourself to potential employers. A powerful résumé and cover letter are the conventional ways to go. Read Chapters 4 and 5 to find out how to create and send these materials electronically.

The next phase in your search is to actively find the companies and organizations that are hiring people like you. Chapter 6 is all about doing online research to help you build a list of target prospects. This is where the Internet and CD-ROMs are most useful.

Then there are the so-called soft skills that can make the whole process run more smoothly. Things like phone and voicemail etiquette, organizing your work-search, interviewing effectively and negotiating an offer are detailed in Chapter 7. Although you may not use these right away, it's best to know about them early on.

Preparing for Self-Employment Those of you who have chosen the self-employment option may need some basic advice. Chapter 6 is a good one to start with because it discusses online research techniques. This can assist you in defining your target audience, scoping out the competition and refining your product offerings. You might also want tips on actually starting and running a business. Plus you'll have to prepare a cohesive, realistic business plan. And what about setting up an office to work out of? These issues are all addressed in Chapter 10.

Your marketing materials are also essential. Business cards are discussed in Chapter 4, and brochures and letterhead are examined in the latter part of Chapter 10.

Stage Three: Securing Work

You've done your self-evaluation, decided which route to pursue, and prepared yourself for your approach. Now it's "launch time," as they say in the world of marketing.

Success from this point on—and the methods you use to achieve it—will depend on whether you're seeking employment by others, or self-employment. When hunting for a job, your objective is, of course, to secure and accept an offer to work for someone else. Whether it's full time, part time or contract-based is up to you to determine. On the self-employment front, success means finding and signing up customers who will pay you for your services. You will decide if it's best to have one or two steady clients, or many smaller customers.

Getting an Offer of Employment There is a definite process involved in securing a job offer. It begins with networking that lets you gather info, create leads and tap into the hidden job market. I have discussed this process in Chapter 8. You can supplement these proactive efforts by reading Chapter 9, where you will learn how to check for published openings and post your résumé (if appropriate) online.

Getting Customers for Your Business There are many ways to woo customers for your products and services. Whether you're a consultant or direct marketer, online promotion is the newest wave. Chapter 10 looks at the World Wide Web as a marketing vehicle. Also covered here is how to manage your enterprise using small business software, from tracking clients to keeping your books balanced.

Finding Other Information Quickly

I've tried to make this book as easy to use as possible. Information has been bundled in specific areas to help you locate it readily. Chapter 2 is exclusively for people who are just starting out. It gives basic instructions and background on how to use the Internet and other online resources.

Those of you who are interested in the future of work and work-searching can go to Chapter 11. You'll find predictions and advice from some leading Canadian experts in career-related matters.

The Appendix provides you with a list of key Web sites that focus on career-related material.

CYBER TIP Don't forget to use the CD-ROM at the back of this book. It gives you free trial access to the Internet via Sympatico, Canada's national Internet Service Provider, so you can check out the sites that interest you right away!

V. WIRED WRAP UP

O.K. folks, here's a recap of the highlights in Chapter 1:

- Our economy is in an unprecedented state of upheaval.
- The whole notion of the traditional job is disappearing.
- You can no longer rely on conventional methods alone to find work.

Am I a good-news kind of guy or what? Sort of makes you wonder what I have in store for you in Chapter 2.

Despite this initial doom and gloom, I doubt that there's anything you've read so far that you didn't already know. Every one of us has been affected by these changes in some way. In all likelihood, that's precisely what motivated you to pick up this book. If you carefully follow the tips and suggestions I've provided, you will come closer to securing the type of work you really want. That's not to say that this book will find you a job or start a new business for you. Sorry—that's where you get to do all the work!

Note too that I don't claim to have written the ultimate work manual. In other words, don't rush out and burn all those other job-hunting books and business-development guides you've plunked down your hard-earned money on. Instead, use the tried and true principles that work for you, and incorporate technology whenever it can give you an edge. That's what this book is all about. Don't read it expecting to be changed into a technical guru, use it for what is—a guide to help you find and secure the work you genuinely want, with the assistance of modern information management tools.

CHAPTER 2

Online Work-Search Tools: A Basic Primer

Virtual Definition: **newbie** (nōō′bē) *noun*

A newbie is one who is considered a beginner, with lack of skill or experience. Mostly used as a label by experienced Internetters, as a way of classifying someone new to the Net or other electronic resources.

I. THE TOOLS, THEY ARE A CHANGING

Welcome to the wild, wired world of work-searching in the 90s. As if downsizing, job-hunting or the changing economy weren't scary enough, now I come along to frighten you with a bunch of technological gobbledygook. How do you like my book so far?

Facing the Music

We might as well start with a few simple truths. That way we can move right into the mechanics of all this great new stuff.

FACT #1: *Technology has already changed the way that people search for work.* Mostly gone are the days when you could pick up your local newspaper, find a job ad that you liked, and phone the company to talk directly with the hiring manager. Today's ads tell you to fax or e-mail your word-processed résumé to human resources. When you call to find out where you stand, you're confronted with a voicemail system that sits between you and the decision makers in the company.

***FACT #2:** Technology has made the work-search easier for those who've embraced it!* Why travel to a distant library to hunt for information on a company you'd like to work for, when much of what you need is available on your computer screen. Is it necessary to pay a company to design and update your résumé when you can use templates and hints from the latest software package? And what if you could actually use voicemail to increase your odds of breaking through the screening process?

***FACT #3:** It's not as hard as it looks.* With a little practice, anyone can use a CD-ROM to track down hard-to-get information when preparing for a job interview. And it's not that difficult to e-mail your résumé in the proper format—once you know how. Best of all, surfing the Net for career links is a breeze when you understand the basics.

Demystifying Technology Let's face facts. Knowing how to leave a simple phone message or send a basic fax may no longer be enough. The name of the game in careers is *getting an edge*. Whether you're a student looking for your first job, or a senior manager thinking of changing careers, there are ways to make technology work in your favour. You don't have to be a technology wizard to use any of these tools effectively.

This chapter is all about taking the mystery out of some of the new work-search tools. It's a general introduction to a few of the technologies that can speed up your career transition. In later chapters, I'll show you how to apply each of these technologies at specific stages of your work-search.

A Few Things to Keep in Mind Take note that it's not just the Internet we're talking about here. When you're looking for a job, or starting your own business, there's a growing range of electronic resources. You don't have to use all of them to succeed—just the ones that will help you! Having said that, here are some resources that you can consider in addition to the Net:

- CD-ROMs and interactive software,
- fax machines, printers, modems, scanners and other office equipment,
- voicemail and answering systems, and
- pagers, Personal Digital Assistants and cellular phones if you're self-employed.

There's one other point I'd like to emphasize: all this technology can be extremely helpful, but it hasn't replaced the *basics*. You'll still need to take your career journey step by step. You should start by knowing who you are, and where you really want to be—then it's up to you to be proactive. Be prepared to aggressively target and research the companies you want to work for, or the markets you want to penetrate with your new business. Nothing, and nobody, can do this hard work for you. With that in mind, let's take a look at some of the key tools that can help you manage your career and find the work you truly desire.

II. INTERNET ESSENTIALS

We might as well begin with that strange new beast called the Internet. It's amazing how much excitement and publicity (and for many of us, fear and misunderstanding) this thing has generated lately. If you haven't used it yet, don't worry, you still have time to learn. In fact, it's far easier to use the Net today than it was even two or three years ago.

Resisting Is Useless

Before I get rolling, I have a confession to make. I avoided learning about the Internet like it was the plague! No joke. Until about two years ago, I thought of the Net as nothing more than a high-tech waste of time. Don't get me wrong, I'm not some sort of modern-day Luddite. Quite the opposite, in fact. I've always used a PC at work, and I like to try new software, if I think it's going to help my productivity. Somehow, though, this Internet thing had me spooked.

Maybe it was the jargon that people were using to describe it. Words like *Gopher Space, Telnet* and *File Transfer Protocol* all sounded so computerish to me. Or possibly it was the people I knew who were using the Net back then: professors, scientists, computer engineers...you know, the people who you think of (rightly or wrongly) as being removed from the daily realities of life. At any rate, I'm not ashamed to admit that this new technology scared me.

A Moment of Truth I remember when I first realized that I'd better go online and see what all the fuss was about. It happened innocently enough. I was attending a meeting of a company that I was doing contract work for. At the break, I took a little stroll and happened to catch two of my colleagues having a discussion. Here's how it went:

Bob: "Did you get a copy of the new Netscape browser yet?"

Cheryl: "Yeah, it makes the Web so much easier to surf."

Bob: "That's for sure. I was even able to download a GIF of our competitor's newest product."

Cheryl: "Hey, what a bonus. The best thing for me is that I can give up my bulletin board and stick to e-mail."

Bob: "Amazing. By the way, what do you think of your ISP?"

Cheryl: "Actually, they're fine. They give me a 28.8 connection and they're thinking of going flat-rate."

A casual (though, at the time, unintelligible) conversation between two businesspeople, but my complacency was shattered forever. What dawned on me—like a ton of bricks—was that suddenly I was getting left behind! After all the years of priding myself on being an up-to-date user of computers and business software, I was in danger of being rendered a techno-dinosaur by this creeping, mysterious force called the Internet. That very day I vowed to check it out for myself. By the end of that week I was signed up, tuned in and surfing away.

What Exactly Is the Internet?

Now, as part of my consulting, I give seminars on using the Internet for career management. One of the questions I get most often is "So what *is* this Internet, really?" The clearest answer I can give is that it has both physical and content components. On the physical side, it's really just a massive network of computers, connected through modems, routers and circuits, where data can be transferred almost instantly to any point on the globe. As for content, the Net offers an ever-evolving collection of information resources and communication tools.

Defining the Net The word *Internet* literally means "network of networks." (Those who find the Net slow and overwhelming insist that the word evolved from an ancient Latin term meaning "information swamp.") In itself, the Net is comprised of thousands of smaller regional networks scattered throughout the globe. On any given day it connects roughly 30 million users in over 100 countries.

One thing you might find interesting is that nobody actually owns the Internet. There are companies and organizations that help manage different parts of the networks that tie everything together; however, there is no single governing body that controls what happens on the Internet. The networks within different countries are funded and managed locally, in accordance with local regulations. Via the Internet, hundreds of thousands of people around the world are accessing and uploading information from their homes, schools and workplaces.

III. KEY COMPONENTS OF THE INTERNET

For career-seekers and job-hunters, the Net has become a veritable bonanza of information. It's also an electronic meeting place for people with similar goals and interests from across Canada and around the world. There are several useful features that you should know about.

Schizo-Net

A common misconception about the Net is that it's one giant, cohesive entity. Not so. In fact, it consists of several disparate parts, each linked in its own way through the Internet's neural network. Each of these elements can be viewed as a tool in its own right. Together they combine to make the Internet a potent communication force. To help unravel the Net, I've provided descriptions of the important components in Table 2.1.

E-mail: The Winged Messenger

The most popular application on the Internet is e-mail. You may already have it at home, and odds are that you've used it if you've worked in an office. But what is it and what can it really do? In its simplest form, e-mail is an electronic message sent from one computer to another. You can send or receive personal and business-related messages with attachments like pictures, word-processing files or other documents. You can even send World Wide Web documents back and forth on some of the more recently released programs.

How E-mail Works Just as a letter makes pit stops at different postal stations along the way, e-mail is passed from one computer to another as it travels through the network. Each computer reads the e-mail address and routes it to another computer until it eventually reaches its

Table 2.1 Key Components of the Internet

NAME OF COMPONENT	BRIEF DESCRIPTION
E-mail	Electronic mail with text and file attachments
World Wide Web	Information with graphics, text, sound and video
Usenet Newsgroups, forums and mailing lists	Discussion groups based on e-mail messages
Internet Relay Chat, Internet Phone, Bulletin Boards	Used to communicate with others instantly on the Net
FTP, Gopher, Telnet, Archie	Older Internet applications that are not often used

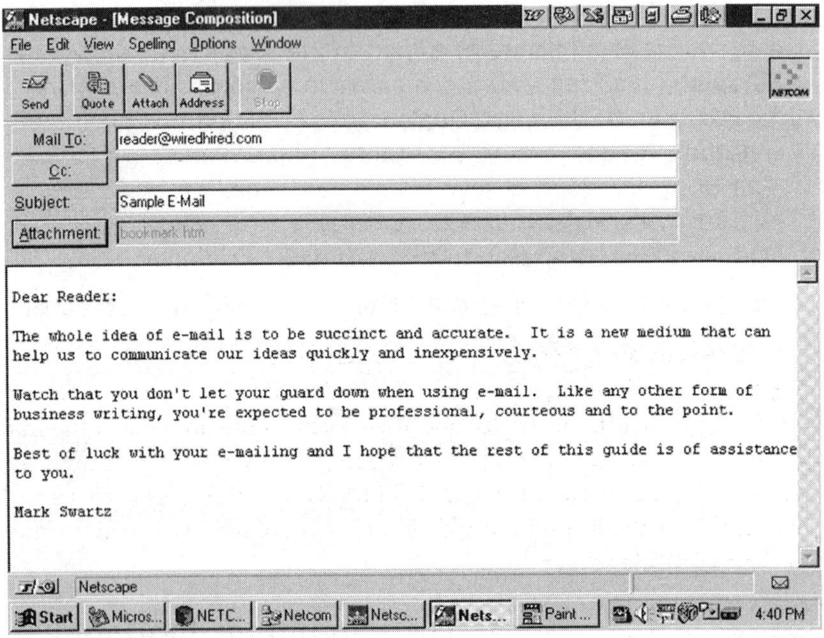

destination. It's then stored in an electronic mailbox, where it waits until you access it with your very own password. With the Internet, the whole electronic mailing process usually takes just a few minutes, allowing you to quickly and easily communicate with virtually anyone in the world who has an e-mail address, day or night, for the cost of a local phone call.

Getting Set Up What do you need to be e-mail enabled? If you're working from home, you'll need a PC, modem and an Internet account (see Getting Access to the Online World later in this chapter). You must also have an e-mail program (which your Internet Service Provider (ISP) will supply you with) and an e-mail address (issued by your ISP). Something else you'll need to know is your username and a password. These allow you to keep the contents of your mailbox private—though not impenetrable. Of course, you'll also need to know the e-mail address of the person you want to send your message to.

> **CYBER TIP** Your Internet Service Provider will usually include an e-mail reader (program) as part of the package. If you want a different e-mail reader, you can always download trial versions for free from the Internet. Qualcomm's Eudora is a popular mail program. A free version can be downloaded at **http://www.eudora.com**. Netscape now includes an e-mail program as part of its browser. You can download a free trial version at **http://www.netscape.com** (try version 3.1 or higher).

Understanding Your E-mail Address Your e-mail address will have the following structure: name@domain. The *name* is your user name (e.g. mswartz or mark), and the *domain* is the address of the mail server (typically that of your Internet Service Provider). You can always tell the difference between an e-mail address and a Web site, in that e-mail invariably has the @ (pronounced as "at") symbol somewhere in the middle and Web sites don't.

Getting Your Mail—The Technical Explanation Downloading mail that you get from other people is pretty straightforward. Just for the fun of it, I'll start with a brief technical overview of how it's retrieved. First you need to enter your POP mail server (where all mail for you is stored). Two commonly used meanings of POP are "Point of Presence" and "Post Office Protocol." A Point of Presence usually means a city or location where a network can be connected to, often with dialup phone lines. Post Office Protocol refers to the way that e-mail software, such as Eudora or Netscape, gets mail from a mail server.

Most mail clients encrypt your username and password, so they are not readable to unauthorized people. To make this work, you first have to configure your e-mail client. That means filling in the details about your e-mail address and, depending on the program you're using, your real name, company, etc. Be sure to specify your e-mail address correctly. Otherwise, responses won't reach you!

CYBER TIP Your password and username should be words that you will easily remember. At the same time, don't make them so obvious that anyone can guess them. This is especially true if you're working on a shared PC (such as a network at the office or home computer used by more than one person).

Getting Your Mail—The Non-Technical Explanation To get new messages, you need to go online first (that is, boot-up your PC and log on to your Internet connection). Once this has been done, you can call up your mail program. (Note: some browsers do this for you automatically.) Then you click on the "Get Mail" or "New Mail" icon.

The e-mail program does the rest for you. It logs in to your POP server, trades usernames and passwords, and downloads any new mail on to your hard disk. Depending on your mail service you will see a status message during this process saying how much mail is on your server and the header for each message. You then click on the message you want to read and...voila!

Sending New Mail Composing an e-mail message is much like creating a regular letter or memo. The difference is that you can send your message across the city—or across the globe—in the blink of an eye. Depending on the program you have, you may be able to type in your message offline (when you are not plugged in to the Net). I prefer this approach because it gives you time to draft and edit before you have to send the message.

Make sure that you fill out the address information correctly. You'll be asked who you're sending the message to, what the subject is, and if there are any attachments. Note that your subject line is very important. It is often the first thing displayed in the mailbox of the person you've sent the message to. Keep it concise and accurate. Having said that, there's nothing wrong with an attention-getting header. Just keep it short, relevant and try not to offend anyone.

The procedure of connecting to your server and uploading your mail is automated by your mail reader. Once you've made your Internet connection, you only have to tell your client to "Send" your new mail. Normally there is no delay. The message is uploaded to the SMTP (Simple Mail Transfer Protocol) server, which sends it right away. It may take a few moments to reach its destination, depending on the size of the message, attachments (if any) and the routing involved.

A Word Of Warning Sending an e-mail message is very easy. Almost *too easy*, in fact. I used to do some teaching at a local university. One day a fellow instructor received a heated e-mail message from one of his students. Understandably distressed, the instructor wrote a hasty reply. The next day, he realized that there was actually some merit to what the student had said. Too late for the instructor, though. Now the student had a permanent record of this faculty member's angry response.

Fortunately, this incident stopped there. But imagine the possible consequences. The student could have made a hard copy of the reply, and sent it to her friends (or even to the president of the university). And it wouldn't have taken much to forward the message online to every single student and faculty member. Think of the potential damage to the instructor's reputation.

Exercise Discretion My point here is that it takes no time at all to compose—and send—an e-mail message. Compare this to a regular letter, where you generally prepare a draft, edit for accuracy, then print a good copy, stick it in an envelope, affix a stamp and physically deliver it to a mail box somewhere away from your home. To me this added time is not necessarily a bad thing. It helps us to make sure that we're communicating properly. We can think things through and check to see that we're saying what we want to say. E-mail lets us circumvent that process. My advice, then, is pretty basic: use discretion when you're thinking of hitting that "Send" button on the spur of the moment!

REAL LIFE *You may find that people send you e-mail written in an informal style. They may get lazy with their sentence structure, or they might not have taken the time to spell-check.* ***Don't be lulled into a false sense of security by this.*** *The e-mail that you send is the same as any of your other formal business correspondence (e.g. memos and letters). Take time to check spelling, grammar and content before you press the "Send" button—your professional image rides on it!*

The Look of Your Message E-mail expert Kaitlin Sherwood has some interesting advice. According to her, "words on a computer screen look different than on paper, and usually people find it harder to read things on a screen than on paper." Some people actually go so far as to print out their e-mail just to read it! There are implications to this timely reminder, in terms of how you put your e-mail message on the page. Remember that resolution on the computer screen is not as good as on paper. Sometimes there is a flicker, or the font may be too small or just plain ugly. This can detract from your message.

Your recipient's mail reader may also impose some constraints upon the formatting of the mail. For instance, some programs that read mail do not automatically wrap the text (adjust which words go on which line). In addition, the mail may be read in a document window with scrollbars. While scrollbars are nice, it makes it harder to visually track long paragraphs. All of this means that an effective e-mail page layout may be different from that of a paper document.

Tips for Improving the Appearance of Your Message To help make your message more readable, consider the following hints:

- Break up your paragraphs to only a few sentences apiece.
- Keep line length under seventy-five characters long.
- Use concise, clear prose instead of big words and elongated sentences.
- Use headers where appropriate to break up your paragraphs.
- Keep the overall message as brief as possible.

Sending Attachments with E-Mail Many mailers support *attachments,* where you can send along a document (or even a binary file, such as a computer program) with your mail. If your correspondent has a mail reader that can handle attachments, this works very well. The file can be opened at the convenience of the reader, in exactly the format that you sent it.

In some ways this is better than a fax. When you send your e-mail message, it gets stored in the reader's mailbox until he or she is ready to open it. With a fax, the message is there for everyone to see. Plus a fax won't go through if the recipient's line is busy. This never happens with e-mail. You can also send your e-mail to anyone who has e-mail access without incurring long distance charges, even if they're halfway around the world. Try that with a fax!

How This Comes in Handy Best of all for work-searchers, you can now send more than just text via e-mail. With the advent of an Internet protocol called Multipurpose Internet Mail Extension (MIME), you can also send formatted documents, photos, sound files, Web pages and video files as attachments. That means you can send your fully-formatted Word or WordPerfect résumé to potential employers, if they are equipped to read it.

MIME and other protocols (such as Uuencode) use a complex mathematical formula to convert files to text and then back to their original form. This conversion process is known as *encoding* and *decoding*. (By the way, don't confuse encoding a file with *encrypting* a file. Encoding a file adds no security. Encrypting changes your data so that only those with the right decoding software can read your file.)

Formatting Is Important One choice you're still given is to send the document "as is" (meaning in its original format) or as a "plain-text" file. When you send a file as is, you are retaining the exact formatting of the document. However, your recipients must be able to decode the file at their end. Plain-text, on the other hand, converts your file to the American Standard Code for Information Interchange (ASCII). This takes out any fancy formatting such as bold lettering, underlining, bullet points and centering. It does, however, make your file readable no matter what type of computer or e-mail reader your recipient has (more on this in Chapter 5, Sending In Work Applications Electronically).

Discussion Groups Via Usenet

In addition to sending messages to specific people, e-mail lets you communicate interactively with other Internet users. The means of doing this

CYBER TIP Before you send attachments, make sure you know what kind of files your recipient can handle. If, for instance, you send a WordPerfect 6.0 or higher document in its original format to someone who only has Word (say, version 6.0 or below), they will not be able to open or read the file. Refer to Chapter 5 to get details on proper formatting of attachments (e.g. when to use ASCII and how to cut and paste on an Internet form).

is through *discussion groups*. These are areas on the Net where people exchange messages about a particular subject. The part of the Net where you'll find many of these areas is called *Usenet*. The discussion groups themselves are called *Newsgroups*.

A discussion group is like a virtual coffee house. If you're the shy type, you can hang back and read what others are posting without responding. This is called *lurking*. Or you can actively post a reply to existing messages. You can even create a brand new topic (called a *discussion thread*).

There are literally thousands of newsgroups covering virtually every topic imaginable—from careers to cucumbers. Career-related Newsgroups often have job postings and self-employment opportunities, as well as advice.

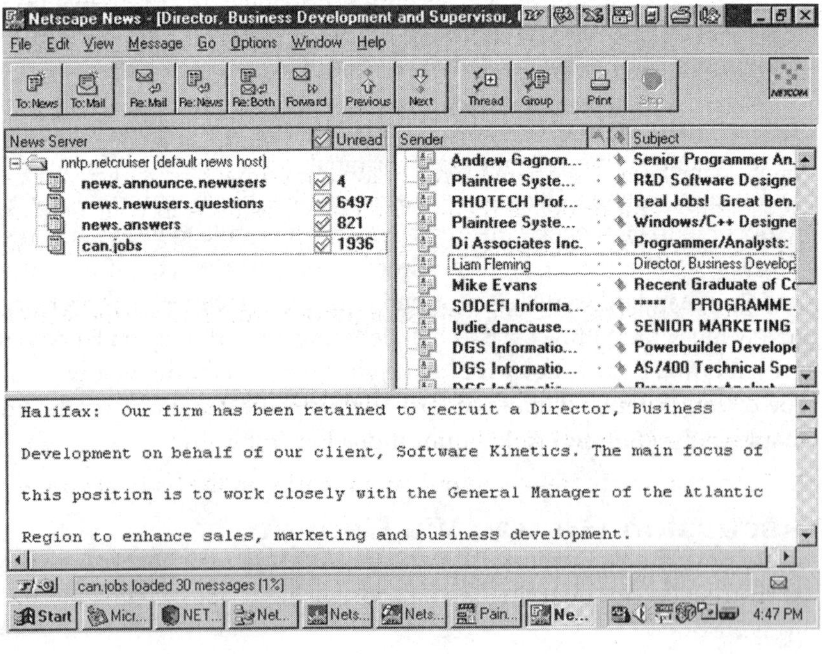

The great thing about Newsgroups is that anyone can participate in them, though not all Internet Service Providers offer access to every Newsgroup. How do they actually work? First you'll need a newsreader program. Your Internet Service Provider will likely provide you with one. If not, Netscape Navigator 2.0 (and higher versions) comes with a newsreader program built in. Next, determine which Newsgroups interest you. Bear in mind that there are so many of them that you will only want to choose the few that really interest you (a few relevant ones are listed in Chapter 8).

You subscribe to (join) a Newsgroup by following the instructions that come with your newsreader. Taking part in discussions requires a certain flair, so you might want to read the section on Netiquette in Chapter 8 to make sure you get off to a good start. Keep in mind that newsgroups used to be the only way to have so-called threaded discussions on the Internet. Today, you can also find discussion groups on a number of Web sites located on the World Wide Web. These are referred to as forums.

Automatic E-mail Notices from Listserves Since we're on the subject of e-mail, one more thing that might interest you is the *Listserve*. This is a mechanism which automatically sends you messages, via e-mail, once you have enrolled (or subscribed). A good work-oriented example is the JobSAT database containing thousands of job openings from across Canada. You access this service by signing up via regular mail, fax, e-mail or Web form.

When you register, you indicate what types of jobs appeal to you in specific geographic locations. Then you receive notification of jobs meeting these criteria. They come directly to your e-mail box, where you can read, store, print or delete them. When new positions in your field are input into JobSAT's database, they are automatically forwarded to your e-mail box.

Getting registered is relatively straightforward. Here are the steps to follow to enroll via e-mail:

1. Send an e-mail to JOBSAT@TOR.HOOKUP.NET.
2. Leave the "Subject" field blank.
3. Enter the word "Help" (no quotation marks) in the body of your e-mail.
4. Retrieve the Help File when it is sent to your e-mail box. Follow the instructions for querying the database using proper commands and syntax.

Untangling the World Wide Web

Once you've got the hang of e-mail, it's time to go surfing. The *World Wide Web* (also known as WWW or the Web) has been described as a wide-area hypermedia information retrieval initiative aiming to give universal access to an ever-expanding series of documents. How exciting!

Alright, so it sounds like techno-babble. What the Web has actually done though, is nothing less than spectacular. It has provided computer users worldwide with a way to access a variety of media in a simplified fashion. Using a popular software interface called a browser, the Web has changed the way people view and post information—it has created the first true global hypermedia network.

How the Web Works Web pages are really just files stored on computers (called servers) located all over the world. The Internet is actually known as a *client-server* system. Your computer is the client, and the Web site publisher's computer is the server. Here's an example: one of the great Canadian career sites is CanWorkNet. When you browse their Web site (**http://www.canworknet.ca**), and you request a page from their

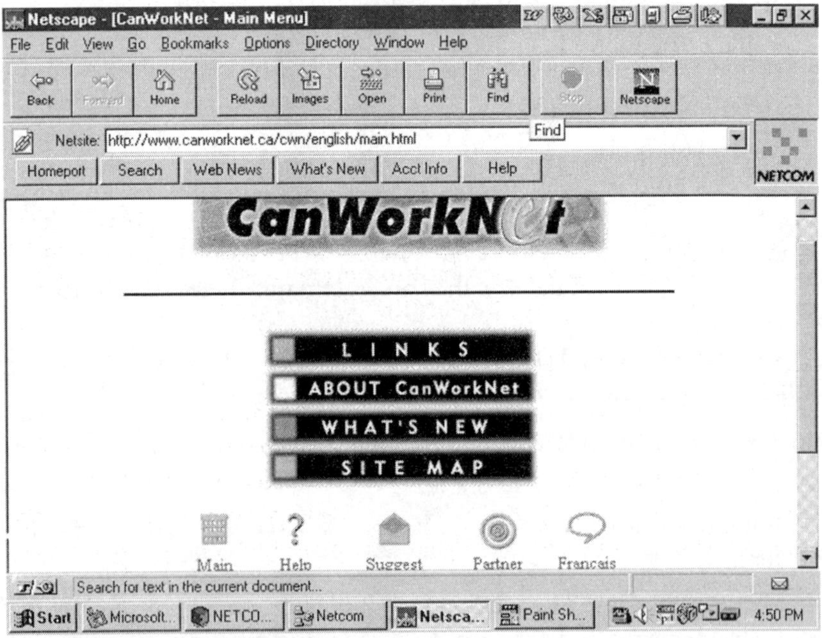

server in Ottawa, the server that is hosting the CanWorkNet site sends the page over the Internet to your computer. Since this Web site has links to hundreds of other career-related resources, you can click your mouse and be in Banff or P.E.I., even Chicago or Norway!

How to Get Hyper The glue that holds the Web together is called *hypertext* and *hyperlinks*. These features allow files on the Web to be connected in a way that lets you easily jump between them. Hypertext is basically the same as regular text. It can be stored, read, searched or edited. There is, however, a critical distinction: hypertext contains encoded connections that can automatically transfer (or link) you to other related documents. This is commonly known as browsing or surfing the Net.

Hypermedia is hypertext with a difference. Hypermedia documents contain links not only to other pieces of text, but also to other forms of media—sounds, images and movies. Images themselves can be selected to link to sounds or documents. Hypermedia simply combines hypertext and multimedia. An example would be if you're using a CD-ROM, and you click on a link that takes you on to the World Wide Web, where you click again to hear a sound clip of a typical job interview.

Just Browsing To be able to access the Web you need software known as a *browser*. The most popular among these are Netscape Navigator and Microsoft Internet Explorer. A browser is the graphical interface between you and all the data that is stored on the World Wide Web.

You generally get a browser with the software provided to you by your Internet Service Provider. Normally it will do everything that you need it to do. It should enable you to view all sites on the Web, access Newsgroups and Chat sessions and support technical developments like frames and Java (new ways to view the Web).

Upgrading Your Browser If you're not satisfied with the browser supplied by your ISP, you can easily get hold of a better program from a variety of sources. Netscape is available in a free trial version directly from the Web at **http://www.netscape.com**. Netscape is also available on diskette or CD-ROM from your local computer or software retailer. It costs about $49 for a licensed copy (which gives you access to technical support, if needed).

The nearest competitor to Netscape is Microsoft's Internet Explorer.

An early version of this browser is included free with Windows 95, and it can be upgraded at no charge on Microsoft's Web site (**http://www.microsoft.com**). While there are many more browsers available, you're better off sticking to the well-known ones when you're first starting out. That way you're assured that they can handle the newer protocols and HTML codes.

CYBER TIP When you download software from the Web (such as the Netscape browser), you are generally asked to select the version you require. It's always tempting to go for the newest, fanciest release. Keep in mind that the latest version often takes up more space on your hard drive and is filled with features that you will never use. Beware, too, of beta-test versions. They're fine for advanced users, but can crash and cause headaches for novices. Stick with the full release when possible.

A Million Channels, But What's Really On? As I mentioned before, the Web is a bonanza for career transitioners. It can help you at every stage from choosing a profession to preparing yourself for your marketing blitz, right up to locating leads for work. That's why it's become so popular with career professionals as well as people who are looking for employment or starting their own small business. The hardest part is finding exactly what you need, precisely when you need it (but then you knew that, otherwise you'd be surfing merrily away instead of reading this wonderful guide).

Where'd I Put That Address? I'm going to make a statement that sounds blatantly obvious at first. The simplest way to find information is to know exactly where to look for it. On the World Wide Web, this means having the correct URL (Universal Resource Locator) for the site you want to browse. A URL is a Web page's Internet address. It typically starts with http:// which means hypertext transfer protocol. Every page on every single Web site has its own distinct URL. That way you can call it up almost instantly with your browser when you're connected to the Net.

Something for Everyone This book gives you all sorts of specific Web addresses to browse. For instance, if you're a student who's just graduating from post-secondary studies, you'll want to look at The National Graduate Registry. It has a job matching service that's free to registered students. The URL is **http://ngr.schoolnet.ca**. For those of you still thinking about which career to pursue, click on over to Job Futures. There's info on all types of jobs and professions, including descriptions of the work involved, educational requirements—even salary forecasts. The URL is **http://hrdc-drhc.gc.ca/hrdc/corp/stratpol/jobs/english/volume1/alpha.html**.

If you happen to be someone who's worked for a number of years, and is currently thinking of changing jobs or careers, you can find a great deal of assistance on the Web. Government programs for work transitioners are outlined at places like Human Resources Development Canada (go to **http://ein.ccia.st-thomas.on.ca/agencies/cec/programs/hrdc_prog.html**).

It Keeps On Growing You can upload your résumé for around $25 (for six months) to the *Globe and Mail's* national job matching service. Get more details at **http://careerconnect.theglobeandmail.com**. And if you're considering self-employment, check out Canadian Business Service Centres for insights and related links. Try it at **http://reliant.ic.gc.ca/english/index.html**.

This is just a tiny sampling of Canadian career-related sites waiting for you on the Web. It doesn't begin to describe the quantity or range of information that is continually being added. You'll find company homepages, with descriptions of the employers you might just want to work for. There are databases containing details on the industries and sectors you'll need to know about. Interested in articles or press releases on specific organizations and people? They're available, if you know where to look. Even career counselling and personality tests are available online!

CYBER TIP If you're having trouble finding what you're looking for on the Web, try using a search engine or directory. They help you to locate information by using keyword searches, or searching by subject category. To get Canadian sites to show up first, try Yahoo! Canada at **http://www.yahoo.ca**, or Maple Square at **http://maplesquare.sympatico.ca**. For generalized searches, head over to Open Text (**http://www.opentext.com**) or AltaVista (**http://www.altavista.digital.com**).

IV. GETTING ACCESS TO THE ONLINE WORLD

To connect with the Internet, you have to sign up with a special service that plugs you in. It's not at all complicated. And your choices have never been broader. In fact, prices keep falling as service levels increase in this very competitive market. Here's what you need to know to get onboard.

Hooking Up at Home

Getting on to the Internet physically has never been easier. In terms of equipment, all you really need is a PC (minimum 386 processing speed) and a modem (minimum 14.4k baud rate). Of course, it's always nice to have the most up-to-date equipment. But you definitely don't need a Pentium Pro 200 processor and a dedicated ISDN (56 kbps) modem and phone line just to do career-related surfing.

The other thing you must have, of course, is a connection to the Internet. This is done by signing up with an Internet Service Provider. You need one of these because you can't just plug your modem into an outlet and be on the Net. (I have to be honest—that's precisely what I thought you could do when I first bought my computer.) First you must tap into a service bureau that's directly linked to the Net's trunkline. In essence, you're renting an Internet connection from the bureau when you pay them their monthly fee.

Finding An Internet Service Provider

Luckily, your choice of Internet Service Providers has increased dramatically. You can select a local provider if you feel comfortable doing so. There are also ISPs with a presence across Canada (and beyond). On top of this, there are full service providers, as well as those with limited features. Then there are the Commercial Online Services. They promote their own content in addition to giving you a gateway to the Net.

To actually find one (or more) of these services is fairly easy. You can start with your local phone book's yellow pages. Look up "Internet," then check for listings of Services or Service Providers. Make a few calls to see which service is best for you (some criteria to consider are listed below).

Buy It and Try It Another way to find a Provider is to go to the closest store that sells computer software. This could be a computer retailer, a software outlet or one of the business supplies stores that seem to be

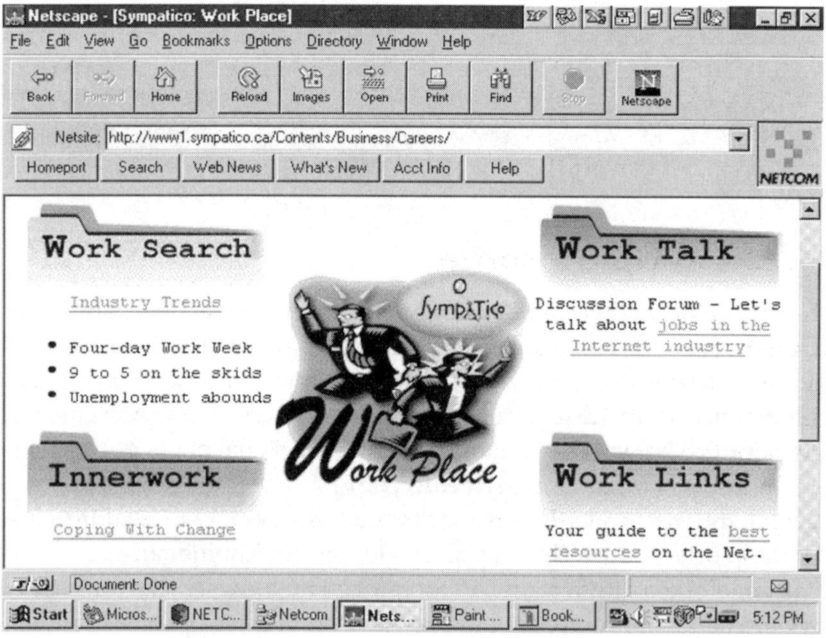

springing up everywhere. Survey the Internet section of the software display. You're bound to see two or three boxed versions of Internet access packages. With these, you'll typically receive software to get up and running, an instruction manual and a free trial period.

Free Trials Are Everywhere! There are even more ways to get start-up software from an Internet Service Provider. For instance, have you checked your mailbox lately? Some of the major Canadian and U.S. services send out free diskettes to households to encourage you to try them and sign on. Shrink-wrapped computer magazines often contain free trial diskettes as well.

Then, of course, there's always the online solution. If you already have a way of getting on the Net, surf over to "the list," at: **http://thelist.iworld.com**. It contains an incredible assemblage of ISPs, searchable by country, province or city.

Choosing the Provider that's Right for You

Your choice of Internet Service Provider should be driven by your intended use. One question you might ask of a potential ISP is if it offers a

REAL LIFE *Before making a long-term commitment to an Internet Service Provider, try a few out for free. Use trial diskettes or CD-ROMs and browse the services that are offered. A Sympatico Trial Kit has been provided for you in this book, free of charge. Load up the CD-ROM from the back of this book and explore the Net today! You can also order free Sympatico diskettes if you need them instead.*

full range of services. Do they give you true one-stop shopping? Can they supply software, manuals, training and 24 hour technical support in addition to the basic service? Can they provide local access connectivity across the country (that is, no long distance charges no matter where you hook up)? And will they guarantee a no busy-signal policy?

In terms of what to expect from your Provider, make sure that you get full Internet access. This includes your own distinct e-mail address, use of the World Wide Web and Usenet Newsgroups, minimally.

Some other nice features to look for? The browser that's included should be capable of reading frames, Java and HTML 3. Some Providers offer you free space to build your own homepage. That can be a bonus for self-employed people who want to promote their services online. (For job-seekers, it probably won't help you). Likewise with Internet Relay Chat (IRC)—it can be fun, but it's not very useful for people seeking work.

REAL LIFE *Nadia signed up for a flat rate Internet Service Provider which had a local dialing number. This meant that she could keep her computer hooked live to the Net as often as she needed. It cost her around $25 month, gave her e-mail and Web access, plus she never had to worry about paying overtime charges or long-distance premiums!*

Commercial Online Providers At the time of writing, there was still somewhat of a distinction between an Internet Service Provider (ISP) such as NetCom, and a Commercial Online Provider (COP) like America Online. That line may have blurred further by the time you read this. Both types of services give you a full gateway to the Internet. Commercial Online Providers have traditionally offered proprietary information as well. This means they've already gathered all sorts of resources and data that may not be widely available on the Net.

Here's what has happened lately. If you check out the Web site of some larger Canadian Internet Service Providers, for instance Sympatico (**http://www.sympatico.ca**) or i-STAR's TrueNorth site (**http://www.truenorth.net**), you'll see that they've been adding content as well. On the other hand, Commercial Online Providers—which used to be much more expensive—have tended come down in price. New, flat rate fees have made them much more competitive with the ISPs.

Despite the diminishing distinctions, there are still some Commercial Online Providers that stand out. The four biggest are all based in the U.S. Some of them have Canadian affiliates (such as America Online Canada) or Canadian content (like Compuserve). Here's who they are, along with their approximate worldwide membership:

- America Online: 7 million members
- Compuserve: 4 million members
- Prodigy: 1 million members
- MSN (Microsoft Network): 1 million members

Why Cheaper May Not Be Better Whether you choose an Internet Service Provider or Commercial Online Provider, make sure that it gives you what you require. Some things to watch for are reliability, user-friendliness, customer-support and simplicity.

The amazing thing is that the gap between the most expensive services (around $25 a month) and the cheapest services (around $15 a month) is negligible. There is, however, one big difference at the higher end that might justify the additional expense: you can be reasonably confident that your Provider won't go belly-up next month. That's a crucial consideration when you've emblazoned your e-mail address on your résumés. You want your address to be valid a few months down the road when it comes time for an employer to contact you online!

V. A FEW MORE WORK-SEARCH TOOLS

I've mentioned several times that *online* means more than just the Internet. As someone who is looking for work, you should at least be aware of the many electronic tools available. I touch upon some of the more helpful tools in this section. You'll find that they're described in a very general way. As the book progresses, I've integrated specific examples of how to use the tools into each chapter.

Computer Software and CD-ROMs

Computer programs that can further your career come in a wide variety of shapes and sizes. Some help you to market yourself, while others take you right back to stage one and let you figure out what kind of work you want to do.

To Market, to Market On the marketing front, you can now prepare professional-looking materials on your own. If you're a job-seeker, word processing programs enable you to put together everything from résumés to thank you notes. Then it's easy to track all the people you talk to, and the interviews you're generating, with a contact management program. The self-employed can create a business plan, brochures and business cards with inexpensive software. They can also keep track of all their customers with a database, and balance their books with an accounting program.

A Peek at Career Planning Online Beyond that, you can also get assistance with fundamental career decisions. There are CD-

ROMs that help you to evaluate your skills and interests. Based on your input, you're presented with potential careers that might appeal to you. Some CDs let you go so far as to explore all sorts of jobs and work options. Others show you how to interview and negotiate effectively—with video clips included! (See Chapter 3 for more details.)

Other Neat Devices

You should know that I don't really like the word *device*. It sounds so clinical. I only use it here because that's what a telephone, or fax machine, or information kiosk is: a mere device. Why then do they strike such fear into our hearts, especially when it comes to our career search? Maybe it's because they operate with such mechanical finality. Who among hasn't left a voice-mail message where, half-way through, we've stumbled or stammered badly—only to have our words recorded for eternity. And what about sending a fax? Press one wrong button in the phone number, and somebody in Tuktayuktuk may get to read the most intimate details of your résumé.

More than Meets the Eye If you can get over this natural reluctance, whole new vistas open up. It's pretty clear that the electronic age has arrived. So much career-related activity can now be done online. Want to send your résumé immediately and impressively? Prepare it with pre-formatted software, then e-mail it as an attached file. How about if a prospect calls to find out more about your new business? Let them order a brochure through voice-mail, or get one sent automatically (and instantaneously) by fax-back.

You can even upgrade your skills to train for a new career via computer. Distance education and computer based training (CBT) bring you the world. This can range from simple "how to" courses, all the way to fully accredited degree programs offered by virtual universities (more about this in the latter part of Chapter 3).

We've Only Just Begun... The possibilities are vast. As more and more technology becomes available and affordable, the potential continues to expand. Some of the upcoming trends for career management and work searching are outlined in Chapter 11, A Glimpse Into The Future. Things like video conferencing, super high speed Internet access and résumé tracking and scanning promise to reshape the work-seeking landscape even further. Until then, we've got our hands full just keeping up with what's already here!

VI. WIRED WRAP UP

Technology has definitely changed the way that we can search for work. Imagine conducting your career journey in the following way:

- Getting initial guidance and career direction in the comfort of your own home, via private Chat sessions on the Net.
- Checking out possible career directions through sites on the World Wide Web.
- Finding details on all the important companies in the industries you've decided to target, using a CD-ROM at the local library.
- Preparing your résumé and cover letter with pre-formatted, expertly-designed software.
- Networking electronically with people across the country to get leads and advice.
- Supplementing your proactive search by viewing advertised vacancies on kiosks at your Canada Employment (CEC) office, or on Web-based search engines that check newspaper career ads all across Canada simultaneously.
- E-mailing your application directly to the decision-maker.
- Leaving voice-mail messages that get people to return your calls promptly.

I wonder how all of this make you feel. Does it inspire you to go out and get started? Or does it just plain overwhelm you? Probably a little of both, if you're anything like me. Don't be surprised if you're starting to feel some resistance, too. For those of you without much experience (either at searching for work or with technology), the thought of all these new options can be dizzying. Even experienced work searchers get thrown off by the range of products, equipment and approaches available today. Keep in mind this simple advice: technology is not the only answer. Yet, it can assist us in many ways. Communication, information and education are a few of the potential benefits.

It's still up to you to do the hard part. Of course, technology can be instrumental in making your efforts more efficient. It can even give you a competitive advantage. But remember that a tool is simply a tool. The

Internet, software, a laser printed résumé—even an online career counsellor—is just something or somebody to aid you in your search and decision making process. You are the one who is ultimately responsible for the career choices you make. No machine (or career consultant, for that matter) can tell you what to do.

In summary, there is a huge (and growing) selection of software, CDs, office equipment, Internet options and other electronic resources to help you with your career search. Used in combination with traditional approaches, your search will become more effective. The rest of this book shows you how!

PART 2

PREPARING TO LOOK FOR WORK

CHAPTER 3

Planning Your Career Online

Virtual Definition: **backbone** (bak'bōn) *noun*

A high-speed line or series of connections that forms a major pathway within a computer network. The term is relative as a backbone in a small network will likely be much smaller than many non-backbone lines in a large network.

I. CAREER LESSONS FROM THE REAL WORLD

This chapter will get you started on the career planning process. It introduces a number of electronic tools and Web sites that can help you rediscover who you really are, and where you'd like to be. You'll also get a chance to embark on some career exploration. There's even an opportunity to find out how to upgrade your skills (if necessary). These tasks will set you on your way to selecting the work environment that's right for you. But first, a little story.

Wired...and Fired!

I vividly recall the first time that I got fired from a job. I don't have to tell you that it wasn't much fun. And the timing—just one hour after being let go, I had to go to my bank for a meeting with the loans manager. My wife and I had bought our first house just weeks before, and I had to sign the mortgage papers *that* morning.

The very first question the bank asked me was, "So where do you currently work?" Imagine how confused and helpless I felt. It's a good thing their vault was locked or else I'd have barricaded myself inside. My embarrassment was, shall we say, profound.

I Wanted Things to Be O.K. Later that day I had this overwhelming urge to restore things to their rightful place. I desperately fought the temptation to pick up the phone, call everybody I knew and try to find a new job—by the next day. The way I saw it, this would save me from having to tell my wife and family the bad news. It would also show people how in control I was (even thought I knew I wasn't).

Time for Some Basic Advice

There was just one little nagging detail. I had hated my job. Well, *hated* is probably too strong a word. But I was extremely unhappy and dissatisfied with my work. Getting fired, as shocking and disruptive as it was, turned out to be a huge relief. It made me realize that it was time to take a hard look at where I was in my life. There was also the rest of my career to consider (not an easy task, by the way, with the bank breathing down my neck). Fortunately, I had immediate access to some excellent career advice. As part of my severance package from the company that laid me off, I was given the benefit of outplacement counseling.

For those of you who haven't heard of outplacement, it's an industry that sprang up in the 1980s. It helps people who have been laid off from their jobs to make the transition to new work. Depending on the package, you get career counselling, assistance with résumé writing, feedback on your interviewing skills, work-search coaching—the whole nine yards. For me it was a lifesaver. I'm forever thankful to the folks at Drake Beam Morin, the outplacement firm whose lap I landed in.

"Tell Me About Yourself..." The outplacement consultant who worked with me was great. On our first morning together, he started with a deceptively simple question, "Tell me about yourself." Without hesitating, I proceeded to do so. I blabbered for about an hour straight. When I'd finished inundating this poor guy with my entire life story, I got up abruptly to leave. I figured the session was over.

"Wait," my consultant said to me. "I have an assignment for you." He reached into his desk and pulled out a sheet of paper. "When we meet next week," he continued, "I'm going to ask you the exact same question that I did this morning. Only this time, you will have just *three minutes* to respond." The expression on my face must have given me away. I thought the guy was crazy.

He then explained, "If you can't tell me about yourself in those few minutes, then you don't really know who you are, do you?" My expression softened. Now he'd piqued my curiosity. "And if you don't know who you are and what you're looking for, how can you begin to plan your next move, never mind the rest of your career?" He handed me the piece of paper and bid me goodbye.

You Mean, I Get Time to Reevaluate? I stumbled out of the consultant's office knowing my task wasn't going to be easy. I looked at the instruction sheet he had given me. It listed the information to include in my self-summary. I'd have to cover who I was, what I had studied (and why), where I'd worked, my main achievements and my future goals—all in less time than it takes to hard-boil an egg.

Something struck me as I drove home that morning: I hadn't a clue how to do what my consultant had asked of me. Of course I understood the premise of the exercise. And the instructions were clear enough. But I'd been so busy in recent years just trying to build my career and hold on to my jobs that I hadn't had time to reflect on important things like who I was or what I really wanted to be doing.

To help me prepare, the consultant had included a series of self-assessment tasks for me. I had to come up with a whole whack of details about my life. What were my strengths and weaknesses? List ten achievements of which I was most proud. What did I consider my strongest values to be? What factors in my work (if any) made me happiest? Which ones stressed me out the most? And the killer question: Where did I see myself in five years, ten years and twenty-five years?

II. WELCOME TO CAREER PLANNING

It turns out that the questions I listed form the basis of the career planning process. This really is the first step in preparing to look for work. It's all about rediscovering who you are, and finding out what career and lifestyle path is best for you.

I can tell you honestly that I was torn by this whole approach at first. On one hand, I wanted to rush right out and start working again. I mean, there were bills to pay and people who relied on me. Plus there was my reputation to think of. On the other hand, this was my first chance as an adult to get back in touch with what I really wanted from my career, and life in general.

Big Questions That Need to Be Answered

As it turns out, I tried to do both at the same time. Most of my days were spent frantically looking for work. But for at least part of the time, I gave some serious thought to the questions my consultant gave me.

My greatest inspiration, by the way, was fear. I was 28 years old with a spouse and mortgage. My friends were climbing the corporate ladder or establishing themselves as professionals; meanwhile, I still hadn't figured out what I wanted to be when I "grew up." Sure I had a general idea of what I enjoyed doing, but who on earth would pay me to do something I liked?

Hey, I'm Not Alone! My consultant at Drake Beam Morin worked with me patiently. I completed my exercises and began talking with some of their other clients (that is, people who also no longer had jobs). And you know what? I realized that, despite our different backgrounds and experiences, we had a lot in common.

Aside from being unemployed, we were all going through a similar process. Initially, every one of us was stunned and angered at losing our jobs. Then came a period of reflection. Some people felt stigmatized and ill-treated by their former employers. Others were delighted at being released from unbearable work situations.

Each of us was united by one overriding quest: to become once again gainfully employed. And while we may have had vastly differing objectives (on any given day I'd be sitting next to an ex-sales manager, a former vice-president of finance, or an aspiring actor), we were all using a similar, though customized, approach.

Inside Out We Go

The process that we were following is the one recommended by career advisors all around the world. We began by looking inside ourselves to see what was really there. This is known variously as *self-evaluation* or *self-assessment*. That's what we'll be doing—electronically—later on in this chapter.

This inward phase creates a foundation for your outward investigation of career possibilities. This is referred to as *career exploration*. You get a chance to check out a variety of work environments and determine which of them will match who you are. This could range from a job in a large company to being self-employed. I will examine this process with you further in the chapter as well.

REAL LIFE *Ideally, both self-assessment and career exploration should begin well before you decide what type of work you want to do next. This allows you to focus your energy as you prepare to market yourself—either for a job or in your own business. It also helps you avoid choosing work that's wrong for you.*

III. SEEKING PROFESSIONAL HELP

There's no doubt that rediscovering who you are can be exhilarating and liberating. It can also be exhausting and time-consuming. If you do it on your own, it's tough to see all the different perspectives. That's why I advise you to seek advice from a professional career advisor, in addition to any online exercises that you do.

Getting Good Counselling

Some people don't really know what a career practitioner does. If you fall into this category, you're not alone. I shudder when I think back to the guidance councellors I had in my early school days. One was a librarian who was given the guidance duties because the *real* counsellor had suffered a nervous breakdown. Imagine how useful this new, completely untrained person was in helping me to choose a meaningful career. (On the other hand, he did show me where some wonderful books were.)

A professionally trained career advisor can actually be of use in many ways. They can assist you in specific stages of your search for work or they can help you to plan and manage the entire process. You're the one who gets to decide. Table 3.1 outlines some of the ways that you could use a career advisor's services.

The Many Ways of Getting Career Advice

It used to be that if you wanted to get career advice, you'd have to travel to a career consultant's office to deal with them in person. The only other option was to buy a book on career management. Then you'd sit at home doing the exercises, isolated from any personalized feedback.

Table 3.1 How Career Counselling Can Help You

STAGE OF SEARCH	WHAT A CAREER ADVISOR CAN DO FOR YOU
Self-Evaluation	• Suggest appropriate exercises and career inventories to use • Work with you to interpret and apply results of inventories (like those described in this chapter) • Discuss personal issues that may affect your search
Career Exploration	• Direct you to specific careers for you to explore further • Suggest creative ways to learn about potential careers • Help you integrate your skills, values, personality and goals when choosing potential career options • Give unbiased reactions when you're deciding what to do
Creating Marketing Materials	• Review your résumé and cover letter before you send them out • Propose strategies to target your marketing efforts
Finding Work	• Give advice on networking and following-up • Prepare you for interviews • Refer you to other relevant resources, as needed • Provide support and motivation during difficult periods

Today you can find career consulting in a wide variety of formats. There is the traditional approach, that lets you work—one-on-one or in groups—with a real, live person. If face-to-face is not your thing, there are online methods too. These range from simple question and answer Web-based services, to interactive CD-ROMs, all the way to live chats with trained counsellors via the Internet. You can select the one that's right for you or mix and match to get customized advice.

What to Expect Although each approach differs in its level of detail and the scope of its services, there are some common features. You may be asked to do some written career interest tests. Then you'll probably review the results and create some ideas about your future.

Sometimes the methods may not seem very relevant. This happened to me when I went for my first meeting with a career consultant back in 1988. One of the tests she gave me was a small wooden puzzle. My task was to put it together as quickly as I could. I tried every trick I knew. Somehow the pieces just didn't seem to fit. After what seemed like an eternity (in actual fact, it was about four minutes), I threw up my hands in defeat. "What on earth is this supposed to be?" I shouted at my counsellor. Smiling, she calmly took the pieces in her hands and within seconds had put together a little wooden elephant.

The lesson here? She advised me (rightly so, as it turns out), to avoid work that required a great deal of hand-eye coordination. There went my dream of being a great brain surgeon!

The Traditional Approach to Career Counselling

Just as methods vary widely, so too can you find traditional career advisory services in many different settings. A lot of these are provided by government and not-for-profit agencies, while others can be found in the post-secondary school system, with more still offered by practitioners in the private sector.

College and University Career Centres An excellent place to begin is with a college or university that's nearby. Almost every single one has a career centre. They often provide a full range of occupational advice to their students and alumni. Many offer fee-based packages to the public as well.

You can quickly find out what's available at your local post-secondary institution by surfing the Web. Almost every college or university career centre now has its own Web site. For a full listing of these Canadian sites, go to **http://www.cacee.com/minisites.html**. This comprehensive page can link you directly to the career centre at the institution of your choice. It's maintained by the Canadian Association of Career Educators and Employers (CACEE).

Government and Not-For-Profit Agencies Traditional career counselling can also be found at Canada Employment Centres (CEC), through Human Resources Development Canada (HRDC). A full list of CEC and HRDC offices on the Net can be found at **http://www.the-wire.com/hrdc/o-hrdc.html**.

You can also get career advice from other government-sponsored programs, as well as not-for-profit agencies. For example, the Parachute Community Employment Centre offers career counselling services. These are described at **http://www.parachute.org.**

Private Career Counellors The private sector is full of consultants who can help you with your career decisions. Some are individuals who work on their own while others are employed by companies. My suggestion is to contact a few and find the one you feel most comfortable with. Because prices and services vary widely, it's best to shop around.

Of course, you could always pick up your local Yellow Pages and look under the Career Counselling heading. Then you can call several services to find out what they offer and how much they charge. This can be just as fast, or faster, than the Web route. But hey, it's not the *Wired* way, now is it!

CYBER TIP To find a comprehensive list of career counselling services in your area, go to Infospace Canada, at **http://206.129.166.151/categ/cancategory.html.** Scroll down the page to "Find This Topic." Enter the word "career." This will take you to the Career and Vocational Counselling section. Select a province and city, then click on "Search." Browse alphabetically. You can have your PC dial the phone number automatically (though believe me, it's faster to do it manually)—click the phone number to find out how.

Going Online for Assistance

Of course, you may want to try the services of a new breed of career counsellor. You won't find them in any phone book. Instead, they're prepackaged on CD-ROMs, hooked up to computers or even live on the Net. This new wave of counselling has some definite advantages (such as round-the-clock accessibility) and disadvantages (you miss the human touch). I'll describe a few of these online methods in this section. The simplest, most generalized approaches are discussed first, moving then to the more personalized.

Basic Questions and Answers On the simplest level, you can get basic answers to general career-related questions. This can be done via kiosk, or on the World Wide Web. This is not as strange as it sounds. Many of the concerns you have are shared by other people. It makes sense to provide responses that can be accessed quickly and easily.

One way to do this is to use an interactive machine called a *kiosk*. This is a touch-screen, computerized device which gives you answers to frequently asked questions. A good example is the Expert Counseling System by Acquired Intelligence Inc. The company describes it as "a friendly and effective way for you to examine your employment problems, and from a list of local resources it helps you address your employment concerns." It's being tested at the Saanich Human Resource Centre in Victoria, B.C. You can learn more about it online, at: **http://vvv.com/ai/counsel/ecs.html#ecs**.

Another method is to go to the Web, where you can sometimes send in your questions and get a free response from a career advisor. An example of this is **http://www.careertalk.com**, the site of Damir Joseph Stimac. He claims to be the Internet's first syndicated career columnist. On Career Talk, you have access to "an international network of career advisors [who] respond to individual job seekers' challenges."

If this sounds too good to be true, that's because it just may be. You can e-mail in a career problem that you have. But don't expect an instant reply. In fact, if you do get a response at all, it's posted directly to Damir's Web site. That way the whole world gets to read it. Not exactly the immediate, personalized attention that you need, but who can complain about a free service?

Affordable Software to Start Your Search

If you're looking for more depth, but don't want to shell out big bucks, you can try the prepackaged software route. At the lower end, there are several CD-ROMs that take you through the career planning process. Most of these sell for about $40 to $70 at your local software store, and tend to be produced in the U.S.

Note that in this range you're purchasing, essentially, a résumé creation package. Since they're on CD-ROM, they have plenty of room to hold self-evaluation exercises, overviews of various occupations and things like video clips of job interviews. Two good examples of this, and Web sites with more details, are as follows:

- Resume Maker Deluxe, from Individual Software Inc.
  http://www.individualsoftware.com/conrdc.htm
- WinWay Resume (Microsoft Exchange)
  http://www.winway.com/winway_resume_4.htm

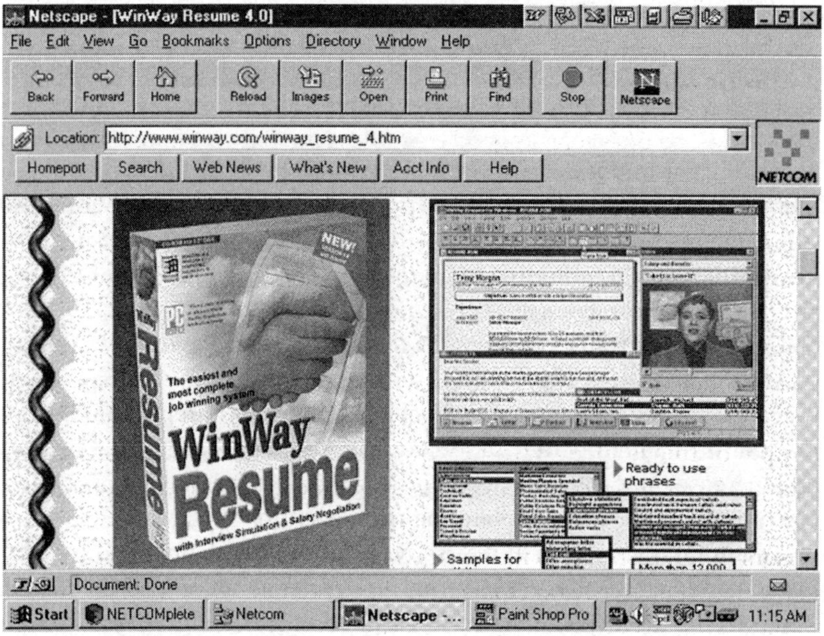

Upscale Software for Greater Depth At the higher end, you can spend from $100 upwards (make that *way* upwards). Here you get a program that is completely dedicated to career planning. I'll give you an example. Upsoftware, a San Francisco based company, makes Jumpstart Your Career. Users "sort through a series of job skills to find their favorites—for proficiency and enjoyment. Exercises afterward help readers understand how to maximize these skills." The suggested price is $99.95 (U.S.). Info and a free demo download are available at **http://www.upsoftware.com/jumpstart.html**.

CYBER TIP If you're really into the software scene, but want it at a low cost (or free), try one of the institutional products. These tend to be purchased by college and university career centres, high schools and employment agencies, which may let you use them on-site. Choices (for high school students and young adults) or Choices CT (for adults) are excellent. Produced by ISM Corporation, an IBM company, trial versions can be downloaded free at **http://www.careerware.com/prodcana.htm**. Also look at the similarly-configured Discover (or Decouverte in the French version), from ITP Nelson. You can learn more and download a free demo at **http://www.nelson.com/nelson/discover/intropg.html**.

The Combo Approach Up 'til now, I've talked about online products or services that, while useful, are lacking the human touch. To get more personal, you can stay with multimedia (if you want to), but add a personal dimension.

One such virtual experience is the Career and Personal Planning (CAPP) course offered through distance education. This course, which is geared directly towards high school students, gives participants "the opportunity to gain a better understanding of their professional futures and increase their confidence" by preparing them for the workforce and teaching the necessities of planning for the future.

When taking the CAPP course, your efforts are supported by connections to a counsellor and peers via telephone, e-mail and the World Wide Web. The cost of the course is around $350, and it even includes a work experience component. **http://www.etc.bc.ca/provdocs/careers/capps.html** is the place to go to learn more about it. It's offered by the Open Learning Agency, a Canadian online learning institution. Their Web site is **http://www.ola.bc.ca**.

Adults haven't been ignored here in PowerSearch, a "self-paced job transition program incorporating videos and audio cassettes, worksheets and an instruction book, quick reference cards and bi-weekly newsletters." This is further supported by 1-800 telephone counselling in situations where it's "impractical or impossible for the candidate to visit the company's offices." It can be checked out at The Focus Group Web site (a member of Career Partners International). The URL is **http://www.hr2000.com/cpi/focus/main.htm**.

More Personalized Equals More Expensive There are, of course, faster (and costlier) alternatives. What you get is a more customized and detailed package that you can do in the comfort and privacy of your own home. One such option is a live, one-on-one chat with an online career counsellor. This service is available on several of the major Commercial Online Providers (e.g. America Online, CompuServe, Prodigy and MSN).

A good example is the Career Center on America Online. Here you can access one of their confidential counsellors. The session is booked in advance with one of their advisors. At the appointed time, you meet online in a private chat room, and your exchange is done through keyboarding.

Convenience does have its price. To take part in one of these sessions, you must first have a paid subscription to the Commercial Online Service Provider. On top of that, counselling fees range from $50 to $100 (U.S) per hour and must be booked with a credit card. So while it's convenient, this may not be your preferred way to go.

REAL LIFE *The cyber-approach to career counselling can be incredibly convenient. However, nothing can replace live contact with a real human being. Making career decisions is of vital importance to the way you live your life. Do you dare trust that process exclusively to a machine? I suggest you use electronic tools to support your efforts, in conjunction with a trained career professional. That way, you've covered all the bases.*

IV. SIMPLE CAREER TESTS THAT YOU CAN DO ON THE NET

The stuff we just talked about covers the full range of career planning. If you're interested in looking at specific areas (e.g. reviewing your skills and aptitudes, or exploring new careers), you can also do this right now, on the World Wide Web. It's fast, simple and—quite often—free.

To take you through the process, I've split the information into two distinct, but related, sections. Part IV below shows you where to find self-evaluation material on the Web. This leads to Part V, which directs you to sites where you can move into the career exploration phase.

Benefitting from the Rest of This Chapter

I'd like to give you a brief refresher on how this book was meant to be used. Remember that it's *not* a conventional career guide. If it were, the next couple of pages would be filled with self-evaluation questions that you'd fill out using a pencil. Along with these would be a manual scoring system. That way you could compare your results to those of other people.

The Web Is the Way to Go This is where my book differs from what you might be used to. You can still use your pencil, but also be prepared to boot up your Internet connection.

For each aspect of career planning, I direct you to some relevant Web sites. In as many cases as possible, I've tried to point out resources that are (a) Canadian and (b) interactive. That means that you get relevant feedback immediately, and automatically, to help you with your career planning process. I found that many sites (but by no means every single one) on the Net give you this interaction. For those that do, the majority are free—for now. If they're not, I've pointed out how much they charge.

A Career Planning Starting Point

Let's begin with a general career planning site on the World Wide Web. There are many, but we can start with a simple one. The site I suggest you check out first is hosted by Charity Village. This Canadian not-for-profit organization is your link to other Canadian charitable and not-for-profit organizations. They have provided some useful material to start examining your career.

I'll point you directly to a lengthy questionnaire that will help you see where you currently stand. You can find it on their Web site at **http://www.charityvillage.com/charityvillage/caras.html**.

A few things to note here: to complete this particular questionnaire, you'll have to print it out first. Then you can use that pencil you've been

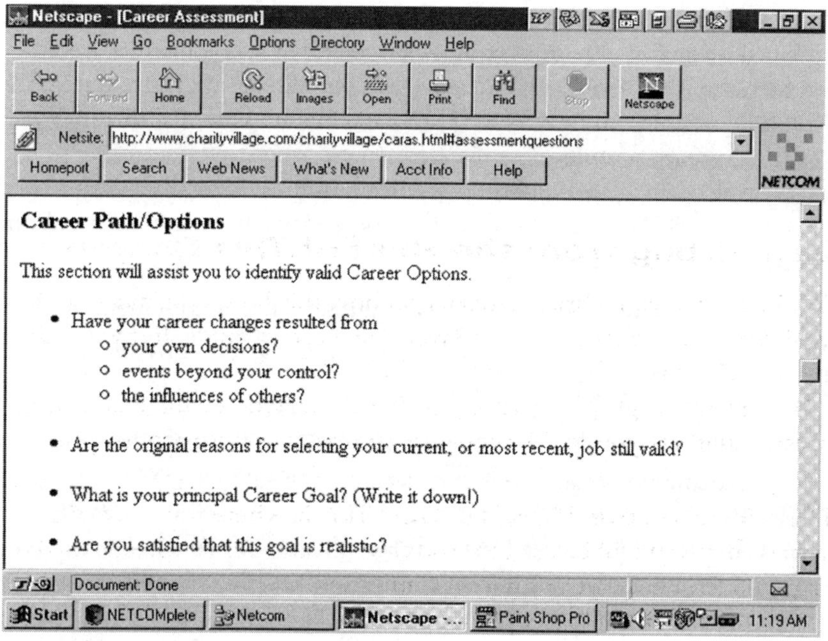

clinging to. Unfortunately, it's a static document. That means that once you've filled it out, it just sits there. You can't get online feedback to your responses. Despite that, it's as good a place as any to get your feet wet.

V. SELF-EVALUATION: THE CRITICAL FIRST STEP

The Charity Village site is a good general starting point. I recommend that you also look specifically at your strengths and weaknesses, likes and dislikes, plus your values and goals. That's the essence of self-evaluation. It can all be done—in distinct stages—online.

Going Back to the Future

Sometimes you have to start with the past in order to get to the future. It's like that with career planning. You need to clearly understand who you are, what you've done and the things you have to offer. Only then can you effectively plot your future.

Why Bother Reflecting? Let's not kid ourselves, though. The process of self-evaluation requires some effort, and a healthy quantity of honesty. You'll need to take stock of your career and life to date. This includes what you've achieved, and a realistic view of the value you bring to the marketplace.

The knowledge you gain here will be used in virtually every phase of your search for work. Here are just some ways that you'll benefit from your newfound insights:

- Knowing how to position your strengths for the employment market.
- Choosing a career and organization that truly suit your style.
- Putting together a targeted résumé that gets results.
- Creating dynamite responses to typical interview questions.
- Increasing your self-confidence and overall self-esteem.

So Much to Look at, so Little Time There are lots of areas to consider when doing a self-evaluation. Everything from past accomplishments to personality traits is fair game. To help make things manageable, career experts often focus on the elements outlined in Table 3.2.

Personal Strengths

Everyone has their unique strengths; however, not everyone is good at everything (in spite of what your mother may have told you). An im-

Table 3.2 Areas to Focus on During Self-Assessment

THINGS TO CONSIDER	WHAT TO LOOK FOR SPECIFICALLY
Personal Strengths	Highlights of your abilities and skills, knowledge and personal traits
Accomplishments	Things you've achieved, and what that shows about you
Interests and Values	What you like, love and hate in your work and personal life
Personality Type	Your moods, ideas and ways of seeing and interacting with the world

portant part of self-evaluation is determining what you do best. This will assist you in choosing an appropriate career. It also enables you to write a powerful résumé and present yourself well at interviews.

Strengths fall into four basic categories: (1) your *abilities* (things you do well); (2) *skills* (how you apply your abilities); (3) *knowledge* (using what you've learned) and (4) *personal traits* (what makes you *you*).

Abilities and Skills Are the Things You Can Do Your abilities generally include the things that you are naturally good at, such as the ability to run very fast, speak in a loud, clear voice or coordinate your hand-eye movements. While you may have to work at these abilities to improve them, they tend to be innate.

Skills are attributes that flow directly from your abilities. That is, you use your abilities in ways that help you to get along at work and in life. (If this all sounds a bit confusing, don't worry. The exercises I point you to next will clear it all up.) Skills come in many varieties. Here's just a sampling:

Leadership Skills

- Initiating projects and ideas.
- Confronting others effectively.
- Making difficult decisions.

Management Skills

- Setting and accomplishing goals.
- Contributing to team building.
- Using time effectively.

General Communication Skills

- Persuading people to adopt your point of view.
- Speaking effectively in public.
- Writing concisely and clearly.

VI. UNCOVERING THE REAL YOU—ONLINE!

Now would be a good time to boot up your PC. If you log on to your Internet service, we can start to explore some useful Web sites that will help you do a self-assessment.

Listing Your Skills and Abilities

Since we're already on the subject abilities and skills, let's jump right to the source. Type the following URL into your browser: **http://www.adm.uwaterloo.ca/infocecs/CRC/step1-skills.html**. You'll find yourself in the very heart of a virtual Career Development Manual hosted by the University of Waterloo Career Resource Centre. This is one of the few places on the Net where, for free, you can do a full-fledged career planning process online. (And it's not just for students!)

The particular page I've taken you to is all about assessing your skills. It lets you list the skills you think you already have, and identify the skills you think you *might* need in the future. This is the basis of a gap analysis. You identify the gaps in your existing abilities and compare them to the abilities required in your future work situations. Then you can go about getting the training or education you'll need to fill the gap.

CYBER TIP Whenever I suggest that you visit a Web site, I've given you the exact URL of a specific Web page. Due to the evolving nature of the Net, sometimes the site will have changed and you won't be able to download it anymore. If this happens, try going directly to the site's homepage, then seeing if the specific page you are looking for is still listed anywhere. Using the University of Waterloo as an example, you could try **http://www.adm.uwaterloo.ca** to see their complete table of contents.

Do You Know What You Know?

Knowledge is critical in our society. We obtain it in many forms and in many ways. Interestingly, it's been estimated that we only derive about 20 percent of what we know through formal education. This includes everything we soak in during high school, college and university courses or vocational training.

The rest we learn through informal means. This could be everything from on-the-job experience to volunteering, to everyday living and reading books, or even from watching T.V. (And to think I actually went back to get a second Masters degree when I should have been home watching Star Trek reruns!)

Knowing Is Different Than Doing It turns out that the old adage is true: it's not just what you know, it's how you use it (or something like that, anyway). Just knowing about a topic itself won't do you much good. You have to be able to *apply* the knowledge in a meaningful way. For instance, knowing that irreparable tissue damage can result from exposing your hands to intense heat is a good start. Not touching a stove when it's hot is even better!

Breaking your formal and informal knowledge into useful bits can be done at the following Web site: **http://www.adm.uwaterloo.ca/infocecs/CRC/step1-knowledge.html**. This page can really help you when you're putting your résumé together. The application of your knowledge will be substantiated by your accomplishments. You can also use this information to help point you in the direction of a career that's right for you.

Let's Get Personal

Personal traits are things we usually take for granted or downplay dramatically. That's because our society tends to value what you can do, not who you are. For instance, think back to your last job interview. Did the interviewer light up when you described yourself as a happy, loving person? Or were they snoozing until you mentioned that you're a workaholic who could single-handedly boost the company's sales by 632 percent?

Let's face it, we are in a fast-paced world with lots of roles and expectations to live up to. Usually when someone asks you to describe yourself, you answer in concrete terms. "I'm a student," you might say. Or "I'm an accountant who lives in Athabasca and I enjoy playing bridge." That tends to be good enough to satisfy the listener.

Can we clear away potential misconceptions right here and now? These superficial, role-driven answers are **not** sufficient for making career decisions! Here's something to consider: When was the last time someone said to you, "So, tell me who you *really* are?" not "Where do you live?" or "What do you do?" What are the qualities that genuinely make you *you*.

Honesty Is the Best Policy When faced with a question like "Tell me who you really are," most people freeze. We're so accustomed to answering in terms of who we think we're supposed to be, or who we'd like to be, instead of who we are.

In career planning, it's important to cut through all the external pressures and accept yourself as you truly are. I enjoy helping people try to get over this hurdle, though it's seldom easy. My clients often start out with ingrained images of themselves that are impressive and acceptable to the outside world. This often shrouds their true sense of themselves.

To Thine Own Self Be True One client I worked with initially characterized himself as a "hard working, get-things-done manager with a staff of 12 employees." Sounds pretty good, eh? Unfortunately, he was absolutely miserable. After many conversations and much soul-searching, this same person came to describe himself as "shy and highly emotional, with a strong desire to nurture and do good." *That's* the level of insight that can help you make the right life decisions.

To assist you in describing *who* you are (not *what* you are), go the following Web site: **http://www.adm.uwaterloo.ca:80/infocecs/CRC/step1-personality.html**. You'll find a list of traits to select from, and space to fill in examples of how you use these in everyday life. Whatever *your* personal traits are, they are vital to your happiness in the work and lifestyle that you select. They can also play a role in your job interviews. One of the basic questions an interviewer could pose is, "What are three of your strongest, and then weakest, traits?"

Accomplishments

The things that you've done in your past (those that you can mention in mixed company, anyway) can be very relevant for your future. Often your achievements tell a great deal about you. Maybe you were president of your high school class. Perhaps you've had one of your poems published in a magazine. Or maybe you've designed some new computer software or increased the sales volume at your last company. All of these things indicate abilities, skills, knowledge and personal traits that you've put into practice. Sometimes they even reveal things about you that you wouldn't normally see.

Showing What You're Capable of Doing An accomplishment is anything you've done that demonstrates your strengths. You can draw upon all of your past experiences, including your achievements from school, work, your personal life or outside activities (e.g. hobbies or social groups). What you're looking for in each accomplishment is:

- *What* you did.
- *How* you did it.
- *Why* you did it.
- *What* the results were.
- *What* you learned from this.

The results of this analysis will be used directly in your résumé and cover letter (see Chapter 4). They'll also assist you in selecting an appropriate career and work environment. If you'd like a guide on listing your achievements, go to the following Web site: **http://www.adm.uwaterloo.ca/infocecs/CRC/step1-achievements.html**.

CYBER TIP The Real Game is a computer program that helps students of all ages make career plans. It is being designed in several formats in conjunction with Canada's National Life/Work Centre. Read all about it at **http://www.realgame.com**. A version for adults, Learning a Living, is also being designed. Interactivity will be provided through SchoolNet.

Interests and Values

"What kinds of things do you truly enjoy doing?" That's another question you probably haven't heard lately, especially at work. I mean, can you imagine your boss coming up to you one morning and saying, "Lisa, you don't seem very happy here. Would you kindly tell us the role that you would like to play in our company? I will gladly adjust your assignment to fit with your expressed strengths and the things you enjoy doing most."

Ha! Nice fantasy, eh? Particularly when most of us are just hanging on to our jobs. Nonetheless, enjoyment and a sense of fulfillment are important, long-term career considerations. So, what *do* you enjoy most about work? Is it the work itself, the people or just the comfort of having someplace to go everyday? Do you find the work you've been doing satisfying? Or is it merely a regular paycheck? And what kind of work do you prefer: something unpredictable and creative, or stable and established? Do you like to work alone or in large groups?

Online Interests and Values Tests

These are some of the questions that you'll ask yourself when looking at your interests and values. They paint a picture of you in terms of the work environment that will best suit your needs.

To help make this picture more complete, career practitioners and psychologists have come up with a variety of tools. Most popular among these are *interest inventories*. Inventories are similar to tests, though they are very different in some important ways. In both cases, you're given a series of questions to answer. Unlike a test, however, an inventory has no right or wrong answers (and you don't get to study for it either).

The idea here is just to give your most honest, immediate response possible. The score that you receive is simply an attempt to measure how closely your skills, interests and values match up with people who are successful in particular fields. Getting a higher score has no correlation with being smarter or better than anyone else. All it means is that your tendencies are more pronounced in certain areas than others.

Web-Based Interest Inventories You can access several interests and values inventories via the World Wide Web. Here are some of the more popular sites:

Self-Directed Search (John Holland) The SDS is a "self-administered vocational interest inventory used in career exploration and selection based on John Holland's theory of personality types and work environments." It can direct you to possible careers for further consideration. It starts with your vocational interests, looks at your work environment preferences and then your personal values. The site is part of the University of Waterloo Career Development Manual at **http://www.adm.uwaterloo.ca/infocecs/CRC/step1-interests&values.html**.

A Homegrown Canadian Personality Quiz (Dr. James Sofia, Ph.D.) Dr. Sofia's Web site, out of Hawkesbury, Ontario, gives you a reasonably priced interest inventory that you can order online. By completing this assessment questionnaire, "you will have taken a constructive step toward learning about yourself, your vocational interests and how they compare to a representative group of people working in a variety of career areas." The cost is $49 and includes a personalized, 12 page report that you receive by mail. The results are based on a statistical analysis of your responses. Visit the Web site at: **http://www.hawk.igs.net/careers/**. Use this tool as a springboard for further inquiry and possible vocational guidance. It would be wise to consider additional sources of information such as your local employment centre, assessing your own skills, examining your values, speaking to a vocational counsellor or to a number of people with hands-on experience in your career choice area.

A Web-Based Values Inventory

The Work Values Arrangement List (VAL-OR) VAL-OR provides 42 of people's most commonly held values. According to this inventory, "Work Values come in two types: Cultural and Operational. Cultural Work Values define the purpose, character and direction of your career and work life. Operational Work Values are those values that you employ more on a day-to-day, short-term basis." The Web site can be found at **http://www.cweb.com/assessment/values.html**.

Personality Type

Each of us has a distinct personality. It consists of our beliefs, values, likes and dislikes, moods, thoughts, genetic disposition and learned behaviours. We can try to change it, flaunt it or hide it. The unalterable fact is that it's deeply rooted within us. Like it or not, this has a tremendous influence on the type of work and lifestyle that we gravitate towards.

They're just Theories, but... Psychologists and career practitioners have been trying for years to bring some scientific credibility to the realm of personality. One way they have done this is through research that segments people into specific *personality types*. There's a huge body of literature on this field. (See for yourself, at **http://www.brad.ac.uk/~mdavarle/faq-mbti.html**.) Still, the theories are just that: potential explanations for the way we behave.

Despite this lack of scientific certainty, doing a personality test can be an eye-opening experience. Keep in mind that they're not really tests, though. They're just another way to measure some of your personal traits.

What You Can Learn About Yourself Your answers can help show how you tend to look at things and how you generally go about making decisions. These can assist you in understanding where your special strengths are and what kinds of work you might enjoy and be successful doing. They can also show you how people with different preferences can relate to each other more effectively.

There are many personality tests to choose from. Some are more popular than others, but no single test can tell you how to run your life. Let me be even more emphatic about this. Personality tests are only one component of an overall career and lifestyle assessment. They should be used with caution.

The Myers-Briggs Type Indicator One of the most common and reliable tools for this is the Myers-Briggs Type Indicator (MBTI). This assessment is based on psychologist Carl Jung's theory of personality, first developed in the early 1920s. It assumes that specific personalities do better in particular careers.

The premise of the MBTI is that our personality can be divided into independent areas or scales. We have a preference for one of two opposites that define each scale. Each different combination defines a particular and unique personality. Sound complicated? It's actually easy to take the test and have it interpreted professionally.

Take a Mini-Test for Free A free, mini-version of the MBTI is offered by Polaris Associates. (By the way, I like their mission statement: "To increase knowledge and options and improve skills of adults and youngsters, by linking behaviors to personal values.") They let you download a pencil and paper test, which you complete at your convenience. You score the test manually with the instructions provided. Then you input your scores on the screen to get a brief printout of your personality. Find it at **http://www.cweb.com/assessment/person.html**.

You can also find the full Myers-Briggs Personality Test online. It may cost you some money, but it could be worth it. Check around and compare prices. Polaris sells a full version for $60 (U.S.). Ordering information is available on their Web site, at: **http://www.cweb.com/assessment/testinst.html#personality**.

The Me2 Personality Asessment Tool If you've got 30 minutes to spare, and you're up for a little entertainment, you might be interested in something called Me2. It's a personality test that bills itself as "the first WWW site which provides you with a tool dedicated to improving your ability to succeed by making you aware of how you invest your mental energy, the stuff that powers your mind." The creator claims that your success and happiness in life are absolutely dependent on becoming aware of how you invest your mental energy. They give you the chance to measure it and learn about it.

REAL LIFE ***Psychological tests should be administered and interpreted by professionals.*** *It's fine to get some preliminary insights from the test you find online but make sure that you check the results with a real-life, qualified career advisor—or you may do more damage than good! For an interesting discussion on personality and typing, try the Usenet news:alt.psychology.personality.*

Note that this inventory was *not* designed by a professional psychologist. Nonetheless, I found it to be fun and revealing. While you won't get the full results for free, you do get several pages of printout. That's enough to give you food for thought. It's at **http://www.me2.com**.

16 Personality Factor (16PF) This well known inventory provides reliable information to use in a job, company or career change event. "The two major areas of information presented are (1) Patterns for career activity interests and (2) Personal career life-style effectiveness considerations. The 16PF interprets personality influences on organizations and careers." The report deals with how people solve problems, cope with stress, interact with others, and match up with different occupational settings.

The 16PF Personality Profile is a 187-item inventory that reveals 16 primary and 8 secondary personality factors. For $60 (U.S.), you can order a five page comprehensive report with personality descriptions, occupational comparisons and vocational observations included in the profile. The URL is **http://www.wonderlic.com/ppspf.htm**. Detailed discussion of the 16PF can be found at **http://www.ic.ncs.com/ncscorp/level4/psych/adoles/sixtpf_5.htm**.

VII. EXPLORING CAREER OPTIONS

Looking inwards was just the first step in the career planning process. If you've used some of the tools suggested in the previous section, you should now have a pretty good idea of who you are, and what you have to offer. These insights are invaluable. They enable you to choose the appropriate career and market yourself to employers, in a very targeted way.

Now you need to decide what the *right* kind of work is. The way to do this is to learn all you can about what really goes in different career settings. Task one is choosing the type of career or job you really want. This is just as true if you've graduated recently and are unsure of the future, or are established in your career but are just plain unhappy with your work.

Seeing What's Right for You

Even if you're satisfied in your current career, you might be wondering what else is out there. Before jumping ahead, you owe it to yourself to investigate some options. Here's where career exploration comes into the picture.

Exploration allows you to do some important information gathering. It builds on all the self-evaluation that you've done. You can now ask such vital questions as: "What kind of work am I genuinely suited for?" "What do you actually do in this type of job?" "How much can I make?" "Should I start my own business instead?" And "Do I need more education to get into this field?"

Why Bother to Look Around?

I can guess what some of you are thinking, "Sure, I'd love to quit what I'm doing and find something I really enjoy. I'd also like to win the lottery and fly to the moon."

It's Tough, But It's Necessary The last thing I want to do is minimize the difficulty of choosing a career direction, or changing your current one. I did it when my wife was pregnant (on two separate occasions, actually, much to her annoyance). It was just about the hardest thing my wife and I ever went through in our lives.

I understand how impractical it can be to take time to look at a new career. We've all got bills to pay and obligations to uphold. The pressure of keeping things afloat can be enormous. But look at it this way: you've got the rest of your working life to deal with!

Your Career Lasts a Long, Long Time Let's assume, for argument's sake, that you'll retire at age 65. How many years of work does this leave you with? 10 years? 25 years? 40 years or more? If it seems like a long time, that's because it is. Therefore, it really is important to find the type of work that you'll enjoy and do well at. This section of the chapter is all about doing just that.

Investigating What's Out There

You can identify potential careers and jobs that interest you with the help of a career advisor, through interest inventories or from your own experience. What you don't want to do is to waste your energy searching in every possible alleyway. By the same token, it would be a shame to miss out on something that might be a potential fit.

Once you've selected a few occupations to investigate, it's time to learn all you can about them. Only then can you prepare your marketing materials and target particular companies. We take a detailed look at that in the next few chapters.

REAL LIFE *If you're already in the workforce, you may want to consider exploring your career options while keeping your current job. This is highly recommended when you can't afford to make sudden changes. While staying in your current career, you can upgrade your education or moonlight in your chosen field (part-time for pay or through volunteering). This way, you can continue to earn an income, build your experience base and create a bridge towards future change.*

Getting to the Nitty-Gritty

For now, you'll want to discover if the potential careers or jobs you've identified are truly right for you. There are lots of unknowns that need to be addressed. Here's a list of some of the main questions to investigate when you're considering a particular career:

- What does the work involve on a day-to-day basis?
- Are there any special educational requirements?
- How do starting and mid-point salary ranges compare to other careers?
- Will it allow me to have the kind of lifestyle that I want (e.g. hours of work, location, stress levels, salary and benefits, security)?
- Is the work itself in line with who I am (e.g structured vs. non-structured, creative vs. predictable, independent vs. team-oriented)?
- What are the best and worst parts of this type of work?

Gathering Information

There are some tried and tested ways to find out about different careers. You can always go to the library and read about them in books on careers, occupation guides or industry trade publications. You can also learn about them on career-related videos, available through school and community employment centres or at your local library. Or you can meet with people who work directly in the field that you're investigating. This is done by means of information interviews (more about this in Chapter 8). You can also try to arrange job shadowing and volunteer apprenticeships, where appropriate.

Online to the Rescue Then you have the electronic methods. Probably the best place to go for this is the Internet. You can start directly at the premiere site for occupational descriptions in Canada: JobFutures. This informative Web site is hosted by Human Resources Development Canada. It includes full outlines of 211 occupational groups covering pretty well all jobs available in Canada. Information on each occupational group includes:

- Job duties and responsibilities.
- Types of employers who hire workers in the group.
- The level and type of education, training and experience required of workers in the group.
- Main labour market characteristics of the group.
- Current prospects of finding work in occupations in the group.
- Job prospects for the next five years.

It's all at **http://hrdc-drhc.gc.ca/hrdc/corp/stratpol/jobs/english/index.html**.

Way to go, HRDC!

On the U.S. side, there's a similar collection called the Occupational Outlook Handbook. It's located at **http://www.jobtrak.com/jobsearch_docs/occhandb.html**. The Handbook describes about 250 occupational groups in detail. This covers about 104 million jobs, or 85 percent of all jobs in the United States. Much of the information is relevant in Canada, too.

Let's Talk About the Bucks Salary information is a little harder to find. Be watchful for median salaries that may not give a true indication of what you can really expect to earn. Your work experience, em-

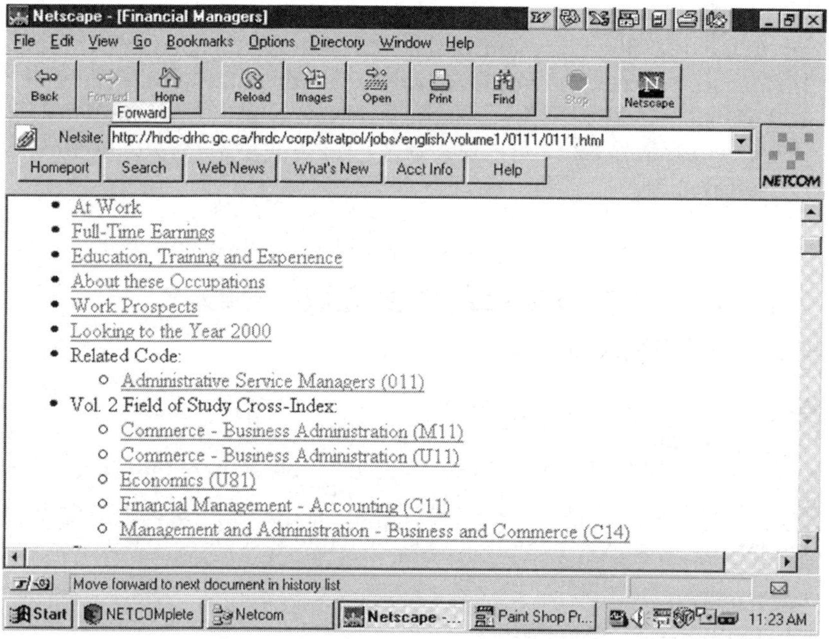

ployability and regional situation will have a major bearing on this. Having said that, try out the *salary assessor* from the Economic Research Institute. You'll find it at **http://vii.com/~rtuengel/cgi-bin/salary.cgi**. It gives you "consensus salary medians and adjusted estimates for many different positions as compiled from various wage and salary surveys." You can also download some free demo software for their more complete database at **http://www.erieri.com/~eri/demodnl.htm**.

Thinking of Relocating? Wouldn't it be nice to work on a quiet tropical island, surrounded by deep blue oceans and the gentle breeze of an eternal summer? Well, stop dreaming—it ain't likely to happen. For most of us, the prospects are somewhat more ordinary. (How does a nice little bungalow in Nippising sound?)

If you *are* considering a geographic move, there are lots of resources available. One terrific Web site is City.Net. It's at **http://www.city.net** and has just about everything you'd want to know about virtually every major city in the world (and many not-so-major places, too). Links to local employment opportunities, chambers of commerce, industry associations and general information can all be found here.

There's even a way to compare the potential salary that you'd need to earn in the new city. Once you've selected a city or town, go to The Salary Calculator. It takes what you currently earn and shows you what you'd need to make in the new destination, based on cost-of-living and real estate price differences. Pretty neat, eh? Find it at **http://www.homefair/cmr/salcalc.html**.

VIII. UPGRADING YOUR SKILLS AND KNOWLEDGE

We've already come a long way in this chapter. I hope that you're gaining insight into the type of work that you really desire. Along the way, you may have discovered that you need to acquire new skills or more education. Some fields require you to have a specific degree. Many others assume that you already possess skills and knowledge specific to that area.

Retraining Options

You'll learn about these requirements while you explore different careers. But what about the actual skills upgrading? Does this mean that you have to go back to school as a full-time student? It may, in some cases. This would only apply, though, to those of you who are switching careers and need a full degree to do so. For instance, you might be working in a bank but you'd much rather be a lawyer (though for the life of me, I can't figure out why). Then again you might want to move into early childhood education or plumbing.

Alternatives to Traditional Schooling Even if you do need a full degree or diploma, you may not have to strap on your knapsack and trudge off to a classroom (tough to do when you've got a kid or two depending on you at home or if you live in the boonies). More and more college, university and vocational programs are being offered electronically.

In fact, Statistics Canada estimates that more than 400,000 Canadians were enrolled in some type of electronically-delivered course in 1994. This evolving mode, known as distance education, takes several forms. There are courses from the World Wide Web, through T.V., over the radio and on CD-ROM.

How Distance Education Works

Learning from afar generally translates into a home-study program. You typically use a variety of resources as educational tools. This can include well-established things like textbooks, workbooks and audio-tapes. (Anyone remember ICS? From a matchbook cover, you could enroll to learn about everything from truck driving to being a medical secretary.)

Nowadays you're just a likely to get your course delivered over the World Wide Web. This gives you hyper-linked text, full audio and graphics. Even video is becoming standard course fare, as Internet speeds increase.

With electronic learning, you get your instruction from a teacher that you'll probably never meet in person. Then your assignments are evaluated by a grading assistant that you'll never see. This can be disconcerting for some, and liberating for others. It all depends on your learning style and social interaction preferences.

Keeping in Touch Online To reduce the possibility of experiencing cabin fever, a number of online schools offer a link to one or more live humans. There could be a phone or e-mail connection with a tutor, and opportunities to talk to other students. Several programs are offered with computer mediated communications support, such as teleconferencing or Internet Chat.

One thing that's made this whole concept more attractive is the ease of signing up. You can frequently enroll in a distance education course online. The faxed application has been with us for years. Now it's possible (in some cases) to fill out a Web-based form, linked directly to the institution's registration office. Talk about virtual convenience!

The Positives and Negatives of Learning Electronically

Before we look at some examples, you should know that there are both advantages and drawbacks to these methods. It's mostly a tradeoff: convenience versus face-to-face human contact.

The Advantages of Online Education The upside of electronic learning, as I mentioned earlier, is heavily weighted to convenience. Here's what I mean:

- In many cases, you can learn about *what* you want, *when* you want to—all without ever having to leave your home.
- The selection of courses and degree programs is expanding all the time.
- You often have the freedom to go at your own pace. That means you can learn at your natural speed, instead of the tempo dictated by a teacher.
- Usually you can start at any time of the year. Thus you don't have to wait until the normal back-to-school periods (e.g. September, January, April or July).
- A growing number of distance education courses qualify for credits or certification. These range from high school diplomas to college certificates, all the way to university degrees.

Drawbacks to Online Education As with just about every new technology, there are some downsides too. With distance education you don't get the benefit of immediate group interaction that you'd find in a classroom. This can have a pretty strong effect. Many people thrive in a classroom setting. The ability to exchange ideas and interact with others directly (and throw little crunched up wads of paper at the teacher's back when they're busy writing on the board) can greatly enhance the learning experience.

Some people argue that distance is no longer a barrier. They claim that video conferencing, phone tutoring and computer networking are starting to eliminate the perils of remoteness. No doubt there's some validity to this line of thinking. What you can't get around is the fact that people are generally motivated and stimulated in the presence of other people. You just don't get that with your Pentium laptop!

Reliance on technology may also mean that you have to spend a large chunk of change just to get the equipment. A computer, modem and software are the minimum requirements to take a course via the Internet. If you have to buy it all from scratch, the price can add up quickly. Not to mention that if your equipment breaks down, you're stranded.

Where to Find Courses Online

For those of you who decide to take a course electronically, there are some excellent educational facilities in cyberspace. One is Athabasca

University, which bills itself as Canada's online university. It's at **http://www.athabascau.ca/html/info/au.htm**. The school offers full bachelor degree programs in arts, general studies, science, administrative studies, commerce and nursing. They even have Masters programs in business administration (MBA) and distance education (MDE). A number of certificate programs are offered as well.

Another Canadian cyber-education institute is The Open Learning Agency. This is a "fully-accredited, publicly funded facility providing a wide range of formal and informal educational and training opportunities for learners around the world." The Open Learning Agency is located in Burnaby, British Columbia. Its Web site is **http://www.ola.bc.ca/ou/ou.html**. There you can see full course descriptions, prices and enrollment procedures.

The Old Reliable Ways I haven't even touched touch upon some of the other possible teaching methods. You can still do televised courses in some areas. The Knowledge Network in Alberta and TVOntario stake their livelihood on this. There are even radio-based courses offered by colleges and universities in some provinces. Of course, if you want to find out about them, you can hop onto the Web and check out your favourite educational institution to see what they're selling.

Investigating Traditional Schools and Courses

If you opt to go back to a regular classroom, cyberspace has not forsaken you. Most Canadian vocational schools, colleges and universities are listed on the World Wide Web. You can visit the site of just about any post-secondary school you'd like to know more about. Once there, you'll see course and program descriptions, departmental activities and overviews of the school itself.

You can start by heading to **http://watserv1.uwaterloo.ca/~credmond/univ.html**. This list includes all institutions that are members of the Association of Universities and Colleges of Canada, as well as a few other degree-granting institutions. Also, there are links to educational sites around the world. For technical and vocational schools and community colleges, sorted by province, try **http://www.sp.utoledo.edu/canctcol.html#ontario**.

Applying Made Easy Here's a feature you might want to know about. Some schools are providing centralized online registration facilities. This can simplify the application process—but you still won't get in if you don't have the grades! If you're thinking of attending university in Ontario, for instance, you can now go to a single site. The Ontario Universities' Application Centre (OUAC) processes applications for each of the nineteen Ontario universities. Their site is at **http://ouacinfo.ouac.on.ca/**.

At the time of writing, some other provinces were working on similar sites. They might be up and running by the time you read this book.

So It's Not a Ph.D. You're Looking For

For many people, getting another degree is *not* what's needed. Often skills and knowledge can be upgraded in a briefer, less formal manner. That's why there are so many workshops, seminars and non-credit courses available.

Locating a General Interest Evening Course That Meets Your Needs Finding evening and non-credit courses at your local college or university is fairly simple. Just access the school's Web site, and look for the link to continuing education (or non-credit) programs. If you like what you see, you can probably register right there on the Web or by fax. It's as easy as that. You'll probably get notified of your acceptance by mail.

The Hunt for Seminars and Workshops As for all the other workshops and seminars out there, finding them may not be quite so easy. As of this printing, only one province has assembled this type of information on one site. It happens to be Ontario (again). They've developed a comprehensive listing of non-credit courses including professional development, general interest and career-related topics. It's available at **http://www.trionline.com/search.htm**.

Computer Based Training (CBT)

It's apparent that education is expanding into new territory. Take a stroll through the software department of your local computer or business equipment retailer one day soon. There are virtually hundreds of CD-ROMs and software titles that are designed to teach you something.

The range is incredible. It stretches from hard skills (like basic computer skills) to *edutainment* (the combination of learning and entertainment), with almost anything else you can imagine. Want to learn how to read or type? Itching to better your math skills? What about gourmet cooking, losing weight or fixing your car? You can even learn a new language or discover ancient history via multi-media—all at your own pace, any time of the day or night. The dawning of the lifelong learning age has truly arrived.

IX. WIRED WRAP UP

Planning your career has never been easier. Today you can undertake a self-evaluation, investigate work possibilities and find out about education options—right in your living room (assuming that you keep your PC and modem there).

Information is easy to come by, and the tools that deliver it are more functional than ever before. All those electronic gizmos that used to seem so frivolous are becoming vital assets for career searchers (and practitioners too). Compare this to, say, three years ago. What were your perceptions then of the home PC, World Wide Web, e-mail and CD-ROMs? To me, they were expensive toys for computer-nerds, or experimental equipment that only big institutions could afford.

Now these gizmos are the tools of my trade. They have become an integral part of my career practice. My clients love it, once they surmount their initial fears of, or lack of experience with, electronics. They tell me that it's helped them tremendously. They are free to do some of the key career planning steps when it suits them best, in ways that meet their individual needs.

Yes, technology is taking the drudgery out of gathering information to help you plan your career. This creates wonderful opportunities to find the work that you really want, and engage in lifelong learning.

But before we go overboard here, let's rein ourselves in for a nanosecond. All these new tools, and the enormous fountain of information they bring us, can easily overwhelm us. We still have to sort through it all to ferret out the material that's relevant to *us*.

That's in addition to all the choices we now have to make, with old occupations and industries dying off, while new ones sprout up almost daily. Job requirements are changing rapidly. At the same time, the need for skills upgrading and education grows constantly. Even with all the available technology, a huge question remains: How do we know which decisions will be best for us in terms of career and lifestyle?

Happily, we still have humans to talk to. Remember that career decisions don't happen in a vacuum. They can affect virtually every facet of your life, so it's vital to get input from others. My advice is to involve people when you're feeling some uncertainty or just want to bounce ideas around. Talk to your family members. E-mail your friends to get feedback. And talk to a career advisor when it comes to the difficult portions. This, in combination with the new electronic tools, will help you to make the decisions that are right for you.

CHAPTER 4 Creating Marketing Materials Online

Virtual Definitior: **java** (jä'və) *noun*

Java is a new programming language invented by Sun Microsystems that is specifically designed for writing programs that can be safely downloaded to your computer through the Internet and immediately run without fear of viruses or other harm to your computer or files.

I. SOME THINGS NEVER CHANGE

Here's a familiar scene: You see an ad in the employment section of your newspaper that catches your eye. It looks promising. Your skills and experience appear to match what the ad is asking for. Moreover, the company is not too far from your home, and the salary looks reasonable. You call them right away to tell them you're interested. And what do they always say in return?

"Send us your résumé, and we'll get back to you."

You Can't Get Around It

So you're thinking of finding yourself a job. It could be a full-time permanent position (whatever *permanent* means nowadays), part-time, or maybe even a contract. The nature of the employment arrangement may have changed over the last decade, but the tools of the trade haven't.

You'll still need to put together a powerful résumé and covering letter as your primary marketing tools.

Getting Back to Basics This chapter looks at how to design and create conventional (non-electronic) self-marketing materials for your work-search. This includes:

- The different types of résumés and which one is appropriate for you.
- Cover letters and thank you notes.
- How to prepare dynamic business cards.

What You're Gonna Get Here

Let's get one thing straight from the outset. I'm *not* here to reinvent the wheel. Résumés, cover letters and business cards have obviously been around for many years. There are all sorts of excellent books out there on how to create conventional self-marketing materials. I don't intend to give you the ultimate guide to the basics here.

What I can do is show you something *brand new*: how to produce these self-marketing tools electronically. This means learning how to design your document by reading relevant articles and looking at examples on the World Wide Web, then utilizing software and the Internet to create professional-looking material that works for you.

Your Roadmap to this Chapter My objective here is to get you psyched and prepared to tackle your marketing materials head on. To start with, I give you a glimpse into the employer's state of mind after receiving your résumé. This puts you in the proper framework to begin writing your résumé. Of course, you'll have to select the format that's appropriate for your situation—a traditional résumé or a résumé alternative. Both of these options are reviewed in this chapter. Next, I move on to specialized letters, such as cover letters and thank you notes. Finally, I provide suggestions on how to use the Internet and software to help create all of these materials, plus business cards as well.

In Chapter 5, you'll learn how to adapt these age-old elements and send them in a variety of ways electronically. It's not all that tough to do, but to do it right, you need to have a strong grasp of the basics. That's why we look at the conventional (non-electronic) versions in this chapter, then the online distribution methods in the next.

The More Things Change, the More They Stay the Same

What first amazed me as I began to write this section is how little these basic tools of self-marketing have changed over the last 30 to 40 years. I guess I can see why. Employers have always wanted to see *what* you've done, *where* you've done it, and *why* you should be selected for a job interview. Thus, they continue to demand a quality résumé and cover letter from virtually every single applicant (unless you happen to be related to the Human Resources Manager).

With all the other changes going on in the world of work, you might have thought that the résumé itself would become obsolete. No such luck. You still have to do the groundwork. This translates into coming up with a powerful, succinct description of your employment history and accomplishments. It could be the traditional two-page version with an attractive, hard-hitting, one page cover letter. Or it could simply be a one-page marketing letter targeted to a specific audience. Whatever the case, it has to be done.

Good News: You May Have Already Done the Fundamentals

Two things can help you out here immediately. One is the work that you did in Chapter 3. If you completed the online exercises described in that chapter, or if you've done a self-assessment elsewhere, you've constructed some of the building blocks that you'll need. If you haven't, it's not too late to skip back to the previous chapter, Planning Your Career Online.

Knowing your strengths, skills and accomplishments is critical for creating your work-search marketing materials. You'll use specific examples of these in preparing a résumé and cover letter. They'll also help you if you decide to go into business for yourself (if that's your interest, look at Chapter 10 too).

How Technology Can Assist You Here The other thing that makes things easier is technology. You can now purchase software programs that pretty well write your résumé and cover letter for you (in your choice of format). All you do is fill in the blanks, and they do the rest. There are also Web sites and Newsgroups that deal specifically with this area. You can get access to detailed articles and relevant examples, or even trade tips with other job-seekers.

Just to show you how far things have come, you can get a draft of your résumé critiqued online—for free—before you send it out to potential employers. You'll find all of this incredible stuff right here in this chapter.

CYBER TIP A wonderful place to commence your résumé preparation is the online Career Manual from the University of Waterloo's Career Resource Centre. The specific Web page is **http://www.adm.uwaterloo.ca/infoces/CRC.** You'll find a series of questions that you can complete right on the Net. Then you can download them when you're through, and use your answers later. There's also a ton of information how to format your résumé, and what to put in it as well.

Before we get into all of that, I'd like to get you psyched for what you're up against. After all, the more you know about the hiring process, the better equipped you are to play the game.

II. BREAKING THROUGH THE WALL

Quick. What's the primary purpose of a résumé? If you answered "to get a job," you're close, but no cigar. The real goal of a résumé is to catch the interest of a potential employer so that they contact you for an interview. If you can't get that far, your hopes of securing employment are, shall we say, somewhat dim.

Understanding the Employer's Viewpoint

Here's a little trick I share with my clients when they're putting together their résumé and cover letter. "Pretend that you are the employer," I tell them, "and write the résumé that you've always dreamed of receiving."

In other words, I suggest that they put themselves in the mindset of the person who will actually be doing the hiring. If you were the boss, what would *you* like to see? Probably a neat, professional-looking document; clear, easy-to-understand writing that gets directly to the point; useful details on the applicant's work experience; and what they can actually do for *your* company. Maybe even no grammatical errors. And would it be asking too much to see your name and title spelled correctly, if only just once?

Screening Meanies

What you really need to appreciate, if you're going to do this right, is the way that employers sift through all the résumés they get bombarded with. The most common process is called *screening*.

This is where some lucky sap gets to open, and read, the hundreds of application packages that are typically received from an ad posted in the paper (or even online).

Do you know what their objective is? I can tell you what it isn't. Screeners are not there to find the best candidate for the job. What they're looking for is a way to weed out every résumé possible. The goal is to present whoever is making the hiring decision with a manageable short-list of potential candidates—maybe 10 or 20 out of all the applications they received.

Screening—Stage One

So what do these screeners look for? Well, it depends on how stringent they are. Many will chuck your résumé right off the bat if they find *any* of the following errors:

- typographical mistakes,
- a single, visible spelling error,
- incorrect title, name or company of the person you're writing to,
- forgetting to include a real person's name (do not write "to whom it may concern"),
- coffee or grape juice stains (e.g. dirt of any kind) on the document.

You might be wondering how these folks can be so cavalier. After all, you've spent so much time putting your application package together. Then, because of one little careless act on your part, they toss it callously into the recycling bin (if they're progressive enough to have one).

It's a Question of Numbers The answer, plain and simple, is that they can afford to. It goes right back to the economic times we find ourselves in. Employers are enjoying a buyer's market out there. The competition for posted work opportunities is huge (which is why Chapter 8 directs you to the hidden job market, where your chances are much better). Odds are that if they toss your résumé out, there are several hundred others to choose from.

To put it more concretely, you might want to try the imagine game I mentioned earlier. This time, pretend that you are the screener. It's 9:40 p.m., you've been at the office since 7:20 this morning, and your daughter is at home running a fever. Meanwhile, your boss has demanded a shortlist of candidates by the end of tomorrow's business day. You're just about to open the 213th application, with another 93 to go. If you saw an obvious error, wouldn't you question the applicant's reliability and commitment? I mean, they haven't even taken the time to get their own résumé right!

CYBER TIP If you really want to understand this process, read an article called "Writing a Résumé for Susie the Screener" (hey, I didn't make up the title). It's written by Douglas Richardson for the National Business Employment Weekly. Find it at **http://www.gsia.cmu.edu/afs/andrew/gsia/coc/student/screener.html.**

Screening—The Next Stages

I won't dwell on the weeding out process. Suffice it to say that employers are looking for any way they can to send you a "thanks, but no thanks" letter. They ask themselves if your skills and work achievements match exactly what they're looking for. If not, out you go. They check if your cover letter is concise and targeted to the reader. If you've sent a form letter, you can probably kiss the job goodbye. The list of reasons to disqualify you goes on and on.

REAL LIFE *To boost your chances of getting past the screening process, follow the first rule of marketing: give 'em what they want. In this case, you can try to reflect back the very words they've used in their ad. You'll also want to give specific examples of how and where you've done the things they're asking for. Finally, this is not the time to be humble. Include as many relevant points as possible, without going overboard (you've got to save a few trump cards for the interview, too).*

Screening—The Future (It's All About *Scanning*)

If you think the process is bad now, just wait. It's going to get worse (or better, depending on your point of view) very soon. What's coming down the pike, and is already here in some cases, is a process known as *scanning*.

It works in a pretty straightforward way. You send in your résumé to an employer, and it gets scanned (electronically copied) into their database. When they want to hire someone, all they have to do is search their database. The candidates with the most relevant qualifications are selected for interviews (talk about dehumanizing). In Chapter 5, I give you some hints on how to format your material for this type of process.

We're Not Quite at the *Key Word* Stage Yet The biggest change to expect is the *key word* résumé, which is reviewed in Chapter 11. At the time of writing, this format was already very popular in the U.S. It hasn't really had an impact on Canada yet, which is why it just receives a quick mention here.

Briefly, it's a whole new way of writing a résumé. The emphasis is on stand-alone nouns, for example the words "manager" and "B.A" instead of the phrases and action verbs we stress today such as "managed a department" or "successfully earned B.A.". The résumé itself gets scanned and is run through an optical character recognition (OCR) program. Then your text can be searched by key word for specific traits, experience and qualifications.

Returning from Cyberspace Before I blow your mind with all these wonderful new concepts (doesn't scanning sound like something out of a David Cronenberg movie?), I'm going to start with a review of the traditional approaches. That's what you'll be using as your foundation, no matter which way you choose to send your résumé and cover letter (plus business cards, which are covered later on).

III. YOUR RÉSUMÉ

One of the main themes in this book is that we need to keep up with the changes that are going on around us. Ironically, even though the way we send out our applications is being transformed, the documents themselves are still pretty much the same. You may have to modify them to send them online, but the core information hasn't changed very much at all.

Some Variations to Consider

Today, there is no such thing as a basic résumé. What you have now are variations on what was once considered the *traditional* version (you know, two pages long, preceded by a cover letter, with your work experience listed in reverse chronological order) along with some newer résumé alternatives. Table 4.1 lists the more common résumés that you will now encounter.

Use the One That Will Best Achieve Your Objectives

Each of the formats referred to in Table 4.1 can be used effectively in different situations. One thing to remember is that there is no such thing as an all-purpose résumé. You need to select the style that will best enable you to achieve your goals. As Tom Jackson, a job-hunting expert has said, "The perfect résumé is a written communication that clearly demonstrates your ability to produce results in an area of concern to selected employers, in a way that motivates them to meet you."

Back to the Employer's Viewpoint for a Moment

Here's something else to keep in mind: No matter which format you decide to go with, your résumé, cover letter and the package you send it

Table 4.1 Variations On The Traditional Résumé

STYLE	NUMBER OF PAGES	WHEN IT'S MOST USEFUL
Reverse Chronological	2 max. + cover	When you have a lengthy, consistent work record
Functional	2 max. + cover	For recent grads or people making career changes
Combination	2 max. + cover	If you're somewhere in between the above two
Résumé Alternative One: Targeted Marketing Letter	1–2 max.	Trying to tap into the hidden job market
Résumé Alternative Two: Broadcast Letter	1–2 max.	When making initial contact with many companies in a variety of fields.

in are the only things (in most cases) that a potential employer will know about you. In other words, your résumé, for all intents and purposes, is YOU; therefore, you should make sure that your materials represent the best possible effort that you can put forward. Keep them neat and professional looking. Eliminate any spelling or grammar errors. Use wording that is interesting, and easy to understand. And always, always keep in mind the needs of your reader.

Traditional Résumés

The traditional résumé is the one that most of us are familiar with. It's usually a one or two page description of your work and accomplishments. For specialized situations (e.g. academia, law, scientific research, or very experienced workers), you may opt for a longer, more comprehensive curriculum vitae. In either case, you'd start with a one page cover letter that's aimed directly at your reader.

REAL LIFE *In addition to your regular phone number, you may want to include your e-mail address (and fax number, which you should try to arrange to have) on your résumé. This gives potential employers the option of contacting you in the way that they prefer. Even if they never e-mail or fax you, it leaves a positive impression that you're up-to-date. Remember: every advantage helps.*

Chronological Versus Functional Most often you would send a traditional résumé when responding to a published job advertisement (such as one you've seen in the classifieds section of your newspaper or on the Net).

Traditional résumés actually come in two main varieties: the *chronological* and *functional* formats. The chronological style focuses on your work history. This is great when you've been working for a while, and have had a steady employment history. The functional version puts the emphasis on your transferable skills such as the ability to organize, plan, communicate and motivate. This can be effective when making a career change, or if you haven't had much formal work experience. A third, less-frequently used variation is the combination résumé, which mixes a little of both the chronological and functional formats.

What Do They Have in Common? No matter which format you choose, there are certain elements that are common in the traditional résumé. They tend to be divided into distinct sections. The headings are generally in bold to show clear demarcation points, and the language is very active and results-oriented.

The following sections outlined in Table 4.2 are often found in chronological, functional and combination style résumés.

Guidelines for Choosing a Traditional Format The style you choose, and when you decide to use it, will depend on your situation. The following sections provide guidelines for selecting the style of traditional résumé that is right for you. You will also find Web sites that show you numerous examples, and provide tips in design and writing.

Chronological Résumé Format

As I said before, the chronological résumé format is used most often, which can be good and not-so-good. On the positive side, employers are familiar with the layout, and it tends to be easy to read. The drawback is that it may not stand out—in a meaningful way—from the rest of the pack.

In terms of format, your jobs and achievements (not just duties) are listed in reverse order, starting with most recent. The emphasis here is on what you have already accomplished, and where you have worked. Some detailed suggestions can be found on the Online Career Centre

Table 4.2 Sections to Include in a Traditional Résumé

SECTION	PURPOSE
Career Objective	Tells the reader what kind of position you're applying for
Highlights	Gives some highlights of your most relevant skills
Employment History	Shows where you've worked and what you accomplished
Education	Lists your degrees, diplomas, certificates and other courses
Additional Qualifications	Describes volunteer experience, awards, computer skills etc.
Personal Information	Lists relevant hobbies and special interests or skills

(OCC) in the U.S., at **http://www.occ.com/occ/DIY/chapter2.html**.

Chronological Résumés Are Best Used When:

- You plan to stay in a similar field as the one you're in now.
- There are no large gaps in your employment history.
- Your work history shows development and increasing responsibility.

Notice that in this type of résumé, it's your work history that really stands out. It tends to show a progression from one level to the next. In fact, it can demonstrate to the reader that you're ready to take on the very role that they are offering.

CYBER TIP To find examples of traditional résumés in chronological format, surf over to JobSmart, at **http://jobsmart.org/tools/resume/res-chr1.htm.** You'll find some résumés from the book Ready-To-Go Résumés, by Yana Parker. They're one page, American résumés, but useful nonetheless.

Functional Résumé Format

The functional format is really just a variation on the traditional résumé. It's particularly effective when you're a freelancer (that is, you have many jobs or contracts instead of a steady employment history), or when making a career change. You should also consider this format when you're just starting out. It focuses the reader on the things you can do, rather than where you've worked.

You actually use most of the same information you would in the chronological version; however, it's arranged in a different way. The functional format uses special headings to emphasize your skills and accomplishments, instead of your work experience. It's less common than the chronological type, but, in the right situation, it can be extremely potent.

REAL LIFE *I've successfully used a functional résumé myself, when switching from a management job in a corporation to a university teaching position. I gathered my information and achievements in sub-headings such as Training And Development Experience and Marketing/Communications to highlight the qualities that were important for my new career.*

Functional Résumés Are Best Used When:

- You are changing industries or are making a significant career change.
- There are substantial gaps in your employment history.
- You have held a series of short-term jobs or contract positions.
- You do not have much work experience.
- Your work history shows little development and no increase in responsibility.

> **CYBER TIP** An example of a traditional résumé in functional format can be found at **http://jobsmart.org/tools/résumé/samples.htm.** When you visit this Web site, take advantage of the other career resources that are offered as well.

Not for the Faint-Hearted A functional résumé requires a bit of creativity. To make this format work for you, it's not enough to just list your accomplishments, or show your credentials. You have to arrange your material in a way that highlights your transferable skills. That is, you want to transfer your strengths and abilities from what you've been doing previously, into something new. Try playing around with the headings so that they show off what you're really capable of doing.

Résumé Alternatives

One question I'm frequently asked is, "When is it best to use an alternative to the traditional résumé?" As it turns out, there are two popular options to consider. One is the *targeted marketing letter,* and the other is the *broadcast letter.*

Alternative One: Targeted Marketing Letters If you're doing your job search right, you won't be spending a lot of time replying to positions that you've seen advertised. Chapter 6 explains that advertised jobs account for maybe 10 percent of all the available vacancies today; moreover, since everyone else gets to see the ads, competition can be ferocious.

Your One Page Marketing Brochure The bulk of employment opportunities are buried somewhere in the hidden job market. This is where a traditional résumé might not meet your needs, or those of your reader. That's why there are résumé alternatives, such as the targeted marketing letter.

For this approach, you produce a one-page, customized selling letter. Your goal is to capture the interest of a specific reader at a particular company: namely, the person who you think can hire you at the place you'd like to work. *You* become the product, and the letter serves as a brief brochure outlining your features.

Standing on Its Own The targeted approach takes a skillful hand at letter writing. It also requires quite a bit of preparation. You must immediately show the reader what you can do for them. And you have to do so in one page, without an accompanying résumé. This is no small feat, considering that the person you're writing to has not, in most cases, advertised an open position.

CYBER TIP Gary Will has put together an excellent Web site that summarizes over 50 résumé writing articles on the Web. He calls his Web site Archeus. Gary deserves our thanks for providing direct links to, and ratings of, these Web-based articles. Check them out for yourself at: **http://www.golden.net/~archeus/reswri.htm.** Find the article that talks about the right résumé for you. Then retrieve the article, download it to your hard disk, and refer to it as a template for your own version.

The Targeted Marketing Letter is Best Used When:

- You are trying to tap into the hidden job market (e.g. no position has been advertised).
- You have done some initial research on the needs of the company, as well as the person who might be in a position to hire you.
- You are going after the top 10 or 15 companies on your target list—they appear to be good prospects, and you think that you would like to do work for them.
- You have been unsuccessful at contacting a key person by phone.

Alternative Two: Broadcast Letters In an ideal world, you'd have the time to customize your letters for every single company in each industry where you might want to work. The reality? Looking for work is a game of percentages. You can't afford to spend too much time chasing too few opportunities. As part of your overall strategy, you *might* also want to do a mass-mailing. This allows you to contact a whole lot of companies at the same time.

Enter the broadcast letter. This one-pager is similar in format to the targeted marketing letter. The big differences are in the content, and the number of copies that you send out. A targeted letter is customized to each particular reader, whereas the broadcast letter is more generic. You may use one or two versions only (instead of customized cover letters). All you really change is the address information to reach senior managers and department heads.

Your broadcast letter might go to 100 or 200 different companies. They might even go to companies in different industries, depending on your career objectives. Compare this to the 10 to 20 targeted letters that you might mail out. No matter where you send it, however, remember that it must be addressed to the *right* person.

REAL LIFE *Since you may very well send out hundreds of broadcast letters over the course of your campaign, try to do it in stages. You could mail out maybe 20 or 30 at a time. This way, you'll be able to follow each one up with a phone call (or an e-mail message) within a week of sending it. This can increase your chances for success enormously. It also makes the process much more manageable.*

What to Leave Out Of Your Résumé

No matter if you choose a traditional format or résumé alternative, there's a definite art to knowing what to put in your résumé. Remember that your main goal is to grab the interest of your reader. You don't want to overwhelm them, yet you want to avoid getting screened out in the initial stages. Here's a rule to keep in mind: put as much in as you need to pique their interest. Use the face-to-face job interview to close the sale.

You May Not Have to Include Every Last Detail Just as there are sections that you must include in your résumé, there's information that you should think about leaving out including:

- Salary expectations and history (unless absolutely demanded by the employer).
- Personal details such as your age, height, weight, marital status, country of origin, criminal record or health.
- Details that are not related to the position that you're applying for.
- Jargon or technical terminology that your reader will not understand.
- The names of any references (you can give these once you're asked for them).
- Outright lies (there's a fine line between exaggeration and fibbing—don't cross it, because it can be grounds for firing).

CYBER TIP Want to get a professional's opinion of your existing résumé—for free? Here are two Web sites that offer free résumé evaluations (of course, if changes are required, they'll be glad to assist you, for a fee). On-Line Career & Management Consulting Services is at **http://www.dnai.com/~career/form_qa.htm**. At the other Web site, **http://bakosgroup.com**, you can fill in the online form to inquire about the free assessment by The Bakos Group. They accept Canadian calls toll free.

IV. SPECIALIZED LETTERS

Wouldn't it be nice if the toughest part was over, now that you've slaved away to create the ultimate résumé. You knew there'd be a catch though, didn't you? It's called letter writing.

In the work-search context, writing letters is as critical as résumé creation. A specialized letter is one that's used in specific situations to achieve particular objectives. There are two basic types that you will run across in your self-marketing campaign:

- Cover letters (sent, with your résumé, before the interview) and
- Thank you letters (after interviews and work-search related meetings).

Cover Letters

Who needs a cover letter? Just about everyone who sends out a résumé does. It is vital to include a covering page that serves as an introduction to your résumé.

The purpose of a cover letter is to immediately grab the attention of the potential employer in a favourable way. If you make a great first impression, the reader may decide to actually flip through your résumé. If not, consider yourself screened.

Because it's often the first glimpse that an employer gets of you, your cover letter is very important. Done right, it gives you the chance to summarize your potential worth to the company, and keeps you in the running.

Helpful Hints for Making an Effective Cover Letter

1. Create personalized stationary with a word processing program. It should include your name, address and contact numbers (phone, fax and e-mail). Try to make it look as professional as possible.
2. Tailor the letter to the person who makes the hiring decisions at the company where you want to work. Show that you know something about the company and the industry. This is where the research you learn how to do in Chapter 6 comes in. No need to go crazy—just make it clear that you didn't pick this company randomly from the phone book.

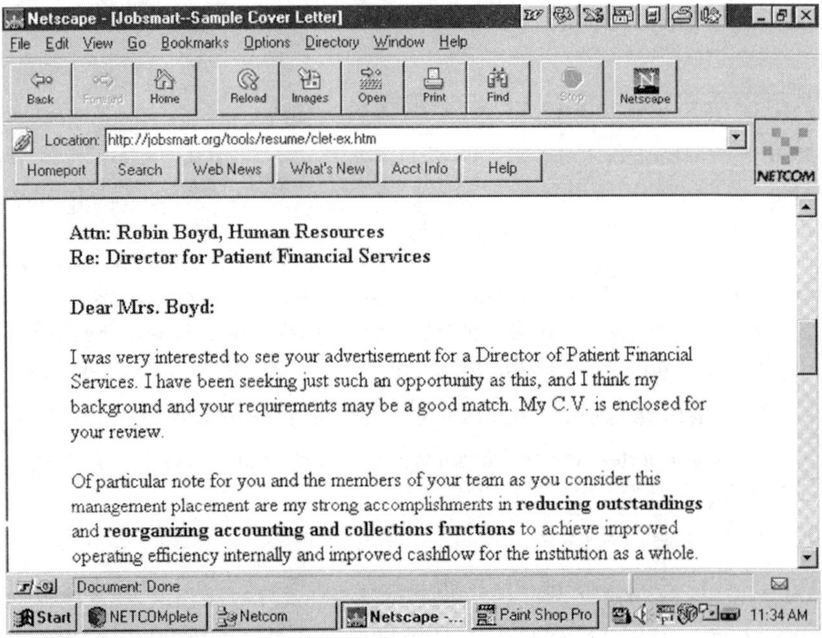

3. Write as much as you can in your own words so that it sounds like you—not like something out of a book. This is a good chance to let the best of your personality show through.
4. Use terms and phrases that are meaningful to the employer. (This is where your industry research, networking and thorough review of the company's employment ad come in).
5. Keep it to one page. If you overload the reader, you just might frighten them off (they have to read all the other letters and résumés too).

CYBER TIP There are some excellent instructions on the Web for preparing a cover letter. Begin with the Canadian perspective, provided by the University of Waterloo Career Resource Centre: **http://www.adm.uwaterloo.ca/infocecs/CRC/step4-letters.html** is the exact URL. The Riley Guide (written by Margaret Riley) gives a U.S. perspective, and can be reached at **http://www.jobtrak.com/jobguide/career.html#writing.**

Thank You Notes

One of the most overlooked components of an effective self-marketing campaign is the thank you letter. Ironically, it's also one of the quickest steps to do.

You should *always* send out a brief thank you immediately after you've done any of the following:

- Met with someone for an information interview (as part of your networking).
- Completed a job interview.
- Spoken to someone who has been helpful to you.
- Read a work-search guide that gives you a competitive advantage (kidding, folks).

Doing It Yourself

Thank you letters are a nice touch. In your continued quest to differentiate yourself in meaningful ways, why not try a more personalized approach. Send them a home-made, customized card.

CYBER TIP A good example of a thank you letter can be found at the following Web site: **http://cardinal.umeais.maine.edu/~career/otherlets.html**. You'll also be treated to a number of other letters that you can use in your work-search, thanks to the University of Maine.

The idea behind a thank you card is simple. If you send a letter, it may be appreciated for a few moments, then it's tucked away in some file or maybe even tossed out. A card, on the other hand, is something that may get displayed. If the person you sent it to puts your card somewhere where they (and others) can see it, you've secured yourself some free advertising.

Some Software To Think About

- Stationery Shop or Greeting Card Maker (Expert Software)
  http://www.expertsoftware.com/soho.htm
- Print Shop (Broderbund Software Inc.)
  http://www.broder.com/PrintShop/aboutps.html

CYBER TIP You can create a thank you note directly from your word processing program, using special card paper (available at business supply stores) and a printer (colour or black and white is fine). For WordPerfect users, go to "File," then "Template." Choose "Publish," then "Thank You Card" (in older versions, the commands may vary). Design it to suit your needs.

V. CREATING RÉSUMÉS AND COVER LETTERS IN A WIRED WORLD

Having reviewed the various types of résumés, it's time to look at how to put them together electronically. Once again you have several choices here. You can do it using a general word processing or publishing software package or you can get hold of specialized software that pretty well writes and formats your material for you, with cut and paste templates. Then there are the Web options, too.

Have Things Really Changed This Much?

One thing became evident as I put this chapter together. There's been a radical shift in the way that we construct out marketing materials compared to five or ten years ago. Table 4.3 takes you on a stroll down memory lane, contrasting how we do résumés today versus years ago.

Electronics Have Made Things Faster and Easier It's obvious from Table 4.3 that we have some new tools at our disposal. What may not be so apparent are the ways that basic computer programs can shave hours off our preparation time, and create startlingly professional results.

Prepackaged Software to Make Writing Simpler

If I had to create my résumé from scratch today, I'd probably run right out and buy a special software package to assist me. There are several résumé and covering letter kits available, both on diskette and CD-ROM. An example is Tom Jackson's *The Perfect Résumé*. It's based on this U.S. career expert's book by the same title.

No Such Thing as an All-In-One Solution. This program, and others like it, gives you almost everything you need to design and produce an excellent résumé. For about $60 (Cdn.), there are exercises that transform your list of skills and accomplishments into an excellent résumé. You're given a selection of templates with various résumé styles. Choose the one you like, cut and paste your text where appropriate, then view it on-screen before you send it.

The program works well. It is, however, U.S. oriented (as are all the similar software packages that I could find). Thus, you'll still want to run your final draft by someone whose opinion you respect. And try not to make your résumé *too* prefabricated. If it looks like it was assembled by a cookie-cutter process (e.g. a professional wrote it, not you), it could turn some screeners and employers off. Inject a personal touch, if possible, to stand out from the crowd.

For More Information To get more details on The Perfect Résumé program, visit the Davidson and Associates Web site (U.S.) at

Table 4.3 Creating A Résumé: Then and Now

STEPS INVOLVED	DOING IT 10 YEARS AGO	DOING IT TODAY
Put initial ideas and rough thoughts down	Write them by hand and create categories that you think are meaningful	Fill in blanks of online preparation exercises described in Chapter 3
Create a draft version	Organize your thoughts and put them on paper to get a rough idea of the layout	Input your text into a word processing program on your PC, and save file on diskette
Prepare different versions to see which one works best	Start from scratch with a typewriter for each new version, or cut and paste using a photocopier, scissors and glue	Cut and paste text with a mouse click. Print out drafts immediately to compare how they really look
Do a good copy	Type in the whole thing manually, from scratch, on your electric typewriter	Make edits, stick some nice-quality paper into your printer and click on "print"
Check for errors one last time before sending your material out	Manually proofread (usually late at night) and hope that you catch any mistakes	Use spelling and grammar programs to correct errors automatically, then get it reviewed for free on the Net
Make final changes to document, if required	Use correction fluid on your paper (nice smell, eh?), or rip it up and start all over again	It's probably perfect by now. If not, insert changes via keyboard and print out laser-quality copies
Send out completed application package	Make a photocopy for yourself, put the résumé in an envelope, attach a stamp, seal it and drop it in a mailbox, then wait days	Send your high-quality original by fax or e-mail directly from your PC for immediate receipt

http://www.davd.com/products/résumé.html. There's even an internet coupon that you can redeem for a discount on the product.

There are other offerings of this type available at your software store. They range in price from $20 to around $70. Look for a program that will make it easiest for you to create a résumé that fits your style. Some examples of software programs (and locations to learn more about them) are:

- Résumé Maker Deluxe (Individual Software Inc.) **http://www.individualsoftware.com/conrdc.htm**
- WinWay Résumé (Winway Corp.) **http://www.winway.com/pages/winway_résumé_4.htm**
- Résumé Writer (Expert Software Inc.) **http://www.expertsoftware.com/résumé.htm**

Always Do a Double-Check A final consideration. Feel free to use your word processor's spell-checker and grammar program. But don't rely on them exclusively. They may not catch everything (especially if you have them set to American English, instead of Canadian). Read your documents thoroughly yourself. You should then get someone whose opinion and language skills you trust (maybe a friend, colleague or career practitioner) to give them a thorough review.

CYBER TIP If you already have the information that you need to write your résumé, you can turn directly to your existing word processing package. The more recent versions of Word and WordPerfect have built-in résumé templates. For Word users, go to "File," "New," then "Résumé Wizard." On WordPerfect, try "File," "New," "Business," and "Résumé." Type in your text, then personalize it to your liking. (Note that the actual commands may vary depending on the version you have.)

Web-Based Résumé Builders

What would this book be if I didn't show you where to go on the Net to create your résumé? Not surprisingly, you can put together an entire résumé for free while plugged in to the World Wide Web.

The first site I'll point you to is called Résumé Maker. It gives you the ability to type your qualifications, work history etc. into pre-defined boxes. Once you're happy with the results, you select "publish key." The site automatically formats your material, then you can print it out to see how it looks. Find the site at **http://www.iguide.com/work_mny/resume/rmaker.htm**.

Another option is the Intellimatch PowerBuilder. This service is similar to the one above, but it also gives you the choice of posting your completed résumé to an online job matching service (more about these, and what to watch out for, in Chapter 9). The Intellimatch site, which is U.S. based, is at **http://www.intellimatch.com/watson/owa/w3.logon**.

CYBER TIP When using a home or office printer to produce your application package, make sure that it comes out professionally. If your printer is an inkjet, use the highest print quality. 600 DPI (Dots per square inch) is recommended, and the minimum is 300 DPI (but I'd suggest you try for better). A laser printer that produces 300 DPI is perfectly acceptable. 600 DPI will be sharper, but unless you're using artwork or pictures, it won't matter much. One other thing: use the best paper available to match your machine's output.

VI. BUSINESS CARDS

A simple, relatively inexpensive way to remind folks of who you are is with your business card. You can use it when you meet new people while networking, as an introductory or concluding piece at an interview, as part of your mailing package, or as a way of advertising your new business.

In any case, your card can be a vital tool in making a positive impression with potential employers. Also, collecting and sorting business cards that your contacts give you will help you to manage your work-search. Once again, you can get computer assistance in both areas.

Getting the Facts Right

Like any marketing piece, your business card should say a lot about you without using too many words. Below is the type of information that you can consider including. Choose only the points that will make the strongest impact on *your* card (feel free to substitute any others that are appropriate).

- Your name and any relevant credentials. This can include your degree (B.A.) or professional designation (C.H.R.P.).
- Area of specialty (e.g. finance, marketing, plumbing, etc.).
- The name of your company and your title.
- A full address where you want any correspondence to be sent to you.
- A phone number where you can easily be reached (preferably one that is hooked up to some sort of answering system, so that you can retrieve your messages regularly).
- A fax number. Remember from Chapter 2, it doesn't necessarily have to be your own fax machine. For instance, a friend might be willing to lend you their fax number while you're looking for work. Or you could use a rented number from one of the many business service companies that have sprung up recently.
- Your personal e-mail address. You'll need this to send and receive messages with potential employers, and to take part in Newsgroups for networking and work-searching.
- The address of your personal Web site on the World Wide Web. (This is not needed for the average person. It is important if you're in the hi-tech field or are running your own business.)

Should You Create Your Own Business Cards?

After a conference I recently presented at, some people approached me to exchange ideas (and business cards). One fellow handed me his card and proudly exclaimed, "I made this myself!"

Apparently he'd used a business card software program, his PC, and a colour inkjet printer. The result was an exquisitely designed marketing piece. It had appropriate graphics, the text was clear, and the colour added a whole new dimension. The trouble, in my opinion, was that it *looked* home-made.

It's Fun, It's Affordable...But Is It Professional Enough?

The manufacturers of business card software are going to hate me for saying what I'm about to say. So far, I haven't found a single program that outputs an end-product which remotely approaches similarly-priced, professionally-printed cards (in terms of feel or quality).

There. I've said it. This is one instance where the home-made version doesn't yet rival that of the printing services. Don't misunderstand me, you can get some very creative and professional looking business cards from a variety of software packages. It's just that they tend to feel, well, inferior.

The Paper Makes the Big Difference I could see immediately what the problem was. The card stock (that is, the grade of paper supplied in the software kit) didn't feel right. First of all, it was substantially thinner than the stock a printing service would use. I later learned that this is done to prevent paper jams in home printers.

The second hitch involved the edges of the card. Printing services use huge cutters to make their cards come out with sharp, even edges. The software-produced version can't do this. Instead, it must perforate the sheets on which you print out your business cards. Then you tear each card off individually once it's been printed.

The End Result What does that give you? Serrated, rough edges and thin paper instead of firm, heavy stock and clean-cut edges. I'm not saying that this is the end of the world. But when so much is riding on the impressions you make in your work-search, you might want to take this into account.

Creating a Business Card Using Software

Despite my negative pronouncements, you may still want to try this for yourself. What you'll need is a PC and printer (definitely not dot matrix), plus software designed to produce business cards. Colour can provide an impressive effect; however, it's not critical if you're looking for something simple. A laser printer still tends to give black and white material greater clarity.

Software and CDs to Consider Here are some programs that enable you to create customized business cards. They generally give you templates, design tips, graphics and font choices, plus sheets of perforated paper to run through your printer. All that you have to do is fill in the blanks with the information you want.

- MyBusinessCards (MySoftware)
  http://www.mysoftware.com/mybusinesscards/index.htm

- Easy Business Cards (Claris)
  http://www.claris.com/software/swcdb.cgi

CYBER TIP Use templates from your word processor to design business cards as well. In recent versions of WordPerfect, go to "File," "New," "Business," then "Business Card." Input your information, select a graphic from your image files, and you're set. You will also have to buy perforated sheets of card stock to run through your printer. These are available at your business supply store.

Managing Your Contacts by Scanning Your Business Cards

There's another *wired* thing that you can do with business cards. When people give you their cards, you can upload them into a searchable database on your PC. This can be extremely handy. One of the keys to finding work is to track your contacts effectively. This can be a very cumbersome task. Look what's involved: in addition to your PC, you have to own a scanner, contact management software (such as Symantec ACT! or Maximizer by MultiActive Group) and card scanning software (like The Smart Business Card Reader by Seiko Smart, which is described at **http://www.seikosmart.com/sbcr.htm**).

A Multi-Step Process Here's what a typical process could look like. Let's say that Cheryl has just come back from a networking session with her human resource professionals association. She met about 15 new people, and collected business cards from each of them (after giving hers out, of course). Now she's back at home.

Cheryl turns on her PC and scanner. Then she calls up the business card scanning software. When it's running, she inserts the first card into her scanner. She does this for each of the cards, then calls up her contact management software. Cheryl transfers the entire file into her contact management program. All the information is automatically stored and cross-referenced for future use.

The Way It Works It sounds straightforward, but this is what actually took place. When Cheryl put the business card into the scanner, it created an electronic image of the card. This was transmitted into the card scanning software. Then, the optical character recognition (OCR) component of the software automatically converted the image into readable text. Each line of text was then put into the proper field (the person's name was read into the name field, for instance). When the file was transferred into ACT!, each field migrated over to the new program.

Is It Really Worth It?

What Cheryl ends up with is a database of contacts that she can search at any time, in a variety of ways. She can now look up people using specific fields (such as their title or company), or with key words (e.g. "networking contact" or "potential job"). This could be a valuable tool in her search for work.

The question is, is it worth the expense and time invested to make this possible? Basically, only you can decide if this method will be worthwhile for you, or if manually writing down the information is sufficient for your needs.

REAL LIFE *You may be saying to yourself "would having a personal homepage on the Web help me to secure work?" Seems that everyone has one nowadays. The truth is, it's practically useless for work-searching, unless you're in a high-tech field where you need to impress potential employers (if so, see the end part of Chapter 11). Otherwise, hardly any employers will take time to search out your site. Why should they, when everything they need is in your résumé and cover letter?*

VII. WIRED WRAP UP

I cringe when I think back to how I applied for one of my first "real" summer jobs. It was with one of the big advertising agencies based in Toronto. The previous summer (after my last year of high school), I had worked for free at a smaller ad agency run by a gem of a man, Reid Bell. He was kind enough to refer me to a friend of his who held a very senior position at the biggest ad company in Canada. All I had to do was write her and set up a meeting.

So what did I do? I guess what every other clueless, arrogant university student does at least once. I figured I was in, so I didn't take it seriously. First I procrastinated until the last minute. Then I hastily typed up a letter without doing a rough draft. In my rush, at least three typos were made. Rather than starting over, I mangled things further by sloppily using correction fluid.

The pièce de resistance, however, was the envelope. I wasn't sure how to spell my contact's name, so I took a guess (I was wrong). Then I wrote down the company name as I thought it should be (not as it really was). Best of all, I handscrawled this incorrect information on an old, wrinkled-up envelope. It actually had a footprint on it from someone who had stepped on it.

Can you picture the reaction of this prominent advertising executive to my misbegotten experiment in self-marketing? And it wasn't enough for me to send this pitiful package to just anyone. It had to be someone who'd spent the last 40 years mastering the art of presenting ideas in a professional, persuasive format.

I needn't tell you that I didn't get the job.

Today you can avoid the spectacular mistakes that I made in my ill-spent youth. With a word processor and some basic advice that you can get for free on the Web, you can create first class self-marketing materials. In fact, it's become so easy that employers now *demand* a very high standard, just as a baseline.

What you need to keep in mind is the way that employers typically hire. Once you understand the screening process and that the needs of the employer are paramount, the rest is simply a matter of tailoring your material to your audience. If you (and the person who has reviewed your material) are happy with your results, then you're ready to learn how to send your materials electronically.

CHAPTER 5

Sending in Work Applications Electronically

Virtual Definition: **port** (pôrt) *noun*

Generally, a place where information goes into or out of a computer. For example, the serial port on a personal computer is where a modem would be connected.

I. SAME BALLGAME, SOME NEW RULES

By now you've probably constructed the ultimate electronically-produced résumé. It has been looked over numerous times by your colleagues, as well as by a qualified career practitioner. You're all set to mail out a few to test the waters—then you see an employment ad that asks you to e-mail your résumé.

The Medium Is the Message

What do you do now? You want the job. And you're computer literate. You realize that if you *don't* respond electronically, it's likely that you'll be screened out. You've also heard from your colleagues that there's more than one way to format an e-mail (and fax, for that matter). If you choose the wrong configuration, you're guaranteed to be screened out. Where do you turn?

You've Come to the Right Source In this chapter, you'll get the scoop on sending your materials in just about every electronic

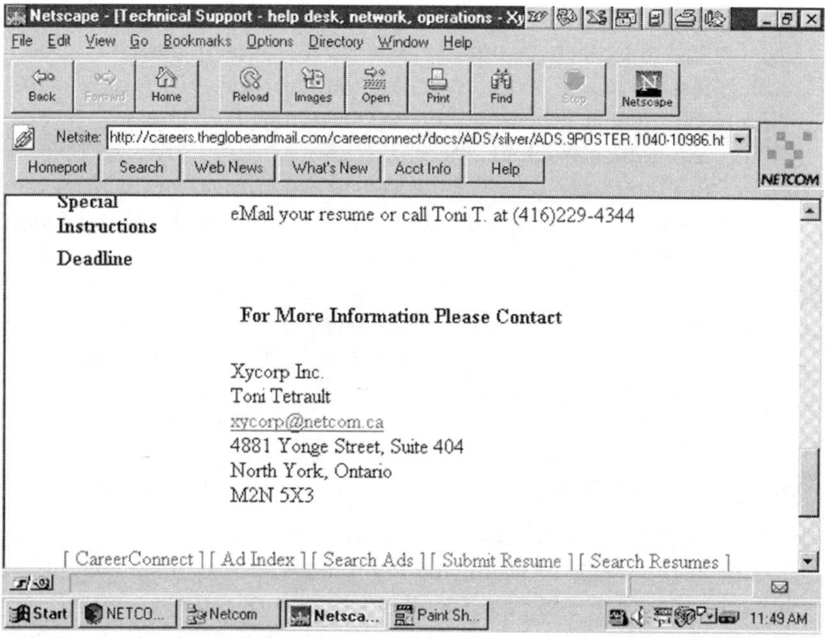

way that's in use right now. Primarily, you will learn how to adapt your cover letter and résumé to send them in their best possible form via:

- fax (both by regular fax machine and PC fax program),
- e-mail (within the body of the message and as an attachment),
- the World Wide Web (by way of Internet form), and
- scanning (image-based and Optical Character Recognition).

The Newest Trends

You may have noticed that employment ads have evolved in the last decade. About 10 years ago, you'd pick up a newspaper and check out the classifieds. The want ads would give you the hiring company's address and phone number, then you'd respond by mailing in your résumé.

Five years ago, that same ad would have the company's address, phone number and fax number. You might have faxed in your résumé, then followed it up with a hard copy by regular mail.

The Modern Age Requires New Skills To see how much things have changed, check out a typical job advertisement today. You'll definitely see the hiring company's name (unless it's a blind ad with just a box number listed), but from then on, there may be some new twists.

Many companies are deliberately excluding their address and phone number from their want ads. This is done to discourage people from calling in or visiting the company itself. They're hoping to protect their switchboard and human resources people from being swamped. Instead, the ad may just have a fax number, or a fax number along with an e-mail address. If you're in the high tech industry, you might only be given an e-mail address and an Internet site (Web Page URL) with no phone number or company location at all.

Adapt or Die

The message here is loud and clear. You'd better learn to adapt your materials to fit the needs of the hiring companies. If that means knowing how to use new technologies to send out your applications, then so be it.

Fortunately, this doesn't necessarily mean that you have to completely reinvent your marketing materials. You can still use the résumé and cover letter that you've worked so hard to develop in the previous chapter; however, be prepared to move things around a bit, and to learn a few new techniques.

Even familiar technology, like the fax, continues to emerge in new ways. It used to be that you had to submit your résumé using a standard fax machine. Today, you have the option of using your PC, modem and a facsimile software program to send your résumé right from your computer. There's no need to own an actual fax machine.

We're Still in Our Infancy There really is a whole new series of decisions that have to be made with your marketing materials. Part of the problem is that this whole electronic thing is just beginning to emerge. Because of this, there are no definitive standards to go by. You can see how confusing this is when you look at the process of e-mailing your résumé package to an employer. Here are some of your options. If you're sending a file, you can type the text into the body of the e-mail or cut and paste from another file. Mind you, it will automatically be converted to ASCII, losing all formatting such as bolding, underlining or centering. You can avoid this step altogether by sending the fully-formatted file as an attachment. Note that your recipient must have a similar program, or else they won't be able to read the file that you send them.

See what I mean by confusing? There's no way to know how to proceed unless you have (a) the right information about your recipient's setup, and (b) easy-to-follow instructions. The employer can give you part (a), but you'll probably have to ask for it. The chances of them providing you with (b) is nil. That's why I've tried to break your options down into manageable steps for each of the new technologies.

II. SENDING YOUR RÉSUMÉ WITH A STANDARD FAX MACHINE

Let's start with a device that most of us are familiar with—the fax. This is by far the most common form of electronic carrier for résumés. No wonder—it's a fast, relatively cheap way to send out applications to potential employers. Did you know, though, that there's a science to sending out the perfect fax?

What You Need to Know About Faxing and Fax Machines

Like many people, I used to think that all you had to do was drop your photocopied résumé and cover letter into the fax machine, dial in the recipient's number, press send and wait for the receiving company to call for an interview. Not so.

Your Image Is Everything It's not quite that simple. First of all, there are some downsides to faxing that you should be aware of. The major concern is the print quality of the document that the reader receives. It is rarely as crisp and clean as your original. This is especially true if the recipient uses a low-resolution fax printer, or a machine that can't handle plain paper.

Then there is the issue of electronic signal degradation (read: ugly printout). Since you may only have one shot at making that all-important first impression, you're going to have to make some adjustments.

Expense and Follow-Up Are Factors Too There are other problems that can also be annoying. What if you're sending out applications across the country, or internationally? A fax sent somewhere far away costs you the same as any other long-distance phone call. Charges can rack up pretty quickly, unless you do it a smarter way.

Another problem is that you can never be sure if your intended reader actually gets your message (and if they do, does it arrive on his or her desk quickly, or after several days?). If the recipient works in a large office, the fax will probably get routed through a delivery system that may be somewhat circuitous. If timing is critical, this could slow things down dangerously.

Some Definite Upsides In spite of these drawbacks, faxing can be a great way to send out your materials. And now you have the choice of using a standard fax machine, or sending directly from your computer and modem. To get the best quality, there are some simple suggestions to follow.

Obtaining the Best Image from a Standard Fax Machine

The standard fax machine is something you encounter in almost any office, be it a big business or home-office. With its built-in modem, it allows you to send and receive faxes through your telephone line. A fax machine converts the image of your message into electronic data, which is transmitted at the rate of your fax modem. The printer output varies widely, depending on whether the machine uses thermal, inkjet or laser technology.

REAL LIFE *You may want to call your recipient to ask if he or she has a laser fax machine. If not, be aware that the images produced by thermal and inkjet machines are generally less than top quality. You can compensate by sending a hard copy of your application package in addition to the faxed version. If your application is going to be photocopied and distributed to others, this becomes even more important.*

Sending It Accurately When sending out a résumé or letter on a standard fax machine, make sure that you know exactly who to send it to. Get the correct name, spelling and title of your intended reader. You can do this by calling the company directly, and asking the receptionist or administrative staff for information. At the same time, ask for the right fax number for the person you're trying to reach. Some larger companies have several fax machines on their premises, and you want to choose the one that your target reader uses.

The Under Cover Advantage No matter how elegant your cover letter or résumé is, it's imperative to precede it with a formal fax cover page. Bear in mind that it will be the first thing that your reader sees. It must be attractive, professional looking, and error free. Furthermore, it should resemble the other material in your application, in terms of layout and font of the text.

The fax cover page gives the reader the basic information that they need to process your application. It tells the recipient who the fax is from, and who it's for. The design itself can be as simple or elaborate as you want it to be. Try to keep the look of it consistent with your other materials.

Some details that you may want to include are as follows:

- The name and title of your intended reader.
- Who the fax is from (include your title and company, if appropriate).
- Your return phone and fax numbers, plus an e-mail address (if available).

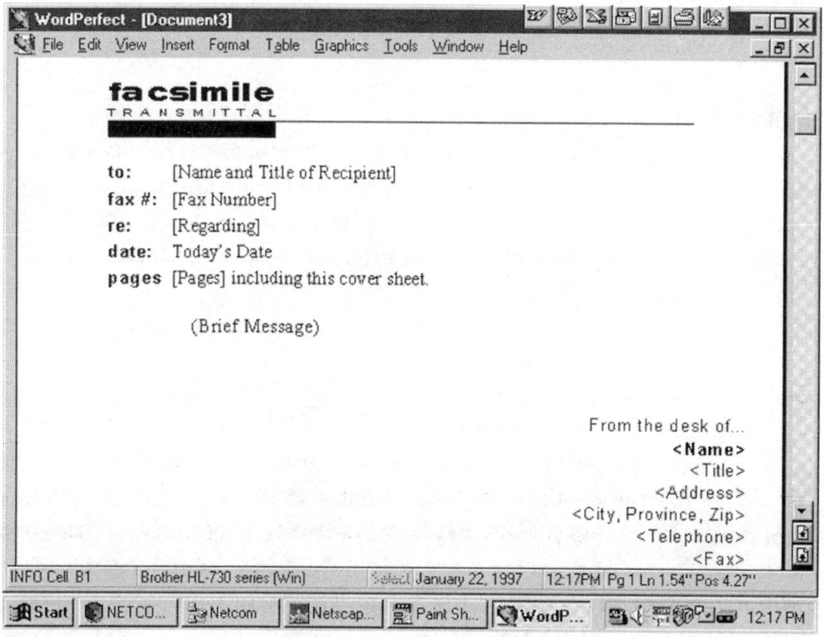

- A very brief description of the subject or purpose of the fax (you're cover letter does the rest).
- The number of pages being sent, including the cover sheet.
- Date and time that the fax is being sent.
- The reference number and title of the position that you're responding to (if provided).
- Who you're sending copies to (if applicable).

Design Hints

Like any other document, a cover page should please the eye of the reader. Make sure that yours is no exception. Go for the professional look: leave lots of white space, but get the important details upfront. Also, consider incorporating some sort of appropriate design or graphic. You can use this to reflect your personality. It may catch the reader's eye, and provide a bit of uniqueness, especially if you can include it on the other pages in your package as well. One word of advice, though. Try not to get too cutesy. It may backfire, by drawing attention away from your main message. Design your page so that it looks business-like, while still capturing your reader's attention.

REAL LIFE *Your fax cover page should reflect the type of position that you are applying for. If you're sending material to a bank, make sure that it looks dignified and conservative. But what if you're applying to an ad agency? Well then, let your creativity (and courage) be your guide. These are not hard and fast rules. The crux of this advice is to know your audience.*

Improving the Quality of Your Output

Before you send your fax, there are several things you can do to enhance the image that your reader will see. First, use high-quality, pure white paper only. Coloured paper can cause the image to come out dark grey. Next, check your original for any marks or blotches (known as hickeys in printing jargon). You may be able to cover these up with correction fluid or correction tape, instead of reprinting the whole thing. If you just leave the hickeys as they are, they are guaranteed to be there when your recipient starts reading.

It Doesn't Take Much Time You can also fiddle with the resolution of your transmission. Many fax machines (especially for home office use) give you the option of standard, fine, super fine or photo transmission quality. I advise you to go for the super fine, which is the highest resolution possible for text such as résumés and cover letters. This increases the dots per square inch of your image, resulting in a sharper version of the final output. Note that it may take longer for your message to be sent, and you might have to play a bit with your fax machine's settings, but it's worth it (make sure to read the manufacturer's instructions first).

Something as simple as cleaning your fax machine regularly can also make a huge difference. In particular, make sure that the scanning bar (the part that reads your documents) is dust and streak free. Check the owner's manual of the machine you're using to see how to do it properly.

Making Sure It Looks Right There's one more thing to watch for, and you may not have any control over it. I'm referring to the shrinking effect. Sometimes when you send a fax, it arrives looking smaller than the original. Suddenly the 12 point type that you chose so carefully looks to your reader like scrunched up, hard-to-read, 8 point type. Unfortunately, there's not much you can do about this from your end unless you know for sure how your image will appear on your recipient's machine.

To get around this, you could speak to the person who will first receive your fax (e.g. an administrative assistant) and enlist their aid. Ask them—politely—if they would quickly view your résumé *before* they pass it on to the intended reader. You want to ensure that the quality is above just

CYBER TIP Recent versions of word processing packages have built-in templates for fax cover pages. On Microsoft Word, go to "File," "New," "Faxcover" or "Fax Wizard" (depending on your version). With Corel's WordPerfect, try "File," "New," "Fax Expert." Type in your text, then customize the design to suit your requirements.

simply acceptable. If it's not, get suggestions on how to improve it, then reformat and resend.

Making Sure It Gets to Your Intended Reader

Just because your fax machine says "Transmission O.K." after you've sent your application, doesn't mean that it will arrive quickly and safely in the hands of the person you're targeting. Ever heard of an in basket? That's where every piece of correspondence and documentation gets dumped on someone's desk. It's pretty easy to have your fax lost (or buried).

Follow-Up Manually Consequently, it can be useful to call the company shortly after you've sent your fax to make sure that it has been received. Note the time, date and name of the person you're speaking to, and keep it in your files. That way if things go awry, you have a confirmed record that your application was indeed given to the right person.

Send a Snail Mail Version for Good Measure Since a follow-up call isn't always a viable option, I strongly recommend that you also send a hard copy of your application by regular mail ("snail mail") or courier. That way, you get two hits at the same target.

By doing this, your reader can get your information immediately by fax. This puts you in the running when responding to a published ad (as long as you meet the deadline). Then your reader can see the high-quality version when it arrives as a hard copy several days later. By the way, this suggestion applies whether you're using a fax, e-mail or Internet form.

REAL LIFE *When you send both a fax and hard copy version of your application, don't forget to cross reference them. Mention on your fax that you've also sent a hard copy by mail, which should arrive in a few days. Likewise, mention on your hard copy that this is a follow up to the fax that you sent on a specific date. Then your application can be processed properly, without creating unnecessary confusion.*

III. SENDING A FAX DIRECTLY FROM YOUR COMPUTER

Faxing a document directly by PC has become my favorite way to send out material. It's fast, cheap and accurate (and hey, let's not forget cool, as my daughter says). There is very little image degradation, since you no longer have to print the document onto paper before you send it.

What You Need

All you need is your PC, modem and some fax software. You do *not* have to be hooked up to the Internet to make this work. Your modem must, of course, be plugged into your phone line. You'll also need to set up the fax program as one of your available printers. (Read the manufacturer's instructions for specific set-up procedures. It's a cinch once you've tried it six or seven times!)

CYBER TIP To save on long distance charges, get a savings plan, or schedule your faxes to go out late at night, when tolls are reduced. This is easy to do with most recent machines, especially those that scan and store the fax image for later use.

Software to Get You on Your Way

There are several popular fax programs on the market. They generally allow you to convert files from your other programs (e.g. word processing, spread sheets, presentations etc.) directly into a fax image. You can also store your faxes under specific categories and view the status, such as time and date sent, if it was transmitted without error, size of file, plus other relevant details.

One such program is WinFax, from Symantec (formerly Delrina, a Canadian company). Winfax comes as a stand-alone product, or as part of a suite of communication programs. The stand-alone version should run you between $110 to $140, depending on the version and where you buy it. It is relatively easy to use, and gives you lots of flexibility. The company's Web site is **http://www.symantec.com**.

REAL LIFE *Don't forget to print yourself a hard copy of any fax you send via PC. You may want to file it for later reference. If you're relying on your PC to store all your fax images, be forewarned that they can take up lots of valuable space on your hard drive, so you should purge these regularly (or else zip them into a compression package). I realize that paper is uncool for some people, but if you think we've reached the era of the paperless office, take a look around.*

Why Shop Retail? Other similar programs range in price from zero (freeware) to $10 (shareware) up to $200 for full-featured, bundled communication packages. Here's a software Web site to search through for information and demo versions: **http://www.download.com**.

Once there, enter "Fax" in the search box. Then look for a program that meets your requirements, download it for free, and see what you think.

Faxing from a Fax Program

When using a fax program such as WinFax (or ProComm, as another example), you can send your document in one of two distinct ways: with a cover page provided by the fax program, or with one you're using as part of the file itself. To clarify this, we'll examine both processes.

CYBER TIP Save the fax number, address, name, title, company and other important details of your recipient in the address book of your fax program. That way, they will always be just a click away for the next time.

Steps to Sending a Fax Via PC Let's say you've just created a winning résumé and cover letter using a word processing program such as WordPerfect. When your material is ready, you can send your document as a fax simply by clicking on the "Print" command. You don't even have to create your own cover page. Most fax programs let you choose from an assortment of predesigned templates. You can use one of their cover pages as is, or customize it to suit your task.

Step 1. When creating your document, include your cover letter and fax as one file. Make sure that the cover letter is the first page in the document.

Step 2. Once you've input your material and are satisfied with it, save it just as you would any other file.

Step 3. If you're ready to send, turn on your modem (make sure it's connected to the phone line).

Step 4. Select the "Print" command from the "File" menu in your word processing program, then select your fax program as the printer. Click on "O.K." and you'll be transferred automatically to your fax program.

Step 5. Input the name and fax number(s) of the recipient(s), as directed by your fax program.

Step 6. Call up the predesigned cover page that you want to use. Your send information (to, from, date, number of pages etc.) will be inserted automatically. You can manually type in a brief message tailored to your reader.

Step 7. Input the time that you want to send the fax (immediately, or delayed until later).

Step 8. View a sketch or image of the fax, *before* sending it. Make sure it looks the way you want it to. If everything's O.K., click on "send" then and there. If your cover letter or résumé isn't right, you have to go back to the word processing program itself, make any necessary changes, and send to "print" again.

Step 9. You can watch your PC screen while your fax is being sent to see if the whole thing goes through properly. Or, you can go to another program and keep working while your fax is being sent in the background. In either case, verify that the fax has been sent by checking on the "send" log screen of your fax program.

CYBER TIP Set the modem command in your fax program to match the top speed of your modem (e.g. a 28.8 modem should be set to 28,800 baud in your fax program). This will allow your faxes to be sent as fast as the receiving machine can load them. Note that this still tends to be at 9,600 baud, since many people are using older or inexpensive fax machines. The maximum receiving speed today is 14,400, but watch for this to increase.

Some Precautions to Ponder

Just like when using a standard fax machine, there are certain safeguards to take if you want your fax to arrive properly in the hands of your intended reader. Again, I strongly recommend that you also send a hard copy of your application by regular mail or courier. That way, your reader will get your application immediately by fax, followed by a higher-quality version. It's also useful to call the company after you've sent your fax, to make sure that it has arrived safely.

REAL LIFE *If you think it's appropriate, don't just send your application to the human resources department. Take the time to find out who the actual hiring person is, and consider sending him or her a copy too. Make sure you spell names and titles properly. This may help you to stand out from the competition. Keep in mind, though, that some recipients might not like having their screening process circumvented.*

IV. USING E-MAIL TO SEND YOUR MATERIAL

The newest way to send your application package is by e-mail. There are quite a few reasons for seriously considering this option:

- You will likely stand out from your competition, because not all of them are using e-mail (yet).
- You may not have a choice. If that's what the employer wants, that's what you shall give.
- You're also showing potential employers that you have the computer skills needed to use e-mail properly. This alone can give you a competitive advantage.
- The version you send by fax or mail will probably be pre-screened and sorted into a pile somewhere. The e-mail version, however, might actually get to the decision maker faster—without being screened.
- The print quality of your résumé is clear when sent by e-mail (though the final image still depends on the recipient's output device).
- An e-mailed résumé remains in the recipient's private mail box until he or she decides to open it. If privacy is a real concern, an e-

mail beats a fax, which could lie around for hours, or days, at an open fax machine once you send it.

- There are no long-distance charges for sending e-mail anywhere in the world, and the transmission is close to instantaneous.

Knowing Which Format to Use Is Critical

When sending information by e-mail, you need to decide which method of transmission to use. You've basically got two main decisions to make. First, you can insert your cover letter and résumé into the body of the e-mail message itself. If you do this, you must decide whether to type in the material from scratch or cut and paste from a pre-existing file. Second, you can append your document as an attachment. Going this route means you have to know which format to save your document in, plain text or fully-formatted, as well as the set-up of your recipient.

Full Formatting Versus Plain Text I talk a lot in this chapter about formatting. You'll recall from Chapter 2 that ASCII is plain text, which means no fancy fonts or elaborate layouts (more about this later). With e-mail, you may find that you have to convert your cherished résumé, with all its artistic flair, into a dull-looking, text-only document. I'll let you know when it's necessary and how to do it.

The Recipient Determines Your Course Of Action Let's put aside your personal preferences for a moment. Otherwise, you'll find yourself choosing the easiest method all the time, namely, attaching a fully formatted file to your e-mail message. This method only takes a couple of steps and your formatting is preserved. The danger here is that your recipient may not be equipped to read the format you've sent. Result? You've got cyber-egg on your face (and no interview!).

Option One: In the Body of Your Message

As I mentioned, you can put your cover letter and résumé information directly into the body of your e-mail message. You might have to do this when your recipient has the ability to receive e-mail, but doesn't have the same word processing program as you, or when you have no idea what kind of set-up your recipient has.

Why It's Good—And Not Good The nice part about this option is that it virtually ensures your message will be readable by your recipient, no matter which e-mail application they use. There is some bad news though. By putting your text into the body of your message, you can only send it as plain text (ASCII), as things now stand. That means goodbye to all your fancy fonts (bold, italic, underline) and attractive set up styles (indenting, bullet points, graphics).

CYBER TIP Don't assume that your recipient can receive and decode your Word or WordPerfect files. They must have a similar program with a version that's at least as recent as the one you're sending your file as, in order to convert what you send them. If they do have the same program, but it's as little as one generation older (e.g. Word 6.0 to your Word For Windows 95) they won't be able to convert your file.

Inputting the Text Manually in the Body of Your Message You would use this approach if you haven't yet created your word processed cover letter and résumé. Otherwise you could use the cut and paste method (described further below) to copy your existing stuff into a new file. The following steps will guide you with inputting the text manually into the body of your message.

1. Call up your e-mail program onto your screen (refer back to Chapter 2 for more details).
2. Click on the "New Mail" icon (or whatever your program uses to create a new message).
3. Put in the e-mail address of the recipient (use the e-mail's address book, if available), and type in the topic of your message in the "subject" line (it should refer to the job being sought).
4. Manually type in your entire message, including your cover letter and résumé. Keep it plain and simple.
5. Review your document for errors, using the e-mail's spell-check program (if available).
6. When you're satisfied, send your message to your recipient.
7. Check your e-mail inbox a few minutes later to see if your e-mail has been returned as unsendable. If it hasn't, that means it arrived safely.

Cutting and Pasting the Text into the Body of Your Message This method is much easier than rewriting your entire application package several times. All you need to do is insert the existing version that you saved in your word processing program earlier. Mind you, there is the little glitch of converting your text to ASCII. I suggest that you do so within your word processing program *before* pasting it into your e-mail. This will allow you to realign the text more quickly and effectively.

1. Go into your word processing program and call up the file that has your cover letter and résumé saved together as one file.
2. Make a plain text (ASCII) version of the file. Start by selecting "Save As," then in the "As Type" box, choose "ASCII DOS TEXT" (if using WordPerfect) or "Text Only" (if using Word). You want your new file to have a ".txt" suffix.
3. Under the "Edit" command on your toolbar, click on "Select All." This highlights all the text in your new file. Then select the "Copy" command to pick up all the text.
4. Repeat steps 1 through 3 from the preceding instructions.
5. Point your cursor to the uppermost, left-hand corner of your message area. Click once to anchor the text, then paste the text into the body of your e-mail by selecting "Paste" from the "Edit" menu.
6. Make any adjustments that are needed to the layout of your text (but don't add anything fancy, or it could throw things off).
7. Repeat steps 5 through 7 of the preceding instructions.

CYBER TIP Use the word processing program's spell-check and grammar-check features to search for errors before you paste the file into the body of your e-mail. If you make additional changes to the text once it's in your e-mail, do a final review using an e-mail spell-checker such as CyberSpell (available as a free add on to Netscape 2 and higher versions).

Option 2: Sending an Attachment

Oh, how I love this option. In my opinion, it's like sending a fax from your PC, only better. If you can send your attachment in its original format (that is, without having to first convert it into plain text), you have a fast, efficient way of getting your materials anywhere across the globe—with the full layout intact.

Sending a Fully-Formatted Attachment When would you use this approach? When you want the reader to receive a fully-formatted version of your cover letter and résumé, complete with fancy fonts and attractive layout. In other words, exactly as it appears in your word processing file.

When else would you use this approach? Only when you're certain that your recipient will be able to convert your attachment properly. If you're not sure, do yourself a favour—call the company and ask the switchboard operator or administrative staff about their electronic set-up. If it's compatible, you may be in luck. If not, it's time for the ASCII (plain text) route again.

> **REAL LIFE** *Always try to find out what your recipient is looking for in terms of e-mail. Even if your programs are compatible, they may not want a fully-formatted attachment. This could happen if the company is using a scanning process or database storage system that requires plain text. (Back to rule number 1 in self-marketing: give'em what they want.)*

To send your résumé package as a fully-formatted attachment you should:

1. Review the word processed file containing your cover letter and résumé to ensure that it's in the proper form.
2. Call up your e-mail program onto your screen. Click on the "New Mail" icon (or whatever your program uses to create a new message).
3. Put in the e-mail address of the recipient (use the e-mail's address book, if available), and type the topic of your message in the Subject line.
4. Manually type in a brief message, mentioning the purpose of your e-mail, and that you've attached your cover letter and résumé (mention the file type and format). Also state the reference number and title of the job you're applying for. Note that this, in effect, becomes your cover page. It's the first thing your reader will see before they open your attached file, so it had better be good.

5. Click on the "Attachment" icon to select the file you want to attach. Browse your files and select the proper one.
6. Choose "As Is" or "MIME" as the protocol, depending on your e-mail client. This will protect the format in its current state.
7. Send your message to your recipient.
8. Check your e-mail inbox a few minutes later to see if your e-mail has been returned as unsendable. If it hasn't, that means it arrived safely.

Sending a Plain Text Attachment You might choose this alternative if your recipient specifically asks for it. I'll remind you quickly that plain text (or ASCII) takes all the special fonts and styles out of your document. You'd probably only do this by special request. It makes your text universally readable, but the recipient still has to have a corresponding word processing program to open your file up and read it.

To sent your résumé package as a plain text attachment you should:

1. Review the word processed file containing your cover letter and résumé to ensure that it's in the proper form.
2. Make a plain text version of the file. Start by selecting "Save As," then in the "As Type" box, choose "ASCII DOS TEXT" (if using WordPerfect) or "Text Only" (if using Word). You want your new file to have a ".txt" suffix. Make any changes to the layout as needed, and resave as ".txt."
3. Repeat steps 2 through 5 from the previous instructions.
4. Select "MIME," "ASCII" or "TEXT" (depending on your e-mail client).
5. Repeat steps 7 through 8 from the previous instructions.

CYBER TIP With some programs, you can create your e-mail off-line (that is, when you're not connected to the Internet). Then, when you're ready, you can dial up your online service and quickly send your completed message, using up very little of your online time. This can save you money (if you're paying an hourly rate), and it frees up your phone line (for potential employers to call in).

Do a Test (Just in Case) Regardless of the option that you go with, here's a neat idea to try. To preview how your message will appear, you can try sending your e-mail to yourself first. This won't guarantee that your reader will see it exactly the same way, because different e-mail packages may have slight variations in formatting. You will, however, be able to catch most major glitches.

V. APPLYING THROUGH AN INTERNET FORM

Some companies are ahead of the game and have tried to make the electronic transmission of your application as painless as possible. One such organization is Canadian Tire. Check out their human resources Web site and you'll see what I'm referring to: **http://www.cyberplex.com/CyberPlex/CanadianTire/CTHome.html**.

There is a lot of useful information on the company and its key business units. There is also a listing of available positions within the company. Each of these can be clicked on for a detailed look at the job description and requirements. These folks have even included a calendar outlining when Canadian Tire will be conducting college and university career fairs and interviews on campus.

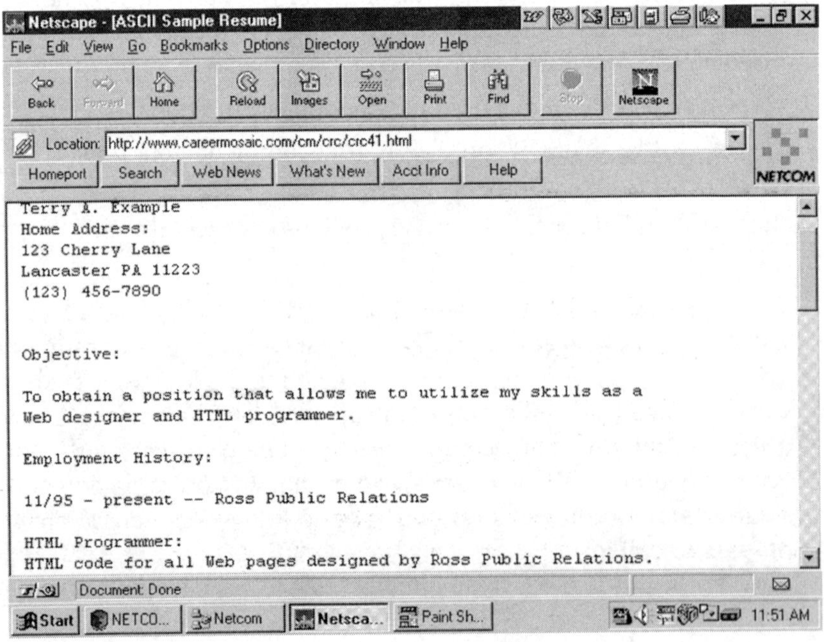

It's All In The Form

One of the things that makes this site user-friendly is an electronic résumé submission form (*Internet form*). Not only can you see the job postings, but you can apply immediately by completing the required information and clicking the "Submit" icon.

To see an example of this, go to "About You. Send Us Your Résumé" on the Canadian Tire site. It allows you to type your name and address into the boxes. Then you're asked to cut and paste your résumé directly into the form. Since it's an Internet form, your only option at this point is to use the ASCII, or plain text, approach.

All you have to do at this point is click on "Submit" and your information is whisked away to Canadian Tire's database. Like every other electronic method, it doesn't hurt to send a snail mail hard copy and follow up with a phone call after a few days to make sure that your application was received.

CYBER TIP If (and only if) you're a high-tech worker, you can strut your stuff to a potential employer with a Web-based, multimedia résumé. It can include hyper-text, graphics, sound and video. When you send out your regular application, make sure you highlight your URL on your cover page, cover letter and résumé, so employers will know where to look. Find examples by going to **http://www.altavista.digital.com/cgi-bin/query?** and using the AltaVista search engine. In advanced search, type in "multimedia and résumé." Choose examples that look appealing and preview them. It helps to have a browser that supports frames, plus a sound and video card in your PC.

VI. SUBMITTING YOUR RÉSUMÉ AND COVER LETTER FOR SCANNING

Scanning—the word chills me to my very core. Isn't this what the aliens did to the humans in that flick *Independance Day*? Well, maybe not. But it *is* something that most of us need to know about. Right now, it's the up-and-coming technology for résumé processing. Already it has become extremely popular in the States (almost every Fortune 500 company is using it). Now our very own companies such as Canadian Tire, The C.E.O. Group and a growing number of others are hopping on board.

Growing in Popularity Every Day It's easy to see why scanning is becoming so popular. Scanning enables human resources departments to easily manage massive numbers of résumés. When résumés are processed using scanning techniques, the image or text itself can be stored in an electronic database, which employers can search using specific criteria.

Although it's expensive for companies to have their own complete system, there are services in Canada that are starting to act as affordable, third-party résumé handlers.

Once Again, It's Not Cut and Dried

Just like the other technologies we've looked at so far, there's more than one way to approach scanning. In this case, you've either got straight scanning, or Optical Character Recognition (OCR).

Image Versus Text In straight scanning, your résumé is stored purely as an electronic image. That means that the computer cannot decipher the text that you've written, even though you've done it on a word processor.

OCR does things differently. It starts the same way, by converting your application to an image first, then back into readable text. This way, the employer can retrieve résumés on the bases of specific words or criteria.

Just like with e-mail applications, it's absolutely necessary to know in advance which version of OCR is being used. You'll have to design your materials a little bit differently for each version (see Table 5.1).

Some Living and Breathing Examples To illustrate the variations in the main methods of scanning, let's look at two leading online employment matching companies in Canada. These are services that accept your résumé, input it into their database, then match you up with positions for companies that are hiring (see Chapter 9 for more details on fees, features and cautions). The first company, JCI-JobMatch, uses straight scanning. The other, CareerConnect, incorporates OCR technology. We'll take a quick look at the application process for each in the following section.

Scanning as Image (Not Converting to Text)

When you go to sign up with JCI-JobMatch, you'll receive a complete

Table 5.1 Formatting for Straight Scanning Versus Optical Character Recognition (OCR)

FORMATTING REQUIREMENTS	STRAIGHT SCANNING (IMAGE)	OCR (TEXT)
Recommended Fonts	Any of the fonts you would normally use in a résumé, including fancy ones (if so desired)	Any sans serif, plain font will do (e.g. Times, Courier, Helvetica, Univers, Optima, Bookman). In other words, no fancy stuff
Text Features	Use the styles you normally would to make your résumé attractive	No bullet points, underlines, italics, bolding, tables or tabs. Also, no hard returns , shading, or lines
Text Size Guidelines	Stick to 12 point for easy reading	Minimum 10 point, maximum 14 point, so that the OCR software can read it properly (try 12 point if it will be read by a human too)
Using Images or Graphics	Use if you feel it will assist you in breaking through	Don't use 'em
How To Send A Hard Copy Of Your Application	Send original by regular mail or courier. Fax is iffy, because it may degrade the quality of the text. Use good quality white paper with print on one side only. Do not use staples	Send original by regular mail or courier. Fax is iffy, because it may degrade the quality of the text. Use good quality white paper with print on one side only. Do not use staples
How To Electronically Send A Copy Of Your Application	If they accept formatted attachments, you may be able to use e-mail	E-mail in plain text only, or Internet form where available (also plain text only)

sign-up kit in the mail. They ask you to fill out some paper-based forms describing your work history, education level and computer skills. They also provide a return envelope, in which you submit the completed forms and a high-quality copy of your most recent résumé.

When JCI receives your package (and your cheque), they take out your résumé and scan it as an image. They also code the data from your completed forms, so that their computer can match you to available jobs. Note that they do not allow you to send your résumé in electronically. See for yourself at **http://www.jcitech.com/jobmatch/index.htm**.

How the System Works Don't worry, I'm not going to launch into a lecture on database mechanics or electronic technology (I'm not a techie). Let's just say that once your résumé gets scanned, it goes into JCI's database. An employer who is registered with JCI can access their database when looking for people to interview. If you have the experience and credentials they're searching for, the employer might ask to see your résumé. If so, JCI will fax them a copy. This is why the quality of the résumé that you send in initially is so important. The employer will then decide whether or not to contact you directly.

Scanning as Text (Converting an Image Through OCR)

With CareerConnect, things work in a slightly different way. You still send in a high-quality copy of your résumé, only in this case, you can choose to submit it electronically. First the company scans it, then they run their OCR software to turn your résumé into readable text, and after that it's saved in ASCII format. Because of this extra step, you must format your résumé in a way that meets the needs of the computer equipment (see Table 5.1). Look this site up at **http://careerconnect.theglobeandmail.com**.

The Employer Has the Final Say Registered employers who are hiring can access the CareerConnect database and search by any combination of keywords that they want (e.g., years of experience, job titles, computer skills). This is not quite the same as a keyword format résumé, which is discussed briefly in Chapter 11. If your résumé comes up during a search, the employer can get a copy. They'll contact you directly if they want to pursue things further.

Hints to Make Plain Text Stand Out

It's not easy to be attractive when you're stripped of all your clothes, makeup, shoes and hair grooming gunk. This is much the same for a plain text résumé. Think of it as sending in your application stark naked (nowhere near as embarrassing as showing up that way for the interview).

All Gussied Up and No Place to Go When your material is converted to plain text (ASCII), it loses much of its special look. Still, there are ways to compensate. Here are a couple of tips:

- Use dashes instead of horizontal lines.
- Substitute capital letters for fancy text (e.g. bold, underlines, shading).
- Replace bullets with asterisks (*).

Here's one more thing to think about. Even when you're putting your résumé on an electronic database, consider including a cover page. It will be scanned along with your résumé. Try to let your expertise and personality show through. It just might be the thing that differentiates you from the other applicants.

CYBER TIP When you know your résumé is going to be scanned, and you're sending it via regular mail or courier, make sure that it's the highest possible quality. Send it in on plain white paper (not too thick); provide an original, not a photocopy (otherwise you start to get text degradation, which scanners hate); print on one side only, and don't use staples; forget dot matrix printers—try for at least an inkjet of 600 dpi (laser printers are preferred); and check to see that there are no errors or smudges (or the scanner will choke).

VII. WIRED WRAP UP

When my three-year-old son sits down to cut and paste, we give him some children's scissors and non-toxic glue. When you do it, odds are you'll be using a mouse, a word processor and an e-mail program. Oh, how times have changed.

I can barely remember the last time that I licked a stamp or placed a folded letter into an envelope. Between faxing, e-mail and the Web, I can reach virtually all of my business contacts—whenever I need to.

The same holds true for your work-search. Now that an increasing number of employers are requesting electronically sent materials, it falls directly on your shoulders to respond accordingly. If you do it properly, there are some definite benefits:

- Your message arrives quickly.
- The quality is high.
- You demonstrate to the employer that you have at least some of the skills needed to thrive in today's economy.

I have to admit that the new rules haven't quite replaced the old ones yet. This can be a pain because you sometimes have to duplicate your efforts. Why, for instance, should you have to *call* an employer to find out the best way to e-mail them? Or that thing about sending a hard copy by mail in addition to the application you filled out on the Web. I mean, isn't that a waste of time?

The answer, at present, is "no, it's not a waste." Whenever a system is in the process of being converted, you have to expect redundancies. That's just what we're experiencing now. Companies are really just beginning to switch to the new technologies. However, most applicants (and most human resources departments) are used to the older, more established approaches. That means you have to satisfy both ends of the spectrum.

If you're thinking that it takes a bit of extra effort to do things this way, you're absolutely right. However, think as well in terms of *results*. If employers are giving you the option of sending your application the hi-tech route, and you're one of the people who can do it, you're automatically ahead.

Of course, it's up to you to ensure that your material is top notch, and that your interview and follow-up skills are finely honed. What you're striving for is integration and consistency. It requires determination and know-how to blend the best of the old with the new, and technology with the human touch. Take the time to learn how to do it properly. It may just lead you to where you want to be.

CHAPTER 6

Researching and Targeting Potential Employers

Virtual Definition: **gopher** (gō′fər) *noun*

An older, text-based method of making material available over the Internet. Gopher is a client and server style program, which requires the user to have a gopher client program to access the information. Masses of data can be stored on gopher sites, though they have basically been replaced by Web sites.

I. DIGGING FOR GOLD

Let's say that you've just finished creating the ultimate résumé. Not only does it accurately describe your every skill and accomplishment, it does so in vivid, dynamic terms guaranteed to capture your reader's attention. And the layout—well, it's nothing less than a masterpiece. To top it off, every single word is spelled correctly and your grammar is faultless. Now there's just one little question left to answer: Who do you send the résumé to?

Passive Is Passé

As it turns out, you've got several options here. You could wait (and wait) until you see the perfect job ad in your local newspaper. Good luck. Or you can mass produce your résumé, sending it out blindly to every company within a hundred mile radius of your home and hope it all works out.

Then there's the proactive option: finding companies that you'd like to work for and going after them directly. This approach, by far the most effective way to search for work, is called *targeting*. It's a process of identifying and learning about potential employers in your field of interest.

The Real Secret to Getting what You Want

There are no crystal balls or coin tosses involved here. Far from it. Instead it takes determination, investigative skills and persistence. Your objective here is straightforward. You're trying to match strengths, accomplishments and interests with the needs of the companies you'd really like to work for. And the basic ingredient is...research.

Going After the Good Stuff Research? Yuck. It's kind of like spinach, don't you think? You know it's good for you, but there's something unappealing about it nonetheless. In this stage of your job hunt, however, information gathering skills become critical. If knowledge is pure gold, research is your best means of sniffing it out. You'll want to know which companies are offering work in your particular field, where they are located and what kind of people they are looking for. Then it's time to narrow down the list. Which companies would you like to be involved with? What kinds of products and services do they offer? What makes these particular companies special? You'll learn how to answer these questions, and so much more, in this chapter.

CYBER TIP You can now hook up to libraries across Canada from your home. On the Web, you can go to **http://library.usask.ca/~scottp/canlib.html** and find the one closest to you. Some libraries are also offering diskettes which enable you to dial in via modem. You can't quite read the books online yet. What you can do is find out which books are available, make reservations and browse the collections.

This Is How It Can Work in the Real World

I'd like to offer a personal example to show how targeting can work for you. A number of years ago, I decided to make a major career shift because I was feeling very unfulfilled as a corporate marketing manager. After extensive career counselling and a great deal of inward and outward exploration, I decided to change fields. The area I really wanted to go into was helping people make career and lifestyle transitions, based on who they truly are. After coming to this conclusion (and believe me, it took a long time), my first task was to find out where I could do this sort of work. I already knew that career counselling was offered in a wide variety of formats (discussed in Chapter 3). But now I had to find out who, if anyone, would hire me.

Making a Broad List of Target Companies And where did I turn first? To my trusty phone book, of course (this predated the days of instantaneous, online info). Under the section on Career Counselling, there were more than 40 companies listed. I also looked under the Outplacement Counselling heading, where I found another 20 companies. To my delight, I suddenly had 60 potential employers as the base of my target companies.

Selecting the Top Priorities My next step was to narrow down the field. I didn't have time to personally approach each one of my 60 prospects. And why would I want to, anyway? It seemed obvious that some places would offer a better fit with my background and skills than others. I then asked myself, "Which of these companies would I really want to work for?" (I must admit, though, at times the question felt more to me like "Which of these companies would ever want to hire me?")

This took me to stage two: developing my target list. Here's where my research kicked into high gear. I went to the reference section of my local library. My librarian showed me how to use search terms to find specific information about the career counselling industry.

Gather Knowledge About Your Industry I discovered a wealth of information. There were articles on how the industry was changing, and who the main companies were. There were even interviews with some of the top people in the field. And there was lots of discussion about future trends, key issues and important past events.

Armed with this overview of the industry, I began contacting some people in the field. It was a lot less difficult than I'd imagined. I started by calling a few of the people who'd been quoted in the articles I'd collected. Amazingly, they were thrilled that someone had taken the time to follow up. Soon I was meeting with some of them in their offices. They graciously spoke with me about their perspectives on the industry. (This process, known as information interviewing, is described in Chapter 8.)

Once You've Got the General, Move Towards the Specific Each time I met with someone, I asked them very specific questions. Who are the best companies in this field? Are certain companies known for their work in particular areas? Where do you think someone with my skills and interests would do well? Can you give me the names of a few people to contact at companies that you would recommend?

By the time I'd met with a dozen or so people, I had a pretty clear idea of the kinds of companies that were out there, and where I might fit in best. This enabled me to prepare a target list of 10 companies. Compare this to the 60 companies I'd started with. My task had become much more manageable. Now I could focus my efforts on these top prospects.

Going for the Kill At this point, my research became much more focused. I tried to find out everything I could about the companies on my target list. I wanted to know if the company was growing (or downsizing), how the company treated its employees, comparative salary ranges and who was responsible for hiring. Now I was ready to start my marketing campaign in earnest (mainly through networking, which I talk about in Chapter 8). Ultimately, my combination of research and targeting started me on the road to a successful career change. I saved time by only pursuing companies that made sense. People responded to my inquiries because I had taken the time to learn about their organization and find out the right person to contact. Best of all, it seemed to me that my competitors were eating my dust. They were sending off hundreds of résumés in the faint hope of finding any sort of work. I, on the other hand, was systematically seeking out my best employment prospects.

REAL LIFE *Let me be the first to concede that the approach I've just described may not suit everyone's needs. A targeted, planned approach takes time and resources. If you're in a situation where you're looking for work—any work—as soon as possible, you still need a plan of action. Simply skip the stage where you ask yourself "what do I really want to do?" and substitute the phrase "who will hire me immediately?" Then concentrate your efforts on the best prospects.*

Today It's Easier than Ever to Be Proactive Now back to the present. As I sat down to write this chapter, I asked myself if there's anything I would do differently if I had to do it all again today. The answer is a resounding "yes." I'd take advantage of all the newest electronic information sources. This includes the World Wide Web, Commercial Service Providers and CD-ROM databases. These tools make the process of researching faster and easier.

Take It a Step at a Time, if You Can You may be anxious to jump in and start researching your target companies. But before racing ahead, consider taking a multifaceted approach. For instance, you could begin with an overview of the economy and how it's affecting the particular sector that you're interested in. You can also track current events to see what kind of impact they're having on your chosen industry.

Then you can move on to the selected industry itself. Look at the key players, understand the trends and overriding issues. This will help you select the companies you want to learn more about. It will also make you far more knowledgeable, which will put you in a great position during networking sessions and job interviews. (It will also help you identify markets and trends if you're considering self-employment.)

II. KEEPING INFORMED ABOUT BUSINESS AND THE ECONOMY

Broadening your knowledge of the economy and current events will help you to understand where the jobs are and how our economy is shifting. Here are some things to look for:

- Local, national and international economic trends that might have an impact on you.
- Government employment initiatives that could help you find work.
- General business news, such as company start-ups or plant closings.
- Current events that may influence the plans that you are making.

Global Is Good

Using the general-to-specific format, you can start with international overviews. For news from around the world, visit the Cable News

Network Web site at: **http://cnn.com/WORLD/index.html**. It gives you headlines and stories from CNN, which are frequently updated. You can click on the headlines to get the details on stories that interest you.

If it's international economic information that you're looking for, consider viewing Industry Canada's multi-cultural information advisor. It's on their Strategis Web site, at **http://strategis.ic.gc.ca/sc_mangb/contact/engdoc/main.html**. Strategis is just about the best site on the Net to find international business and economic information from a Canadian perspective.

CYBER TIP Don't worry if you have trouble locating specific details your first few times out. If you're not getting what you want, go back to a search directory such as Yahoo Canada (**http://www.yahoo.ca**), and look through the categories. With a bit of practice, and a lot of patience, you'll get the hang of searching in cyber-space.

Oh Canada

You can also get purely Canadian info from many sites on the Web. National news stories can be found through the *Globe and Mail* (**http://www.theglobeandmail.com**). You'll see some headlines and a few detailed articles, but not the entire paper—yet. Or check out Canadian Online Explorer (Canoe), a Web site developed by Maclean Hunter. It's got 24 hour news, with articles that can be easily downloaded. You can also link to *Maclean's* magazine, *The Financial Post, Chatelaine Magazine,* and all the *Sun* newspapers. The great thing about the Canoe site is that there's a vast range of information and services (including online forums) in one place.

What's Up in the Economy (Besides Unemployment)

When it's Canadian economic data you're looking for, it's there on the Web. The Strategis site from Industry Canada has a microeconomic monitor. This is a detailed review of economic activity, produced on a quarterly basis. Included is sector-specific information (see **http://strategis.ic.gc.ca/sc_ecnmy/engdoc/homepage.html**).

Then there's the Statistics Canada look at our economy. StatsCan has gone to great lengths to produce some extremely useful information on its Web site (**http://www.statcan.ca/Documents/English/Pgdb/economy.htm**). This particular portion includes general economic conditions, the international trade picture, and industry performance.

Looking at It Provincially

Just to show you how much information there is on the Web, you can also find detailed data on every single province in Canada. For example, the Strategis site provides provincial industrial overviews at **http://strategis.ic.gc.ca/sc_ecnmy/mera/engdoc/05.html**. It looks at each province from an overall perspective, and by specific industry as well. Moreover, it's updated on a regular basis.

CYBER TIP Listen to this (literally): you can now hear the news directly on your computer. You'll need a RealAudio program, available for free downloading at the 680 News Radio Web site. Your PC must also have a built-in soundcard. Try it out at **http://www.canoe.ca.**

Newspapers Go Online For provincial news coverage, Maclean Hunter offers Planet Sun. This is where you'll locate stories from newspapers in different regions under the Sun banner. Choose from Edmonton, Calgary, Toronto or Ottawa. Planet Sun can be found at **http://www.canoe.ca** and your host is Rogers Multi-Media Inc.

The *Toronto Star* is also available, to a large degree, on the Web. When you go to their site, you can read the news just as you would your morning paper. Scroll to the section you want and find the articles that appeal to you. If certain articles can help you in your work search, print them out and file them. It beats stepping outside your house on a cool winter's morning to snatch the real thing.

There are more publications going online every day—and it's not just the big guys anymore. For an up-to-date list, check out the Yahoo Canada search directory at **http://www.yahoo.ca.** Under the News and Media category, click on "Newspapers." Select "Canadian Categories," then choose a province to see which newspaper links are featured.

CYBER TIP You can now get automatic updates on all your favourite topics. **News gathering agents** collect the information on subjects that you select. They travel all over the Internet and bring it directly to your computer. There are free services such as The Pointcast Network. Pointcast, hosted by the Globe and Mail, has Canadian content and is located at **http://www.pointcast.com/whatis.html.** For a more customizable, fee-based service, try IBM's Infosage, at **http://www.ibm.com.**

Off the Net, on to CD-ROM

Time to disconnect from the Web and fire up your CD-ROM drive. Well, it's probably not *your* PC you'll be using. More than likely you'll have to head out to a local library that's equipped for the task. What you're looking for are CD-ROMs that contain enormous amounts of news bits and articles—all of it *searchable* by subject, name or industry. You can't buy them in stores, but if you have anywhere between $500 to $3000 lying around, you might be able to obtain one for home use (otherwise you better head to the library).

Abstracts or Full Text? The number of CD-ROMs with useful information for work searchers continues to grow. Something to watch for is the depth of content that you'll find on each. Many of these provide abstracts or citations only. What this means is that the text of the article itself is not found on the same disc. All you get is a brief summary of what the article is about.

The more direct path is to use a full text CD. You get all the news you can handle in a searchable, downloadable format—information heaven. The tradeoff is that you don't get as many citations, and they don't go back nearly as far.

Abstract and Citation CDs for News Articles There are several excellent news-oriented CDs which are bursting with abstracts. One example is ABI/INFORM. It contains more than 550,000 abstracts for articles appearing in approximately 1,000 American, Canadian and international periodicals. This covers business, management, trends, corporate strategies, competitive and product information.

Magazine Index Plus is another wide-ranging guide. It has periodical articles from a variety of Canadian publications. This complements the Canadian Business and Current Affairs (CBCA) disc, which claims to provide instant access to over two million articles in over 600 Canadian magazines and eight daily newspapers, over a ten year period.

Full Text CDs for News Articles Could there be anything more convenient than getting access to all the articles you've ever dreamed of at the click of a button (well, perhaps not *every* article)? Interestingly, the ABI/INFORM disc I mentioned earlier also comes in a version that has the complete text of each article from 550 major publications since 1991.

Canadian NewsDisc is great for newspaper articles. You'll find the complete text of articles from seven major Canadian newspapers, plus *Maclean's* magazine. You may be able to uncover revealing info about trends and historical happenings that will help you with your planning.

III. FINDING OUT ABOUT PARTICULAR INDUSTRIES

From the extended economic overview, we can now start to taper our information hunt. This brings us to the industry (or industries) where

REAL LIFE *When was the last time you asked a real live* ***librarian*** *for assistance? Yes, I said librarian. Remember them? The people who are highly skilled in helping you locate the precise information that you need? They're located in many forums: public or reference libraries, academic institutions (colleges and universities), even your trade association may have one. Many librarians have become experts in helping you locate the exact piece of data that you need—electronically.*

you're thinking of working. These are some of the details you might want to know:

- The names of companies in a given industry in the region where you'd like to work.
- The kinds of products and services offered in this field.
- Names and profiles of key people in the industry.
- Names, addresses and contact information for the associations representing the industry.
- The main issues and trends that the industry is faced with.

To the Web We Go

You can commence your search for industry data on the World Wide Web. Why not start with a complete list of all the companies in your field. Jump to the Canadian Yellow Pages, as presented by InfoSpace at **http://206.129.166.101/categ/cancategory.html**. This is truly an incredible resource. It's like having every phone book and every fax number list from each city in North America. You can look for all companies within a particular industry, cross-referenced against city or province.

REAL LIFE *A word of warning: you might want to double-check your cyber-data against traditional sources. For instance, don't rely exclusively on Web-based telephone numbers and addresses. This free information tends to be up-to-date, but you can never really be sure. Check your "old-fashioned" paper phone book to ensure that you haven't missed anything. Not everything gets captured in cyberspace (yet)!*

Name Your Sector

The Strategis Web site offers a thorough industry overview called Industrial Perspectives: Key Sectors in Canada. You can review this site at **http://strategis.ic.gc.ca/sc_indps/engdoc/homepage.html**. There's a wealth of data here that can give you insight into how your industry is doing.

Spotting the Growth Industries How about some advice from one of Canada's best known economists, Nuala Beck. She's assembled an excellent site that shows you who the winning industries are, and where the losers are headed. It's a great way to gain an understanding of the sector you've targeted. It's all at **http://www.neweconomy.com**. And on the American side, go to **http://www.jobtrak.com/jobsearch_docs/indoutlk.html** for the American government's overview of the major industrial sectors.

Industry Associations Another terrific source for sectoral information is the association that represents a given industry. It's possible that you already belong to one (or more) already. Now they're moving to

the Web. An example is the Canadian Banker's Association. It has news releases, publications and hotlinks relating to the financial services industry. You can find it at **http://www.cba.ca**. For links to other Canadian associations, try **http://www.clo.com/~canadainfo/assocon.html**, the Associations Canada Online Web site. It gives you a searchable list of associations, segmented by category. Unfortunately it's not the full list. They'll gladly sell you a copy of their complete list, but you'd be better off going to the library and using their copy.

CD-ROM Solutions

As for CD-ROMs, there is a great deal of industry-specific information here. The *Canadian Business, Trade & Technology* CD is just one example. It offers the full text of 120 Canadian industry and professional periodicals and newsletters. The publisher is Micromedia Limited. It allows you to search by industry, as well as other sub-categories. You'd be amazed at what you can find.

There are at least a half-dozen other CD-ROMs containing data on Canadian industries, 20 to 30 on industry in the U.S., and more for international material. Use them selectively to gain quick insight about what you're getting yourself into.

REAL LIFE *Not all the information you need will be found electronically. Your local library, for example, is an excellent source of printed material. There are business directories and local chamber of commerce magazines. Reading newspapers, journals and business newsletters can also be helpful. And don't ignore the human touch. You can often get information from your colleagues and networking contacts that you will never find in published sources.*

IV. GENERAL INFORMATION ON SPECIFIC COMPANIES

It's time to narrow down your base of potential employers to those that appear most promising. In creating this target list, the kinds of things you'll want to know about a company include:

- Location of head office, branches, plants, corporate parents and subsidiaries.
- Financial status of the company (including profit history and future forecasts).
- The operating style and corporate culture.
- Names, titles and background information on the people who are in a position to hire you.
- Products and services offered by the company, and areas of specialty (if any).
- Salary and benefit packages as they compare to the competition.

Home Sweet Homepage

Start by going to the Web site of a company that interests you. Odds are that if they're well-known enough for you to recognize their name, they have a site. The type of stuff you can find ranges from information on the company's products and structure to key people, corporate history and financial details.

At the time of this writing, more than 75 percent of large Canadian companies have a presence on the Web. Over 50 percent of medium sized companies are there as well. Many smaller companies are coming on board too, because it's a relatively inexpensive method of connecting to a potentially large audience.

Finding Your Way Home With all the junk out there in cyberland, how do you navigate to the companies that interest you? I'll harken back briefly to my *Wizard of Oz* analogy by saying that you *don't* tap your ruby red slippers together and repeat the words "There's no place like home." What you can do is follow one of two searching methods: keyword and directory.

1. **Keyword search**
   Let's say, for argument's sake, that you wanted to work in the publishing industry. You could go to your favourite World Wide Web search engine (e.g. Open Text at **http://index.opentext.net**). If you typed in the first publishing company that popped into your head, like Prentice Hall for example, you'd get a big list of sites that may or may not match your criteria.

Within this list, which may have hundreds or thousands of URL citations, there likely lies a hyperlink that takes you straight to the Prentice Hall Web site. Fortunately there's a rule that can help you narrow down the choices. In the list of sites, look for the URL that has the company name as part of main address (e.g. **http://www.prenhall.com** for Prentice Hall). Click on it to connect to the site. Once in the company's Web site, follow the links and navigation tools to surf away.

2. **Directory search.**
   This approach works best when you know the industry you want to explore, but aren't sure which companies you're looking for. The Yahoo search directory gives you a great big list of links to company homepages from coast to coast. They're all arranged by industry category, to make it less confusing. There is now a Canadian Yahoo directory, in addition to the big U.S. version, available at **http://www.yahoo.ca/Regional/Countries/Canada/Business_and_Economy/Companies**.

   Another Web-based resource comes from Strategis. They've put to-

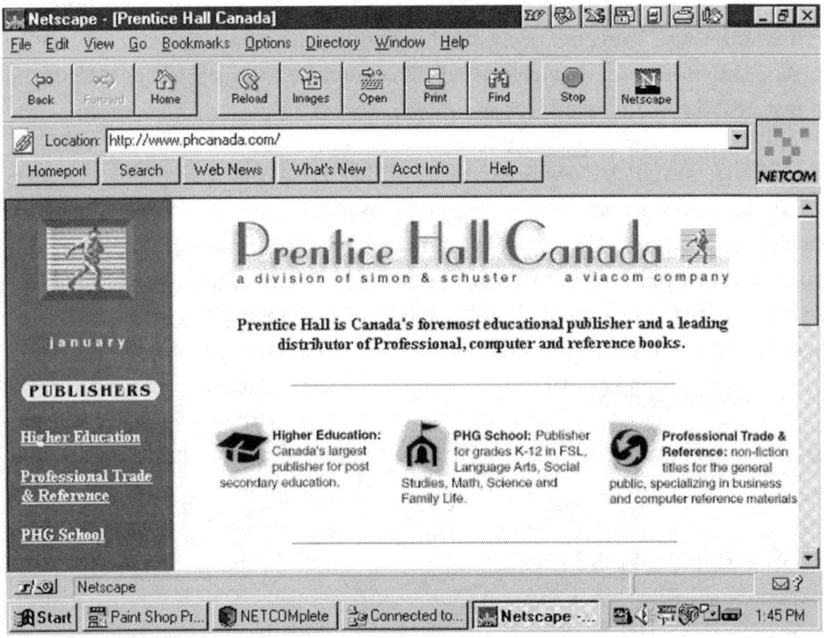

gether a series of links on their Canadian Company Capabilities site **http://strategis.ic.gc.ca/sc_coinf/engdoc/homepage.html**. Basically, it's a searchable grouping of Canadian companies. By clicking on the company's name, you are magically transported to their homepage.

It's Apparent Who the Parent Is Bear in mind that many Canadian companies are subsidiaries or divisions of larger conglomerates with a head office in the U.S. or other parts of the world. If that's the case, they may not have a separate listing for the Canadian Web site.

In these circumstances, your best bet is to find out who the parent company is. You can do this by checking out the CD-ROM entitled Inter-Corporate Ownership, which lists more than 75,000 corporations. Published by Statistics Canada, this resource basically tells you who owns whom.

Once you know who the parent company is, you can get back on the Web and find their homepage. The U.S. version of Yahoo has links to over 120,000 companies. You'll find it at **http://www.yahoo.com/text/Business_and_Economy/Companies**. From the parent's Web site you might just find a link to the Canadian subsidiary. Minimally, you'll be able to gather important details on the main company itself.

> **REAL LIFE** *When in doubt, pick up the phone. Once you've exhausted your online searches and still haven't found a company's Web site, call them and ask if they have one yet. But try at least three or four search engines first (e.g. AltaVista, Excite, InfoSeek and Maple Square).*

Philanthropy: A Different Route For those of you considering a career in the not-for-profit sector, go to the Charity Village Web site. It has links to many Canadian and international not-for-profit organizations. There are discussion forums to exchange ideas and make contact with others in this field. They've also provided a career guide.

Even if you're not thinking of a job in the nonprofit world, you can consider doing volunteer work. I often recommend this to my clients who want to give something back to society. It can also be a great way to expand your experience and increase your marketability. You can often develop your skills and credentials in new areas by doing project work for a not-for-profit institution. Everything you want to know is at **http://www.charityvillage.com/charityvillage/bus.html**.

Just The Facts Please Sometimes you need only the most basic of information on a company or organization. This would include things like the address, phone and fax numbers, e-mail address and 1-800 numbers. All of this is conveniently arranged for you at the InfoSpace Web site. You can easily search Canadian or U.S. companies. Try it at **http://www.infospace.com**.

V. HONING IN ON THE DETAILS

There are times when you might be seeking very specific information. Some occasions that come to mind are job interviews, networking sessions with targeted individuals and salary negotiations. The more you know about the company and people you're dealing with, the better your chances are to:

- Impress potential employers with your knowledge.
- Demonstrate your initiative and seriousness about working with their firm.
- Understand the realities of what you're getting into.
- Beat out your competitors.

The Free Versus Fee Debate Revisited

Can you believe all the free stuff on the Net? I used to wonder how all these companies could afford to put up detailed information without charging for it. Now I know better. Almost everyone's out to make a buck online. If the material you're using is free, it's probably just another form of marketing that the company is experimenting with, such as giving you a sample or demo of the full version of their product. The rationale is that if they give you a taste of their product without charge, you'll gladly fork over the bucks to get the real thing.

Consider the Source It's time for another of my little cautions. I think the Internet is great for gathering general information from all over the world. As a starting point, it's hard to beat. But it's not like having a private research company at your beck and call. The free information tends to be somewhat superficial, or biased in favour of the sponsoring company. It's just like everywhere else. You usually get what you pay for, so buyer beware. If you do shell out some money, you should demand value. The quality of the information you retrieve should exceed that of the free material. Look for data to be more recent, with greater scope and depth, as well as being quick and easy to locate. Moreover, it should come from a reliable, independent source.

Free and Clear

The corporate Web sites that provide free material may not give you everything you need, but they are a solid start. And anything that gets you moving toward your target is fine, in my mind.

Company Capsules on the Web The World Wide Web is full of free information on companies and organizations. The most popular form of data is a *capsule*. Typically, this is a very brief summary which includes the company's address, line of business, annual sales, and contact numbers. Basic data, but not bad for a freebie.

Hoover's Online, for example, gives you information capsules on more than 10,000 companies worldwide for free. Try **http://207.13.58.34** and you can search by industry, location and annual sales. In many cases they also provide a hyperlink directly to the company's Web site, and to online news services which automatically search for articles on that company (but don't expect *too* much, since it's free).

Another terrific source of capsules is the Thomas Registry. It provides details on nearly 55,000 industrial products and services, as well as information on thousands of manufacturers. In all, more than 1,500,000 individual product and service sources are included for companies in the U.S. and Canada.

The nice thing here is that they let you register online at no charge. Then you can immediately search their database by product/service, company name and location (state or province). You can take advantage of this at **http://www.thomasregister.com:8000/member.html**. The Canadian listings are somewhat limited; however, they also offer a demo version of their software that has more substance.

Company Profiles on the Web A *profile* of a company gives you much more depth than a mere capsule. Generally, you're provided with company background, history, range of products and services, key contacts and full financial disclosures. The problem is that, because it is free, your choices are somewhat limited. Having said that, look at what is available. Want to check out the Fortune 500 companies, by name and location? **http://www.search.com/Single/0,7,150400-50068,00.html** is the place to see American material, but interesting if you're looking at parent companies.

How about the *Financial Post* top 50? You can get them broken down by ranking on assets, revenues and all sorts of other criteria at **http://canoe2.canoe.ca/FP_Top50**.

Annual Reports on the Web Company annual reports are also tremendously useful for researching. They are produced by publically owned corporations, and contain a large amount of relevant information including company overviews, mission statements and full financial results.

Some of the larger companies have begun to provide their full reports online. Rogers Communications, for instance, has its report at **http://www.rogers.com/RCI/annual1.htm**. Note that you may have to use Adobe Acrobat Reader to view the files in their full format, but the site provides you with instructions on how to do this. One site to find some samples of online reports is the Investor Relations Information Network, in the U.S. Their Adobe-based annual reports are at **http://www.irin.com/acro30.html**.

CYBER TIP You can also order **hard copies** of annual reports via the Web. This saves you from calling the individual companies themselves (handy in terms of saving time and potential long distance charges). Two URLs to scope out are **http://www.prars.com/newform2.html** and **http://nt1.irin.com**.

Press Releases on the Web In addition to capsules and profiles, the Web contains a wide variety of press releases. Companies often announce new products, quarterly sales results, shifts in key personnel and other major happenings via their own news releases. Since the companies or their public relations agencies writes these releases themselves, don't look for dirty laundry here.

Press releases are accessible, by company name or subject, through several sources. Try Canada Newswire, a great example, at **http://www.newswire.ca/htmindex/organizations.html**. Not only can you peruse actual up-to-the-moment press releases, you can even use their Listserve feature. This allows you to get automatic updates on the companies that interest you the most. Select your favourites and news releases are instantly sent to your e-mail box when issued.

Canadian Corporate News provides similar services at **http://www.cdn-news.com**. I would suggest that you use both of these providers when necessary. Once or twice I've searched Canada Newswire for a particular company, but have found nothing. Then I went to Canadian Corporate News and there it was. The reverse also happens, so be diligent.

REAL LIFE *Many of my clients use press releases to get just-in-time information. An example is interview preparation. A day or two before they go in for the big interview, they check the Web to see the company's latest releases. Often my clients find valuable news that they can inject as part of their meeting. It shows the employer that you have real initiative and technical skills.*

Detailed Company Information Via CD-ROM CD-ROMs are your best choice for finding specific company data for free. They are easy to use and contain vast amounts of detail. You can find extensive company profiles, including lists of managers and executives, products offered, annual sales estimates, number of employees and other pertinent points, on the Compact Disclosure Canada CD. Produced by Micromedia, they have even described it for you on the web at **http://www.micromedia.on.ca**.

The Canadian Financial Statement Infobase (CFI) is another worthwhile disc. It features the top 500 public companies in Canada. You can find it, along with other info-packed CDs, at a library near you.

Fee-Based Services

Most people will find more than they need for free using CD-ROMs and the Web (and by talking with other people, of course). For those of you seeking the ultimate in convenience and more specific details, they are definitely available online—for a fee.

Cheap and Cheerful—At a Flat Rate For the budget minded, there are pay-per-use information services that focus on company information. Profiles of more than 11,000 U.S. companies can be found at

http://www.sec.gov/edgarhp.htm. These are the filings for the Securities Exchange Commission. It'll cost you $9.95 (U.S.) per month to read all the 10K reports you can handle.

Another relatively affordable route is an information service bundled with a Commercial Online Provider. An example is America Online, which charges you around $10.00 (U.S.) for five hours of online time. This monthly fee also gives you free access to Hoover's Company Reports. Here you can quickly look up detailed profiles on close to 4,000 major companies.

Hoover's is also available separately on the Web. For about $10.00 (U.S.) per month, you can access up to 100 reports. The depth of these reports is incredible. A free sample is stored at **http://207.13.58.34**.

The Pay-Per-View Option Dun and Bradstreet offers online access to their Business Background Report. It provides useful information on a company's history and operations, business background, special events and recent newsworthy items. At present, only U.S. companies are profiled, and it costs $20 (U.S.) to retrieve a report. There are, however, millions of companies to choose from. Their homepage is at **http://www.dbisna.com/dbis/product/secure.htm**.

Watch Those Fees Climb Higher Let's move up the scale a notch in terms of price and depth of information. Now we're getting into searchable databases that give you full text articles on the company (or subject) of your choice. One such service resides on CompuServe, a Commercial Online Provider. In addition to the monthly CompuServe subscription fee (around $10.00 [U.S.] for five hours), you can take advantage of *DataBase Plus*. This is an extensive collection of articles and reports that you can search by keyword. You get charged a couple of dollars (U.S.) for every article that you choose. I discovered the hard way that it doesn't take long to rack up large bills using this method. If it's any consolation, the service works well. I was able to find hard-to-get information immediately.

And Higher... For the info-junkies among us, there's even more. The *Globe and Mail* offers a searchable database that you can access from your computer. It's called the InfoGlobe Personal Edition. To use it, you'll need a communications software package, such as Symantec's WinComm, plus a disk provided by the *Globe and Mail*. It will cost you abut $40 a month to connect with the *Globe and Mail* database and download the article archives.

Highest! If this isn't enough for you, it's time to seek professional help. No, not that kind (though you might want to ask yourself why you need all the info that you're gathering). What I mean is, you can hire the services of a trained researcher, who will go online for you, to sophisticated databases such as Lexis, InfoMart or Dialog. The detail that can be found here is mind-boggling. But be forewarned: you get charged on two fronts. First, the database company may charge you simply to search each database, plus an additional download fee per article chosen. Moreover, the researcher will definitely charge you in the range of $25 to $100 per hour of their time. My suggestion: use this approach only in emergency situations, or if you have very little time and extremely deep pockets.

REAL LIFE *While research is important, so is taking action. Try not to spend so much time gathering information that you ignore other parts of your work-search. Find only as much data as you need to help you make an informed decision. Meanwhile, keep up your networking, letter writing and interviews.*

VI. WIRED WRAP UP

The information age is truly upon us. It has given us some incredibly powerful research tools for work-searching. We can explore corporate homepages on the World Wide Web, scan databases on Commercial Service Providers and locate detailed news stories on CD-ROMs. This gives us tremendous insight into the industries, companies and people who are doing the hiring.

When done properly, research builds the foundation for a targeted work-search. Rather than the shotgun approach of applying to every company possible, we can actually be proactive. Of course, it takes a bit of effort. Identifying the industries we'd like to work in and the companies who are hiring is no small task. And matching our strengths to meet the needs of the companies we'd like to work for takes some definite creativity.

The effort is worth it—you have my word. There is no more effective way to find work than by actively pursuing companies that you've targeted. How to approach these companies is the subject of Chapter 8. For now, it's enough to know that relevant information is a critical part your work-search. And electronic resources can help put you in the driver's seat on the road to securing employment.

CHAPTER 7

Assorted Skills for the Wired Work-Search

Virtual Definition: **fire wall** (fiər wôl) *noun*

A combination of hardware and software that separates a local area network (LAN) or other network into two or more parts for security purposes. Deters external users from penetrating a company's intranet or private internal data.

I. PREPARING TO MARKET YOURSELF

If you've been plugging away through each chapter, you're well on your way to finding yourself a new position. Here are some of the things that you've already accomplished:

- Completed a detailed self-examination.
- Explored a variety of career possibilities.
- Developed a targeted résumé and cover letter.
- Researched and pinpointed the companies you want to work for.

The next major stage is to launch your marketing campaign. Your goal is straightforward: try to secure work that is right for you. No matter how you decide to approach this stage, it gets very involved and time-consuming. The good news is that everything you've done so far has prepared you to market yourself effectively. And the bad news? Well, let's just say that, unless you enjoy the stress of job interviews and the occasional rejection, the worst is yet to come.

Increasing Your Effectiveness

Finding work can be a real grind. There are calls to make, meetings to schedule, letters to write, interviews to prepare for and sweat through, thank you notes to send—and that's just for starters. Then, when you finally get an offer, you still have to negotiate the best deal.

Before immersing yourself into your marketing campaign, there are certain skills that you should consider brushing up on. Basically, you want to go into the active selling stage with as many tools as you can to make the process easier, faster and more efficient.

Thankfully, there are several things you can do to maximize your chances for success. This chapter looks at four specific areas, and the ways that you can use technology in each.

- **Organizing:** Keeping your work-search on track and running smoothly.
- **Interviewing:** Polishing your techniques for formal interviews and networking meetings.
- **Phone Management:** Using the phone and voicemail professionally.
- **Negotiating:** Arranging an offer of employment to your advantage.

REAL LIFE *No marketing campaign is complete without a plan. This includes your work-search. To read about how to prepare your own personal strategy, check out "Conducting a Successful Job Search." This is a Web-based article written by Taunee Besson, which was first published in the* Wall Street Journal: National Business Employment Weekly. *You can find it at* **http://www.cweb.com/dimensions/Career_Dimensions3.html#Search**.

II. THE ORGANIZED WORK-SEARCH

Let's start with the issue of keeping on top of your work-search. Scheduling meetings, maintaining a record of who said what and following up properly—it all takes time. One of the more useful skills that you'll need in searching for work is the ability to organize your efforts. (O.K., so it also helps if you're good at networking and can write a decent résumé.)

Making Order from Chaos

Organizing means approaching your work search in a deliberate, orderly fashion, and managing the process in an efficient way. The end product? Better results, sooner, with less energy squandered.

One way to speed things up is to use your computer. There are all sorts of software programs designed exclusively to help you manage your time, schedule your activities and be more productive. They enable you to keep tabs on all your contacts and, in some cases, produce and file professional correspondence. Programs of this type tend to fall into the category known as Personal Information Managers (PIMs).

A Case Study in Getting Organized

Here's a good example of the power of PIMs. A client I worked with, let's call her Helene, was looking for a job as a marketing manager. She was used to using a paper-based time management system. For her work-search, she chose to supplement this with an electronic version.

Helene purchased a PIM program for around $100. Her first step was to create an overall plan for her marketing campaign. For this, she used the electronic scheduler function. She was able to plot out her entire approach to work-searching in one-month chunks. This included approximations of how much time she'd devote to résumé preparation, networking, cold-calling, Internet searching, interviewing and follow-up.

Scheduling a Marketing Plan Next Helene scheduled her meetings and activities. The overall plan was converted into daily "To Do" lists. She could have used the PIM's electronic calendar; however, she chose to write the information out in pencil on preformatted schedule sheets (available at any business supply store), so that she could carry them with her in her briefcase. Helene also prioritized her daily activities

REAL LIFE *Using PIM software can be helpful, but what if you're always on the go? No need to carry your laptop with you everywhere, just print out the sheets that you need and take them with you. Once your back at your terminal, you can input any new notes or activities—that way you stay portable and organized.*

from most important to least important—an excellent time-management technique.

The thrust of her campaign was networking—both in-person and online. To keep things manageable, she electronically diarized all of her contacts. Whenever she was referred to someone new, that person's name was input into the PIM's contact manager. Helene also stored the person's company and title, address (regular and e-mail) and other relevant information. Even details of each meeting, conversation or e-mail session were kept here. This gave her a customized, fully-searchable database to draw upon.

Instant Access to Valuable Information Three months into her campaign, Helene was on the verge of success. She had met with, spoken to, and exchanged e-mail with close to 90 people! Can you imagine the trail of paper that would have normally piled up? Instead, most of the vital information she needed was packed away on the hard drive of her home computer. Best of all, she had fast access to the details she really needed. She could keyword search at any time to find relevant peo-

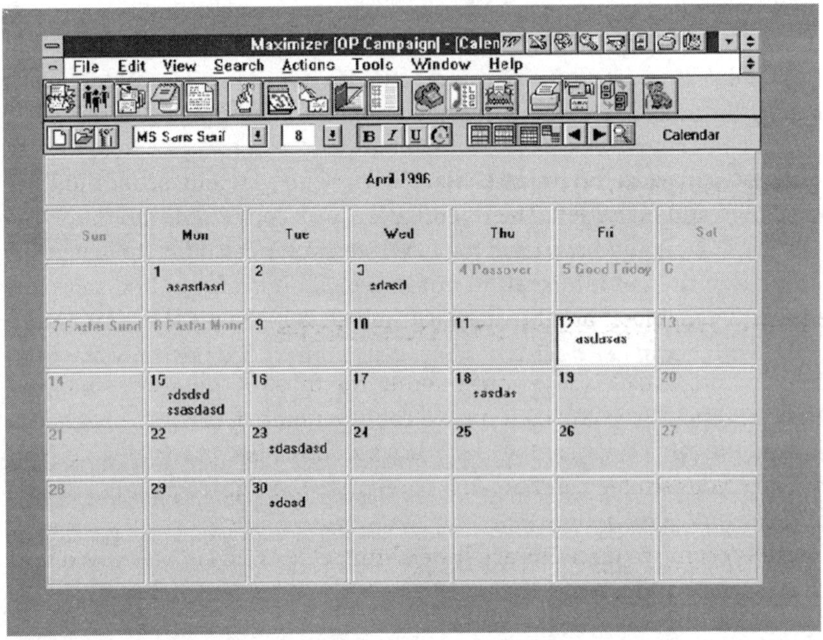

ple. When she wanted to look for, say, everyone she'd met with a marketing background in the banking industry, all she had to do was query her database. By entering the words "marketing" and "financial services," all the relevant names, phone numbers and information about previous contacts appeared!

What to Look for in a PIM

To be honest, not everyone will be comfortable working with a PIM. They can be limiting, in that you must use your computer to take advantage of the PIM program. This can be irritating if all you need is a person's phone number. Plus you always have to update your information to stay current.

If you do choose to make use of a PIM, there are several things to consider. You'll want to decide early on how you intend to use the program. Remember that the two main features of a PIM are time management and record keeping. If the product you're thinking of buying is weak in either of these two areas, I suggest you shop around.

REAL LIFE *Don't get sucked into buying bloatware. The PIM you choose should have a good electronic scheduling system and a customizable database. Some PIMs also come with complete word processing and other programs as part of the package—thus, they're bloated. You're better off keeping it simple. Use your existing software (e.g. word processor) where appropriate, otherwise you may spend more than you need to, and take up valuable space on your hard drive.*

Hints on Managing Your Time

Time management is all about making the most of whatever time you have. It generally involves some upfront planning, followed by detailed scheduling. This is where the electronic scheduler becomes valuable. You can take your strategy and break it down into an achievable daily routine.

For some excellent articles on time management, try **http://www.daytimer.com/resource/library/index.html**. One of the articles you'll find there is called "15 Ways to Save Time," by Lucy H. Hedrick. Here are just two of the tips that she gives:

> Do you keep "to do" lists that run on for pages? If you often feel discouraged by what's not crossed off your lists, make them shorter. The most effective managers identify only three top priorities each day. And their self-esteem is stroked repeatedly when they cross off all three tasks, day after day.

There are two reasons way you should group tasks by category (calls, errands, things to do). First, it allows you to focus your efforts and get momentum going. Second, looking at a grouped list of tasks makes it easier to prioritize the important ones first.

You can even take a quiz online to test your time management skills at **http://www.daytimer.com/cgi-bin/quiz.cgi?src=tmq**.

CYBER TIP Keeping on schedule is a breeze when using a PIM. Try using the audible alarm function. Your computer will notify you, musically, shortly before your next meeting. If it's visual reminders you prefer, use the electronic note feature. A little note (it looks like a sticky note) will pop onto your computer screen at a preset time to tell you what "To Do's" or appointments are next.

Tips on Keeping in Contact

If the first side of staying organized is managing your time, the other side is contact management. As you meet more and more people in your hunt for work, you need to remember who's who. That way you can refer to these people later when you absolutely need to. Contact management breaks down into two essential tasks: list creation and record keeping.

List creation is somewhat self-explanatory. It means that every time you plan to meet someone or are referred to someone in your networking, you add their name to your list. With a PIM, it's easy to keep track of hundreds of people. The beauty is that you can also cross-reference people using a wide variety of criteria and keywords. This can include who referred you to that person, what clubs or organizations they belong to, their title or industry affiliation—you name it.

On the *record keeping* side, you'll be most effective if you note the highlights of the transactions you have with each person you meet.

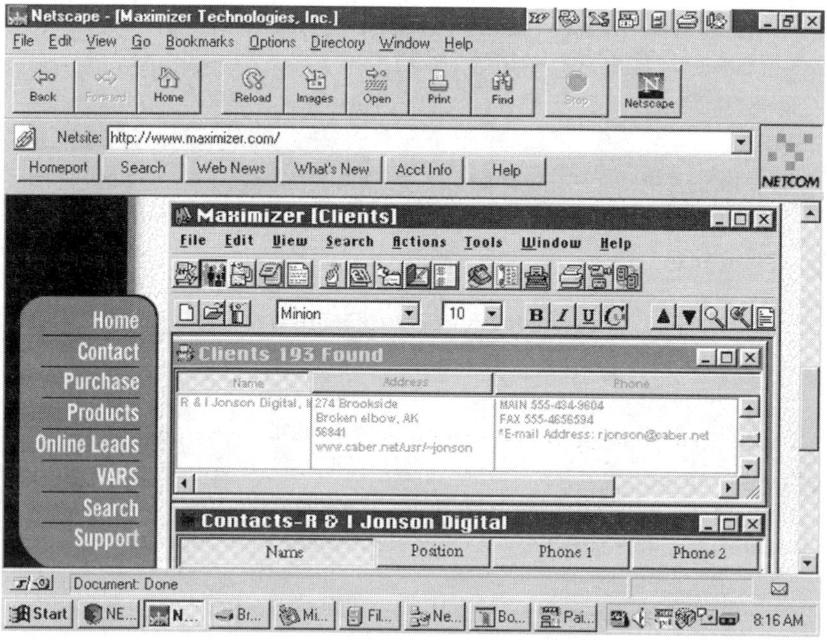

This includes when you saw them, what was said, your impressions and thoughts, how you followed up and what's next (e.g. who needs to do what by when). Doing this enables you to keep your marketing campaign going strong. Keep in mind that you'll want to refine your tactics as you go along. You can only keep effective records if you know what's working and what isn't. This will help you make any necessary changes. Of course, you can then record these changes on your electronic calendar!

Some PIM Software to Consider

Personal Information Managers come in a variety of formats and price ranges. Some can also be obtained online as shareware or freeware. I obviously can't cover every single software package available. What I offer in Table 7.1 is a representative sampling from the more popular programs. You can learn more about the product and its features at the Web sites I've listed, and even download a free trial version directly to your computer.

Table 7.1 Examples of Personal Information Manager Software

MANUFACTURER	PRODUCT NAME	WEB SITE	WHAT'S FREE
Day-Timers, Inc.	Day Timer	**http://www.daytimer.com/comp/tech.html**	Trial version
Janna	Contact	**http://www.janna.com**	Trial version
MultiActive Group	Maximizer	**http://www.maximizer.com**	Maximizer Lite
Symantec	Act!	**http://www.symantec.com/offers.html**	Trial version

The Shareware Alternative Of course, you don't have to rush out to your local computer store to get a hold of a decent PIM. If you want some shareware, try **http://www.shareware.com**. Choose "Selections," then "Business." A list of available PIMs will appear (you can choose from IBM compatible or Mac). For those of you who subscribe to a Commercial Online Provider, type in the word "shareware" under Keyword. Then navigate to the business software section of your provider and make your selection.

CYBER TIP You could always consider a portable database and time manager in the form of an electronic organizer. These calculator-size wonders have telephone directories, calendars, schedulers and expense forms. They range in price from $20 to $200, depending on features and memory. Try for one with at least 128K storage (256K is better). I suggest that you spend in the $50 plus range to get the features you require. To see what Sharp Electronics has to offer, go to **http://www.sharp-usa.com/products/wizard/index.html**. Or see Casio at **http://www.casio.com/cgi/index.cgi?cat=pdas&ser=BOSS/Digital+Diaries**.

III. THE ART OF INTERVIEWING

Keeping track of your interviews is all very well and fine, but what about the interview itself? Are there ways to prepare and increase your effectiveness electronically? There sure are. Quickly think back to your last job interview. (I've blocked most of mine out to protect myself from the emotional trauma.) How'd it go for you? Were you able to answer the interviewer's questions quickly and naturally? Or did you sound artificial and over-rehearsed? And what about your level of nervousness—a bit hard to take, n'est-ce pas?

Personally, I hate interviews. They get me all wound up. For days beforehand, I'm so anxious that I can barely sleep at night. And then comes the dreaded interview day. When I drag myself out of bed (kicking and screaming), I get a queasy feeling in my stomach that always seems to peak just as I'm escorted into the interviewer's office.

Torture or Triumph?

Let's face it, going for a formal job interview is one of the scariest, most nerve-wracking things that you can do. Unfortunately, it's still a necessary part of obtaining work for most of us. If it's of any consolation, the interviewer also tends to experience some discomfort. Of course, if the interviewer blows it, *they* don't go away without a job.

Differentiating Between Interview Types Let's just review the basics of an interview for a moment. There are two essential types. The first kind is the networking interview, which we will look at in Chapter 8. Basically, it is a means of building contacts and meeting informally with potential hiring managers. The stress level is relatively low, since both sides are less guarded and more relaxed.

The second—and more feared kind—is the formal job interview. It's typically a face-to-face meeting with key people from the organization you're hoping to work for. This type is widely used with traditional jobs and contract positions. Here's something to keep in mind: while the main goal of your résumé was to obtain the interview, the primary purpose of the formal interview is to secure an offer of employment.

Beating the Odds

You can greatly improve your odds for success in an interview, be it informal or formal, by preparing thoroughly. The key is to practise the three Rs: reviewing, researching and rehearsing.

You can start by *reviewing* the material you compiled earlier in Chapter 3. Go over your strengths and accomplishments. Make sure that you can answer typical questions such as "What are your greatest assets?" and "Which achievements are you most proud of?"

Then picture your next interview. What will happen when the interviewer says to you, "Tell me what you know about our company?" Will you smile blankly and reply, "Gee, I was hoping you could tell me that?" Or will you reel off an impressive response, citing the company's products and services, market niche and most recent quarterly results. *Research* provides you with the power to do this. Go back and review the techniques shown in Chapter 6.

For the actual interview itself, there is a ton of advice available online. So much so, in fact, that it can be overwhelming. Thankfully a fellow Canadian has taken the time to catalogue this information for us. Gary Will, author of *How to Prepare For an Employment Interview,* created the Archeus Web site at **http://www.golden.net~archeus/intres.htm**. Once there, you can choose from over 50 articles on interviewing as well as sample chapters from Gary's book. Here are some examples of what you'll find at the Archeus Web site.

If you'd like to know about the latest twists in behavioural interviewing, surf on over to **http://www.occ.com/occ/NBEW/Interviewer Techniques.html**. How about answers to the toughest questions you may get asked? They're here at: **http://www.adm.uwaterloo.ca/infocecs/CRC/step4-interview.html**.

What questions should *you* ask of the interviewer? Gary Will recommends that you prepare a list of relevant questions for the employer. Otherwise,

> if you don't have any questions, the interviewer will likely be left with one or more of these impressions of you:
>
> - You're not really interested in the position or the organization.
> - You're so lazy you couldn't be bothered to put any thought into it.
> - You're so desperate you'll go anywhere.

Read more about preparing questions for the interviewer at **http://www.golden.net/~archeus/int-ch14.htm**.

Practise Makes Perfect

Possibly the best way to prepare for the interview is to *rehearse*. Ideally, you would do this well in advance of your meeting, with someone who's qualified to help you. But it's not always possible to work with another person. Once again, technology can come to the rescue. This time, it's in the form of CD-ROMs, Chat lines and video cameras.

Talked to an Interesting CD Lately? There are several good CD-ROMs to help you get ready for an interview. Tom Jackson's *The Perfect Resume* is one example. It takes you through a practice interview step-by-step. There's even interaction. An animated interviewer asks you questions. Based on your responses, the program rates your success as a job applicant. (See it at **http://www.daud.com/products**).

Chat Someone Up If you're not into conversing with a cyborg, there's always the live (or almost-live) option of Chat. You can hold a role-play session with one of your contacts from your favourite Chat line (described in more detail in Chapter 8). Try to choose someone who knows about your field. As a reminder, the Chat route is not recommended for novice Internet users, due to its speed and complexity.

CYBER TIP There's a great example of an interactive interview session on the Web. Go to **http://www.kaplan.com/hotseat**. You'll find a fun but educational game called Hotseat, from Kaplan Interactive. It lets you "brave the interviewers' questions and choose the best responses"—for free.

Video and Audio Assistance

One final suggestion on this topic. If you have a video camera, or can get hold of one, tape yourself in a mock interview. This works best if you have someone to read out prewritten questions and respond to your answers. If you have to do it solo, pretend that you are talking to a real person. You can then review the tape and critique your performance. Cast a critical eye on your posture, eye contact, facial expressions, seating position, where your hands are and professionalism of dress. Also, check to see if you smile occasionally (reportedly other human beings respond well to that).

If video is a problem, try at least for some audio feedback. Even an old tape recorder can be of assistance. Record your mock interview. When you listen to it later, go through it carefully. Are your responses targeted and concise? Does your voice sound confident (or is it wavering and barely audible)? Do you finish what you have to say without babbling on? Also, is your tone sincere or contrived? You should also try to let the interviewer do much of the talking.

Following Through after the Interview

Your quest for work doesn't end after the interview. Immediately after your meeting, it's time to update your records. Go back to your PIM and enter the details. What were the important points? Does it look like a good prospect? Make sure that you schedule in any follow-up activities. These include things like sending a thank you note to the people who interviewed you and providing any other material or information that you were asked for.

Ensure that you send the thank you note within 48 hours of the interview. If you like, you can use your PC and printer to design your own card (refer to Chapter 4 for instructions). In it, mention how delighted you were to meet the interviewer. Try to subtly inject how your particular skills fit the requirements of the job you've interviewed for. If you're rushed, try faxing or e-mailing a thank you note. Otherwise, send a hard copy—it may have a longer impact.

IV. USE THE PHONE AND VOICE MAIL LIKE AN EXPERT

Now let's move on to two things that are so basic, they are often overlooked as powerful work-search tools: the telephone and answering system. We all have a phone. And is there anyone left who hasn't had the pleasure of communicating with an automated voice on an answering service?

If You Think You're Already A Pro, Here's A Little Quiz

I realize that basic telephones and answering services are not exactly leading-edge technology anymore. But how many of us really know how to use them effectively as part of our work-search?

Here are a few deceptively simple questions to see where you stand:

REAL LIFE *The following is a prerecorded message. Phone techniques and voice mail can make or break your campaign. The way we speak and the messages we leave count for a great deal when employers form their impressions of you. Please press the star key to exit and return to the book. Have a pleasant day (click).*

1. When are the two best times during the day to make direct contact with a potential employer?
2. What are three ways to reduce your fear of cold-calling?
3. How many calls does it take, on average, to contact the person you've targeted?
4. What is the best method of minimizing that ever-so-annoying telephone tag?

Phone Tips for the Well Prepared

As you read on, you'll find the answers to these questions. Let's begin, though, by tackling some of the common perils of using a phone as part of your work-search.

Taking the Terror out of Telephoning Like picking up the phone to ask complete strangers for a job, do you? If so, you're in the minority. Most people hate phone prospecting as much as they do the interview itself. Gary Ames recognizes this fact. He is a licensed psychologist and director of consulting with the R.L. Stevens Career Development firm in the U.S. Gary wrote a useful article called "Overcoming Phone-A-Phobia" and posted it on the Web (**http://crm21.com/ames2.html**). Here's how it starts:

> Your heart is pounding, the phone seems to weigh 200 pounds, your palms are sweaty as you grip the phone, your mind is reeling with vague catastrophic expectations as you ask to speak with an executive about a job prospect. These are but some of the symptoms of phone-a-phobia.

Gary goes on to explain that many people are terrified by the idea of calling strangers to sell themselves and that most everyone has some phone-a-phobia. As a result, "they procrastinate and decide to do other things, even when they know that a phone call would aid their job campaign."

Two sound pieces of advice from the article are (1) work with a career counselor to overcome this aversion, and (2) try some "desensitization exercises," where you make some "safe" calls first to people who know you and understand your situation.

Preparing Professionally Why stumble through another conversation with someone who can hire you when there are simple steps that you can take to prepare yourself. It's not like you get a whole lot of opportunities to make a solid first impression. Nor does it take an extensive amount of time to get ready.

One article that's out there on the Web delves into the ways that you can sound your best each time you pick up the phone. Entitled "Telephone Tips," it's offered by the All Business Network at **http://www.all-biz.com/26.html**.

These are some of the things that they suggest you do *before* making an important call:

- Plan what you are going to say.
- Set clear objectives of what you want to accomplish.
- Write out an actual script, including the points you want to make and potential responses from the person you're contacting.
- Rehearse until you feel comfortable.

Voice Mail and Answering Services

I can barely remember the last time I called someone for business purposes and actually connected to a live person. I'm so used to speaking to some sort of answering service that I actually get flustered when a human being picks up the line.

Today the majority of businesses and organizations use automated answering systems. These range from machines, to voice mail, to live answering services. Sooner or later, you're going to encounter one when trying to get hold of a potential employer or networking contact. It can either further your cause or frustrate your process immeasurably.

Your objective, when leaving a message, is to be professional yet natural. That way you convey to a potential employer the image that they're looking for, while still being yourself. The "Telephone Tips" article I cited earlier recommends that when you leave a message on someone's answering service, you should remember to cover the four Ws: who called,

REAL LIFE *When you're looking for work, everything counts. With that in mind, make sure that you return all calls promptly. When an employer is ready to hire, that's when they want to hear from you (not two days later).*

why you called, what you'd like the receiver to do and when you're available to receive a return call. A specific request with detailed information increases your chances of a reply.

Answering the Call *You* need an answering service too. Wouldn't you kick yourself if you were out at a networking session and "the big call" came but no one was at home to pick it up? Why put yourself at risk?

Here are some tidbits of advice for your own answering service from the pros:

- To avoid telephone tag, the "Telephone Tips" article suggests the message on your answering machine direct callers to leave you answers to the four Ws: Who, Why, What, When.
- Mind Tools at **http://www.mindtools.com/phoneskl.html** says that if you get an answering service and you're not prepared for it, hang up and call back. "When you get taken surprise by, you can sound stilted and off-balance. It is much better to hang up, prepare a message, and then deliver it smoothly."

REAL LIFE *There's no need to plunk down hundreds of dollars on an answering machine with all the bells and whistles. If money is tight, call your local phone company to see if they offer an automated answering service. It doesn't cost a lot (between $5 and $10 a month, depending on where you live and the features you order). As a bonus, it takes messages while you're talking on the same line, rather than giving the caller a busy signal. Plus the caller can leave as long a message as they need to without getting cut off.*

Now that I've shown you how important the telephone and answering systems are to your work-search, here are the answers to those "simple" phone questions I asked you at the beginning of this section:

1. Try calling your targeted employers before 8:30 a.m. and after 5:15 p.m. when calls may not be screened and employers tend to be more reachable.
2. To reduce nervousness, call friends and family first. Rehearse until you're comfortable and set clear objectives before you make your calls.
3. On average it takes three calls to make contact, so be persistent.
4. Reduce telephone tag by leaving a simple, coherent message, indicating the best times you can be contacted.

V. NEGOTIATING AN OFFER

The other big skill that you'll be using towards the end of your search is negotiating. Once an offer of employment has been presented to you, you're expected to respond to the employer in one of three ways:

- An unconditional, absolute acceptance of the offer as it stands.
- A counter-offer, where you add or change things and re-present it to the employer.
- A flat-out, "Thanks, but no thanks."

Why Negotiating Is Important

Many people are reluctant to ask for anything more than what is in the original offer. Given the uncertainties of our economic climate, this is understandable. One thing to be aware of is that employers (or companies who award contracts) often use negotiating as a final test of your self-marketing abilities. They figure that if you can't stand up for yourself at this stage, maybe you'll be prone to backing down while on the job.

Try not to misconstrue my message here. I'm not recommending that you storm in and make unreasonable demands. Instead, think of it as a give-and-take process. You're looking for certain concrete elements and the employer has their own position to maintain. Striking a happy balance is usually considered to be the right approach.

What to Look For

Once again you'll find many useful articles on the Web to get you going. An example is "Getting an Offer — Nine Negotiating Tips" at **http://**

REAL LIFE *The best time to negotiate is shortly after a formal offer has been presented to you, and certainly before you accept the position. Once they give you an offer, it means their interest in you is confirmed. If you start negotiating too early, you might scare off the employer. After accepting the offer, you're no longer negotiating—you're asking for a raise.*

www.tms.tribune.com/rjt_job/offer0.htm (Tribune Media Services). The author suggests that you "know exactly what you're willing to settle for *before* the offer comes in, and what perks or benefits may substitute for a lower salary. Keep in mind that it's crucial to be flexible."

Some of the components of an offer to consider haggling over are:

- compensation (how much, how often, flat salary vs. commission on sales),
- benefits, sick leave and vacation allowances,
- training and education expenses,
- travel (frequency and duration, plus expense coverage),
- performance evaluation (how often, on what basis will you be measured, minimum and maximum pay increases), and
- other perks that may be appropriate for someone at your level.

The Tribune article mentioned above has some additional advice for when the offer actually comes in. They suggest that you ask yourself several key questions before deciding whether to accept an offer.

> Is the offer solid? Sometimes it's easy to look at any phone call as a positive sign. Be sure the offer you're getting is real and that the person is not just saying, "You're still in the running." If possible, get the offer in writing.
>
> Does the job fit into your long-term career plans? You may not want to accept something completely unrelated to the field that interests you most. On the other hand, any work can be good work if it enables you to move gradually towards your real goals.

Tips for Students and Recent Graduates When I've spoken to students, I have found a significant polarization in their attitudes towards negotiating. At one extreme, there are people who believe you might as well ask for the world. Sometimes they go in and make preposterous requests that end up blowing them out of the running. At the other end of the spectrum are those who take whatever's handed to them. No matter how frugal or basic the offer is, they say, "Yes, thanks. When do I start?"

What I propose is an approach somewhere between the two extremes. This is illustrated well in an article called "Negotiating the Right Deal," by Stephen Kaplan, past president of the Canadian Association of Career Educators and Employers. The article states that "While it is true that they have less negotiating power in today's market, students, while basking in the ecstasy of getting a job, should not forget that one of the most crucial components of launching a successful career is the art of negotiation."

Kaplan goes on to say that students often believe that "negotiating the terms of an employment contract are the sole domain of the agents' high draft picks of professional sports teams—nothing could be further from reality. It is the responsibility of every employee and employer to ensure that every aspect of the job and the expectations of both parties are clearly understood." The article is at **http://www.cacee.com/negotiat.html**.

CYBER TIP Be as informed as possible before you start your negotiations. On the salary side, you can get some rudimentary info at Salary Comparisons for Various Careers (**http://vii.com/~rtuengel/cgi-bin/salary.cgi**). Then use the Web Forums to network and find more answers online. Try **http://www.canoe.ca/ChatelaineSourcesWork/home.html** for Chatelaine Work forums. Best of all, meet with people in the field to find out about industry standards.

Make It a Win-Win Situation

Whether you're a student or the president of a billion dollar company, the art of negotiating is all about leaving both sides relatively contented. I use the word *relatively* because neither side gets exactly what they want. Note that the word *contented* also snuck its way in, indicating that there is some degree of satisfaction on both sides.

Do not be afraid to leave something on the table. This means that you may have to give up something you want a little bit to get something you *really* want. On the other hand, both you and the employer lose if you accept a lowball offer. You will not be a happy employee and odds are that you will be constantly looking for something better. This could ultimately affect your performance.

Remember that after all the bargaining is over, you have to work together with your new boss. So while you may not get the new Porsche and the condo in Spain you'd asked for as part of the package, take comfort in knowing that your new employer had to pay you more than the $1.70 an hour that they had hoped to get away with.

VI. WIRED WRAP UP

Baseball coach Casey Stengel is famous for his quote, "It ain't over 'til it's over." Searching for work is a lot like that. There are so many stages involved that it becomes a full-time job in itself. Each phase requires planning, execution and follow-through. And until you've negotiated and accepted a firm offer of employment, it ain't over!

We've now looked at many of the steps you have to go through to get to that final stage. If you've been through a search before, you know how exhausting all of this can be. The process is wide-ranging. From self-assessment to writing your résumé, a full-out job search takes an incredible amount of energy, and a great deal of your time.

Staying organized will undoubtedly increase the effectiveness of your marketing campaign. It allows you to keep on target and track your success. Think of your competitors drowning in a sea of scribbled-on papers and sticky notes while your search proceeds smoothly. You have everything under control—electronically.

Consider, too, how much better your interview will go when you're fully prepared. Once you understand what's expected, you can use a variety of electronic tools to help you get ready. Chat lines, Web sites with advice, interactive CD-ROMs and video cameras all give you an edge. And in today's employment market, you'll want every advantage you can get!

PART 3

LOCATING EMPLOYMENT—THE WIRED WAY

CHAPTER 8

Networking into the Hidden Job Market

Virtual Definition: **Sysop** ('sis äp) *noun*

The system operator or sysop is the person responsible for the physical operations of a computer system or network resource. Also someone who administers discussion threads, as found on Bulletin Boards, Usenet Newsgroups or Web Forums.

I. HEY, WHO HID ALL THE JOBS?

Seen any good want ads lately? I used to flip through the employment classified pages in my local paper every single day, hoping (or praying, more likely) to find *the right job*. It never appeared. On those few occasions when I did see a job that seemed fairly well-suited for me, thousands of other people were seeing it at the same time. So by the time my résumé landed on the poor human resource manager's desk, it was buried along with those from hundreds of other hopefuls.

How Do People Really Find Jobs?

Please don't accuse me of suggesting that you abandon the job ads in newspapers and trade publications. I've personally secured some excellent work by these means. What you need to have is a proper perspective on this. Fewer than ten percent of all jobs are typically found through posted advertisements in newspapers, trade journals, the Net or anywhere else. (Note that this percentage varies by field, but even high tech workers must also use other sources to cover all the bases).

The Other Ninety Percent So how do the other jobs get filled? Good question. Recruiters, placement agencies and executive search firms account for some. Mass mailing your résumé and cold calling can have some effect as well. Both of these together account for approximately 10 percent of all vacancies filled.

But here's an astonishing statistic: on average, 60 to 80 percent of all jobs are found through something called *the hidden job market*. And the best way to access these jobs is through the process of networking.

So what exactly is the hidden job market, and what does networking really mean? Just as importantly, how can going online assist you here? That's what this chapter is all about.

II. WHERE IS THE HIDDEN JOB MARKET?

The hidden job market is a term that's been around for many years. When I first was told about it, my reaction was predictable. "Do you mean to tell me that someone out there has thousands of jobs available, but is keeping them under wraps?" I was indignant that no one had invited me to join this secret club. Then I learned the truth.

Hidden Is a Misnomer

The hidden job market refers mainly to upcoming vacancies, work postings and business opportunities that are known only to *insiders*. In many cases the vacancy doesn't even exist yet. A position may be about to come open, but the company doesn't want to let anyone know about it just yet. In other cases an employee suddenly leaves the company, creating an unplanned opening.

It's Hidden Because It May Not Be Real Yet Perhaps an example will clarify this. A pharmaceutical company in Moncton was unhappy with the performance of its finance manager. The company decided that it was going to fire this manager (or declare him "redundant," as they sometimes say). That put them in a bit of a dilemma. The finance department was very busy, so they'd need to fill the position immediately after they let the manager go. The problem was, they couldn't advertise the position yet because technically, there was no vacancy.

How did they deal with this? In several ways, actually. First they worked with a confidential executive search firm to discretely canvass potential candidates, without revealing who the company was. What they also did was review their files for anyone who had recently shown interest in this position from within the company.

Best of all for you, as someone seeking work, they looked for outside people who had shown interest in that company, and in the finance manager's position, through networking.

When Else Do Hidden Opportunities Appear? Not every hidden vacancy comes about due to someone being turfed. They can also arise when a company is about to launch into a growth phase. As they open up new areas, they'll need more staff. But they may not want to advertise this to their competitors.

Additionally, it's not just openings for jobs or contracts we're dealing with here. If you're starting a business, there are also hidden opportunities and hidden customers. They too can be accessed by a process that's discussed in the following section called *networking*.

III. NETWORKING THE TRADITIONAL WAY

With all the changes that companies experience on an ongoing basis, there is often a turnover of staff. The trick is to take advantage of these changes, by being at the right place at the right time. That's where networking works best.

The Basics of Networking

At it's most fundamental level, networking is about making contact with a variety of people who can assist you in your search for work. By creating a critical mass of contacts, you get known by the people who are in a position to make hiring decisions. Then, when one of these hidden openings springs up, guess whose name is forefront in their minds? Yours!

I won't go into too much detail here because networking is explained in almost every career manual around. Here are some highlights of how it works in the traditional sense.

1. You start by making a broad list of people you know. This could include friends, relatives, colleagues and professional contacts.
2. From these, you make a short list of people that you want to meet with first. These are your warm and fuzzy contacts, the ones you know well and who don't intimidate you.
3. You can call or write them to secure an initial meeting. You explain that you're not asking them for a job, you just want to share some ideas about your work search and get their advice.
4. When you meet with them, you exchange information and make a positive impression. Then you ask for a couple of referrals to other people in the industries and companies you really want to work in. Soon you'll have a broad range of contacts in a variety of companies.

CYBER TIP To find out (in elaborate detail) about how to build and nurture a successful network, try the following articles that are based on the World Wide Web: "Grooming Your Granfaloon" at **http://server1.pa.hodes.com/cm/cm29.html** and "Networks That Work" at **http://www.globalx.net/ocd/prospects/tools/networks.html.**

Understanding the Different Types of Networking

One suggestion I have is to set your objectives clearly before you contact your prospects. It helps if you understand that there are two distinct kinds of networking in work-searching. One is to gather information, while the other is to secure work. There may be some overlap, but you'll want to be certain about your goals in advance.

Type 1: Information Interviewing The first type is called *information interviewing*. This is appropriate for people who are switching industries, just coming out of school or making a radical career change. What you're looking for is information that will help you decide which path to take with your career. One of the best ways to do this is to speak informally with people who are already working in the field that interests you and get their candid opinions. Note that you do not expect this person to hire you or refer you to someone who can. This is simply research conducted with a live resource.

What you're hoping to find are details on what it's really like to work in this industry (or this type of company). You'll want to confirm the research you've done previously in terms of who's growing, what your prospects are and how you can fit in. You'll also want to know about the people who are doing the hiring.

CYBER TIP There are some very good articles and instruction manuals for information interviewing that can be found on the Web. Here are two sites to consider: **http://www.adm.uwaterloo.ca/infocecs/CRC/step2-infoInterview.html** (University of Waterloo Career Resource Centre) and **http://danenet.wicip.org/jets/jet–9407–p.html** (Dane County Community Information).

Type 2: Networking to Secure Work The second type of networking can be called the *targeted work search*. This is where you use all those wonderful techniques that you learned back in Chapter 6. What you're actually doing here is seeking work, although you don't come right out and say so.

You start by focusing your attention on companies that mean the most to you. Try to develop contacts who can refer you to the decision-makers at each of these companies. Make a positive impression with these decision-makers, then keep in contact. When a potential opening becomes available, you'll be among the first people to be considered. For a useful list of other networking material on the Web, go to **http://www.golden.net/~archeus/othres.htm** and scroll through the articles.

REAL LIFE *When getting ready for a networking session, keep in mind that the only thing you really leave behind is an impression. These sessions, as informal as they may be, are your professional route to finding work, so come prepared. Do some research on the company, as well as on the person you'll be meeting with. Bring along a list of well thought out questions to ask. Plus have a hard copy of your résumé ready, but give it only if asked. You can also send it after with a thank you note.*

Benefits of Traditional Networking

There are many reasons to carry out a well-planned networking program. Foremost, of course, is the exposure it will give you to the 60 to 80 percent of job openings in the hidden job market. As well, you can create an edge for yourself, even when a position is widely advertised, by being referred by someone relevant.

Careful—This Could Be You If you're not convinced, consider the alternative. You can wake up each morning after 10:00 a.m. and rummage randomly through the want ads. Maybe you could call a few search firms too. They'll gladly talk to you the first time around. When the afternoon comes, you can sit back and watch your favourite talk show. Possibly you might think of how nice it is to be in your pyjamas.

As time passes, you begin to experience growing pangs of anxiety. Still, the phone stays hauntingly silent. Eventually you sink deeply into a miserable state of hopelessness and utter despair. (And you never actually figure out that talk show episode that dealt with parents who sleep with their children's same-sex teachers.)

—Or *This* Could Be You You rise bright and early to attack the target list you've concocted. You feel great because you've selected the companies you'd like to work for, instead of waiting to see what's been posted in the papers or on the Net. Now you're networking your way in to meet the decision-makers.

What a difference. Not only do *you* get to choose the companies and people to network with, but you're also active and way ahead of the game (plus you could always videotape the upcoming episode of your favourite talk show and watch it after you've accepted your next work offer.)

REAL LIFE *As a bonus, networking allows you to meet with people in a far less stressful atmosphere than you'd find in a formal job interview. With you and your network contact more at ease, the odds of you making your best impression increase dramatically. And if you're planning it right, you'll get to meet directly with the people who have the power to hire you. There really is no more effective way to secure the kind of work that you really want!*

The Downsides of Traditional Networking

Of course, every silver lining has its dark exterior. Networking is no exception. A full-fledged networking campaign can be time-consuming and exhausting. You have lists to write up, people to call, visits to schedule, research to prepare, meetings to attend and thank you notes to send.

The physical travel alone can take its toll, not to mention the expense of attending dinner meetings, breakfast sessions, downtown parking etc. On top of this, you have to keep track of who you've seen, what they've said and what you plan to do next. It's easy to burn out if you're not careful. Not surprisingly, this is where online resources can make a real difference.

IV. INTRODUCTION TO NETWORKING ONLINE

Going online to do some of your networking is a great way to increase your efficiency. If you have even minimal keyboarding skills, you can take part in electronic *discussion groups*. This enables you to exchange information with people locally, nationally and all around the world. The idea here is to make contacts that you might not otherwise be able to. Since you're not limited by time, geography or expense, vast new realms become available to you.

A Quick Review of Discussion Groups

You'll recall from Chapter 2 that discussion groups come in many formats. They can be located on Usenet (where they're known as Newsgroups), or on the Web (where they're called forums).

Different Types of Discussion Groups Discussion groups can be very large, involving tens or hundreds of people. They can also be small and private—just you and one other person. In some you correspond by e-mail messages. Others use Chat, which allows you to hold real-time conversations (via keyboard). You even have a choice of how to post your messages. You can send a private message to a single person at a time or you can broadcast to an entire discussion group.

What to Expect There are many things that you can do in these groups. From a career standpoint, you can swap strategies about writing your résumé and get it critiqued by people in your field. Or ask advice about changing careers, interviewing or work-searching. Sometimes you can just share your joys or frustrations with a sympathetic ear. (Or is that pair of eyes when it comes to keyboarding?) Essentially you can learn some valuable information while making new contacts. Details on careers, industries, companies and people that interest you can all be exchanged online.

REAL LIFE *Do not expect to find a job or get referrals through discussion groups. I've actually heard of people doing so, but that sort of thing is rare. Networking online (or live) takes time to build up relationships to this level.*

Making the Net Work for You

Electronic networking differs from the traditional methods. You don't approach your targeted companies or specific people, directly. Instead, you identify discussion groups that centre around your field of interest. Then you make contact, exchange information and gradually develop individual relationships. Table 8.1 breaks down the key steps.

Table 8.1 Steps To Networking Electronically

KEY STEPS	ACTIONS INVOLVED
Identify relevant discussion groups	Use the methods outlined later in this chapter
Get a feel for the group.What are the key topics and what is the tone?	Sign on and monitor discussions for a while (don't post a message immediately)
Decide if this group truly meets your needs	See if discussion threads and level of detail are relevant to what it is you want to know
Check to see if your questions or comments have been answered in earlier postings	Review the forum's stored conversations (discussion archives) or use a search engine to find specific topics
Make your first contact	Post a private message to a group member who seems particularly approachable
Respond promptly if contacted	Answer in a timely and professional manner

The Good and the Not So Good of Electronic Networking

The online world can definitely broaden your reach; however, it doesn't completely replace the meet and greet networking that most of us are used to. Keeping this in mind, here are some things to consider.

The Main Benefits of Electronic Networking

- It allows you to contact people from a wider variety of fields and industries than you might normally have access to.
- It can be a quick, inexpensive way to meet new people and get advice.
- Geography poses no limits: you can speak to anyone, anywhere (if they're online).
- The anonymity of e-mail may allow people to give you brutally honest opinions.

Sounds wonderful, doesn't it? But there are limitations.

The Drawbacks to Electronic Networking

- The intimacy of face-to-face contact just isn't there. Even when video-conferencing becomes widespread, the human element will still be lacking.
- You can't see the other person's body language or hear their voice intonations through a keyboard, thus you can sometimes miss a person's real message or intended tone.
- Whatever you say in cyberspace can leave a permanent record. Even private conversations aren't 100 percent secure.

CYBER TIP Newsgroups are notorious for the viruses they can harbour. Make sure you're using effective protection software that works with your e-mail too. Scan your files often to ensure that they're not infected, and update your files regularly with new virus codes. To get trial versions of two of the most popular products, go to Macafee's Virus Scan (**http://www.mcafee.com**) and Symantec's Norton AntiVirus (**http://www.symantec.com/offers.html**).

- If you happen to make a mistake when posting to groups, everyone gets to see it!

A Word About Netiquette

Discussion groups are really just small communities of people. To help groups run smoothly, informal rules of conduct have begun to evolve. Collectively these are known as *netiquette* (Net etiquette).

Casual Is O.K., Unprofessional Is Not Just as with any form of business communication, you'll always want to be as professional as possible. For instance, don't just barge in on a discussion group. Hang back at first. Get to know the main topics and frequent contributors. Then approach people individually (that's how networking relationships are built).

Try not to post a message to the entire group unless it's really necessary. Throwing out something to the group like "Can you help me find a job?" is considered poor form. That's not to say that you shouldn't occasionally ask for advice from the group. First, though, follow all the steps outlined in Table 8.1. If you still haven't received a satisfactory response, then you can try a general post.

Other Informal Guidelines for Discussion Groups Following up is also extremely important. If someone helps you out, send them an individualized thank you note by e-mail. And don't forget the law of reciprocity. When someone asks you for information, try your best to respond. Otherwise you could earn a reputation as an info-hog. This is a sure way to get frozen out of a group.

CYBER TIP Paul Agre, from the University of California, San Diego, has written an excellent article on **electronic networking.** He states that "electronic mail is part of a larger ecology of communication media and genres—telephone conversations, archival journals and newsletters, professional meetings, paper mail, voice mail, chatting in the hallway...job interviews...visits to other research sites, and so forth—each with its own attributes and strengths." See the full article at **http://communication.ucsd.edu/pagre/network.html.**

One final note about discussion group decorum. On a rare occasion, you might unintentionally (or intentionally) annoy or offend someone. If this happens, and they send you a scathing e-mail (known as a *flame*), show some restraint. If you whip off an emotional reply, you could fall victim to a flame war. That's when everyone gangs up on you and floods your mailbox with nasty e-mail. You can't win a flame war. It's likely that you'll just end up looking hot-headed—not the professional image that you want to convey.

V. FINDING THE RIGHT DISCUSSION GROUPS

It's not hard to find a discussion group online. There are virtually thousands of them, covering practically every subject you can think of (yes, even *those* subjects). The trick is to locate the groups that will help you to further your work-search.

The Technology Differs

The variety of technologies that you can use complicates matters (review Chapter 2). Usenet Newsgroups and Web-based discussion groups use e-mail; whereas Chat groups, (discussed later in this chapter) use Internet Relay Chat (IRC). This allows you to hold virtual conversations with one or more people, just as you would on the telephone (except you're using your keyboard). And Listserves are like mail robots that you can join to get automatic updates on your favourite newsgroup topics.

Keep It Simple For most people, I'd suggest staying with discussion groups that are based on e-mail. They tend to be easier to use than Chat. You also have more time to consider your questions and responses. Plus the depth of the discussions is generally better. In the next part of this section, you'll find a sampling of Canadian career-related groups you can take part in.

Where to Begin?

New Usenet and Web forums are opening up (and closing) every day. I've tried to give you some active sites to get you started. The first one I'll suggest is hosted by Canada's Ministry of Labour. The Conference Centre

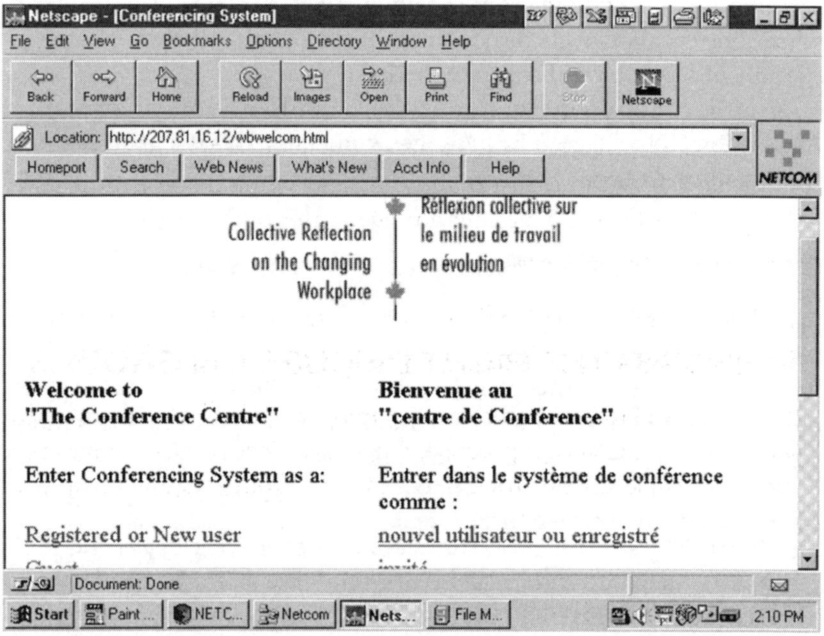

is a series of interactive forums. They are grouped around a document that I referred to way back in Chapter 1: Collective Reflections On The Changing Workplace. You can find it on the Web at **http://207.81.16.12/wbwelcom.html**.

Exploring Association Discussion Groups To start with, you can go to the Web site of the association that represents the industry you're interested in. Often these areas include a forum. This is where you'll find people in the industry exchanging e-mail messages back and forth. The better forums are broken into categories (e.g., Job Search or The Economy), allowing you to choose the themes that suit your needs.

There are some good examples of association-based forums. The Society of Management Accountants, for instance, has specialized discussion groups through its Web site. You can find them at **http://www.purdyswharf.com/CMA**. For this particular forum, you'll need a password to get in. That's not unusual for professional associations with restricted membership (thankfully, these tend to be in the minority).

A good open forum (one which does not require a password) can be found at the Charity Village Online Discussions Page located at

http://www.charityvillage.com/charityvillage/stand.html. There are conversations on all aspects of not-for-profit and philanthropy-related issues, including jobs and contract work.

Another interesting venue is the Canadian Women's Internet Association Home Page at **http://www.women.ca**. This is a great place for sharing ideas on work and life.

Career-Related Forums on the Web

In addition to the associations, there are many other places where career-related discussions take place online. For Canadian content, go to the Online Discussion Forums at B.C.'s Work Net (**http://WorkInfoNet.bc.ca/newuser.htm**). Topics include traditional and electronic job hunting techniques, and it's part of the CanWorkNet portfolio.

> **CYBER TIP** In the U.S., there's a site called Hard@Work. It's main focus is networking on work-related issues. To make contact with our American counterparts, check out the Watercooler forum at **http://www.hardatwork.com/Cooler/Cooler.html.**

Talk to Your Magazine and Connect with Your Newspaper Some of the best forums for employment networking are located on the Web sites of Canadian magazines and newspapers. This makes sense when you realize that these are the most likely media in which to find career-related topics.

Maclean's is as good as any place to start. The online version has a spot called Canada Linkup. It includes a category for careers, and is found at **http://www.canoe.ca/macleans/linkup/forumsetup.html**. *Chatelaine*, meanwhile, has created discussion areas geared towards Canadian women. Their work category is at **http://www.canoe.ca/ChatelaineSourcesWork/home.html**.

The *Globe and Mail* has put together a collection of forums at its CareerConnect Web site. If you go to **http://199.246.67.180:9000/cgi-bin/owa/JobForum.careerconnect** you can choose from four distinct categories:

- *Searching for a Job:* Deals with issues on finding employment, which may include writing a résumé, required qualifications, the interviewing process, and background information on employers.

- *Workplace Issues:* Topics may include the workplace environment, legal issues, employer benefit plans etc.
- *Life Between Jobs:* Discusses issues concerning unemployment and preparing for a new job.
- *General Job Issues:* This category includes any issues that are not covered in the other topics.

Going Commercial

A number of well-structured discussion groups can be found on the Commercial Online Providers (e.g. American Online and CompuServe). They have put together special interest groups that focus specifically on work. It's easy to find a discussion in your field. Of course, you have to subscribe to a Commercial Online Provider first if you want access their information.

America Online Canada, for example, has assembled a series of message boards. If you look in the Business and Finance section, you'll find discussion threads that could be of interest to you.

They've also got *Canadian Business* magazine online. Within this section, there are forums that centre directly on Canadian work issues. You can also try the About Work message centre. Although this one is mainly American, it has a broad reach.

Compuserve also gives extensive access to work-related discussion groups. There don't seem to be any that focus exclusively on Canada. However, here are a few that you can investigate:

- *Career Management Forum:* Read "reviews of career books and headhunting services in the online libraries, attend the live scheduled conferences on career topics in the conference rooms." Share tips through interactive forums.

CYBER TIP There are also thousands of local bulletin boards and chat services across the country. They tend to be very informal, and the content is much more recreational than employment-oriented; however, you're welcome to see for yourself. An extensive list of Canadian bulletin boards is provided by the Yahoo Canada directory at **http://search.yahoo.ca/search?p=bulletin+boards.**

- *Careers Board:* "Funeral directors are talking to other funeral directors, and chefs to chefs." The mix of career discussions going on here means that you're more likely to find messages on Mary Kay consulting or selling Tupperware than teaching or practising law.
- *Organizations' Message Boards:* These bring together members of influential clubs to network online.
- *Professional Groups and Talent Bank Message Boards:* Pick just about any career, and "ask men and women working in the selected field about their jobs." What do they like and dislike? What hours do they work? Which personalities succeed and fail? How much money do they make? How did they get started?

Locating an Appropriate Group

As I said before, finding a discussion group is a cinch; finding one that's right for you is another story. My suggestion is to try the general career-related groups described earlier in this section. Then try to find those that are directly related to your field of interest. It's here that your most effective networking can really get done. Thankfully, other people have created comprehensive search engines for just this purpose. All you have to do is check specific search engines to find relevant groups. These search engines are updated regularly (some even daily). They are divided into several categories, based on the type of Internet technology that they use. Table 8.2 provides a brief description to help you sort things out.

Chatting Your Way to the Top

Men and women do not live by e-mail alone. Sometimes you get the urge to converse with someone else on an immediate level. In the online world, that translates into the realm of Chat.

The principal advantage that Chat has over e-mail is that it's instantaneous. As soon as you type in your message, the person (or people) you're connected to see what you've written. They can then respond immediately, as they would in a real conversation.

Think Before You Press "Enter" Ironically, speed is also the main drawback of Chat. You often don't have time to think carefully about what you want to say. You're expected to respond quickly, as in a normal conversation. This is a real barrier if you don't type well.

Table 8.2 Search Engines For Exploring Discussion Groups

	USENET NEWS-GROUPS	WEB DISCUSSION GROUPS	LISTSERVE MAIL DEPOTS
Search Engine Name	DejaNews	Forum One	Liszt
Purpose	Internet discussions by topic	Searches 23,000 groups	Finds Listserves by subject
URL	**http://www.dejanews.com**	**http://www.ForumOne.com**	**http://www.liszt.com**
Sample Discussion Group	General job postings and articles about careers at the **can.jobs** newsgroup	For Trainers and Human Resource Professionals **http://www.trainingnet.com/chat.htm**	For Performers and Artists **http://homer.ic.gc.ca/capprt/mail_e.html**

And as for spellcheck? Forget about it. What you type in goes out right away—no chance for proofreading or revisions. This can be frustrating when dealing one-on-one. In a group Chat with many participants, it can be mayhem!

Now you know why I recommend Chat for advanced Internet-users only. As always, this doesn't mean you shouldn't at least try it. I'll even give you a tip for finding some groups to check out. On the Web, go to **http://www.yahoo.ca**, and click on "Options" beside the word "Search". This will take you into the advanced search page. In the space to the left of Search, enter "chat" followed by a space, then "and" followed by "career" (without the quotes). You'll get tons of the most recent groups to choose from.

CYBER TIP The Commercial Online Providers all offer Chat sections too. For example, America Online has the About Work section. There are numerous Chat sessions here relating to employment. Likewise the Kaplan Career Centre, also on AOL, is geared to college and university students and recent grads.

A Final Cautionary Note on Chat If you are going to use Chat to network, my advice is to stick to one-on-one conversations as much as possible. You can follow the same steps as outlined in Table 8.1. You'll have to invite someone to chat directly with you. Don't be put off if your first efforts are rebuffed. Chatting is not for novices. But used effectively, it can be helpful.

VI. WIRED WRAP UP

Networking could very well be the most important tool of your work-search. With the rapid changes in today's workplace, it's more important than ever to create and maintain professional contacts. Career experts agree that it will continue to be the most effective way to find jobs at every level in the economy.

The process of networking takes practice. It also requires finesse, plus a thorough understanding of your goals. Being in the forefront of the hiring person's mind when they're ready to hire is your objective. The secret is to focus your energy on the companies and people where you really want to work. It will probably take some initial, unrelated meetings. In the end, however, you'll be much farther ahead.

Electronic resources can definitely make your path easier and faster; however, you should *not* rely on them to the exclusion of face-to-face meetings and phone sessions. Instead, use online forums to broaden the scope of your traditional networking. Sharing information and building relationships are also your objectives. Remember too that behind the fancy e-mail addresses and electronically transmitted messages are people just like you and me. Treat them with respect, and they may just help you to find your next work opportunity.

CHAPTER 9 Job Hunting Online

Virtual Definition: **server** (sûr′vər) *noun*

A computer or a software package that provides a specific kind of service to client software running on other computers. The term can refer to a particular piece of software, such as a WWW server, or to the machine on which the software is running.

I. NEEDLES IN ELECTRONIC HAYSTACKS

Let's start this chapter off with a quick show of hands. How many of you have thoroughly read Part 2, as well as Chapter 8, before jumping to this chapter? Come on, let's see those arms go up.

If you're sitting there with you're hand in the air, congratulations! (Unless, of course, you're lying). It's likely that by now you're extremely close to finding the work you really want. If not, read the next few paragraphs carefully. You're probably thinking that online job hunting is the quick, easy solution we all crave so dearly. I'm here to show you how to do it, while telling you simultaneously not to get your hopes up too high. Whether your browsing for job postings, or uploading your résumé for employers to see, the odds are not yet in your favour. And for those of you looking for self-employment or small business opportunities, Chapter 10 describes your best online approaches.

Remember the Process

A quick review is in order here. If you read the previous chapters, and did some of the recommended exercises, you should now be able to do the following:

- Describe your interests, skills and accomplishments with great clarity.
- Create a professional quality résumé and cover letter electronically.
- Send your application material in a variety of ways—online.
- Pinpoint the exact companies and organizations where you'd fit in best.
- Network your way into contacting decision-makers at your targeted companies.

All of these skills will assist you with locating work, be it a full-time job or contract-based employment.

For Those of You Who Didn't Raise Your Hands Go back and read Chapters 3 through 8! I know, I know, you've got places to go and things to do—just like all the other job-seekers that you'll be competing against. A quick word of advice: you are very unlikely to find work by reading this chapter alone. Matching yourself to job opportunities via the Net can be like looking for a needle in a haystack. Both you and the employer must dig through an enormous amount of hay to find something remotely worthwhile (if indeed it was ever there in the first place).

Why do I put up these warning flags here? It's mostly due to what I talked about in Chapters 6 and 8: researching, targeting and networking. You'll recall that I described the hidden job market, where up to 80 percent of all jobs are found. The remaining 20 percent of jobs are secured through classified ads, recruiters and employment search firms, cold calls or mailings, and nepotism (my personal favourite, but I haven't had much of a chance to use it).

REAL LIFE *If you're in the hi-tech field, such as computers or engineering, it's becoming imperative that you integrate the Net as part of your work-search. If you fall into this category, make sure that you look at the Jobs for Hi-Tech Workers section later in this chapter.*

The Frenzied Twenty Percent The chapter you're reading now deals almost exclusively with this remaining 20 percent of jobs (with the exception of nepotism). The vast majority of these fall into the category of open postings. By open, I mean that they're postings you'd normally see advertised in some way. You can find them all over: in newspapers (career or classified sections), trade publications, Canada Employment Centres, company newsletters, and—increasingly—online.

Know this: seeking job vacancies that are published online, or uploading your résumé to the Net, may not give you the edge that you're looking for. That's the downfall of these open job postings. Everyone else knows about them at the *same time* that you do. When you realize that most job seekers are fighting for only 20 percent of all potential jobs, it kind of puts the networking process into its proper perspective.

What to Expect in This Chapter

None of this means that you should completely shun online job postings or avoid putting your résumé into some of the better résumé banks. It does suggest, however, that you focus your efforts on networking and use electronic job searching as just one more weapon in your electronic arsenal.

In the next few sections you'll learn how to best use your time (and money) if you decide to look for work opportunities online. You will discover that the vastness of possible choices can be mind numbing. To help provide an initial framework, I've outlined the three main ways of using technology to seek out job postings and contract positions in Table 9.1.

Table 9.1 Searching For Work Opportunities Online

BASIC METHOD	YOUR PRIMARY OBJECTIVE
Searching for Posted Job Openings	To find actual work opportunities that you can apply for directly
Displaying Your Résumé on the Net	To capture the eye of employers who are looking to hire people, so they will contact you for an interview
Using an Employment Matching Service	To secure interviews with companies who are ready to hire by means of electronic matching

II. FINDING POSTED VACANCIES ON THE WORLD WIDE WEB

I have this fantasy (well, several actually, but just one I can discuss in this book). Wouldn't it be great if you could turn on your computer, press a few buttons and get your dream job? You'd boot 'er up, put in all the things you want in your next position, then press "Enter." Out would come a list of brand new vacancies that precisely fit your specifications. Then, by clicking on "Submit," your video résumé would be automatically sent to the employers you've chosen.

Reality Bytes

This is pretty far from the way things are today. You can, however, use the Internet to locate a variety of existing positions. This includes everything from entry-level postings, right up to those for presidents and CEOs. There's full-time, part-time and contract jobs available. Many industries and occupations are covered, too.

The trouble is threefold. First, these jobs tend to be posted widely. As we discussed previously, this means that there's no great advantage to finding them online. Since everybody else can see them in their newspaper, what does that leave you with?

There's No Centralization The second problem is that these job postings are scattered all over the Net. It's not like there's one, mammoth repository that you can search with ease. Nope, you've got to dive right into not just one, but an ever-increasing number of haystacks.

This makes it hard to find what you're looking for. Picture this—you're seeking a job as an administrative assistant, and you want to work in or around St. John's, Newfoundland. To locate relevant openings on the Internet, you'd need to look in company homepages, assorted job Web sites, a variety of newsgroups and e-mail listserves. You could also post your résumé on Web-based résumé banks and Usenet job Newsgroups, then cross your fingers and wait for someone to stumble across your material.

Techies Rule on the Net To make matters worse, jobs posted electronically still tend to be geared towards workers in the hi-tech sectors. Likewise, employers who take the time to look for résumés posted online tend be from hi-tech companies or from technical departments in mainstream organizations (e.g. the systems department at a life insurance company).

If you're an insurance agent, or accountant, or marketing representative for a food company, chances are you'll see far more openings in traditional media than on the Net. If, however, you're a techie who wants to work in the systems department of an insurance company, accounting firm or food manufacturer, you've hit a gold mine.

Obviously, you can't rely exclusively on electronic job postings. Having made my point, let's look at where you *can* find positions that are being advertised on the Internet at this very moment.

REAL LIFE *The driving force behind electronic job postings is cost effectiveness. Companies are finding that it can be relatively inexpensive to list their job openings online, in addition to advertising in conventional ways. That's why this approach is starting to reach traditional positions, not just the hi-tech folks. Watch for this trend to spread in the near future.*

1. Company Web Site Homepages

A good place to start is with the companies that you targeted back in Chapter 6. An increasing number of companies with Web sites are starting to list some job openings on their site. If they're there, you'll generally see a hyperlink on their homepage which says something like Employment, We're Hiring or Positions Available.

This is a cheap way for companies to post their openings. Since they're already paying for the Web site, there's very little additional expense. For you, the benefits are as follows:

- You might find an opening at the precise company you want to work for. Used in combination with your networking, it's definitely worth a shot.
- The postings tend to be current, unlike at some other places on the Net.
- Postings are usually accompanied by very detailed job descriptions.
- Often your résumé can be e-mailed directly to the company (see Chapter 5).
- You can review the Web site immediately and get useful info on the

company. You could even use some of this in your cover letter when replying to the ad.

Plan on Seeing More of This An excellent example of a company doing some hiring on the Internet is Canadian Tire. Their site offers a number of features that can assist the typical job seeker. Not only do you get some useful history and background on the company, but there are current job vacancies as well.

You'll see some really nice touches on the Canadian Tire site that other Canadian companies are just beginning to incorporate, like breaking out the job postings by category. The listings you'll find are under Information Systems, Finance, Marketing, Logistics and Other. The jobs themselves range from technical (e.g. Senior Programmer / Analyst) to traditional (Real Estate Manager).

You can even cut and paste your résumé directly into their Web page to send via e-mail. (Hint: see Chapter 5 for tips on posting résumés electronically.) The Canadian Tire Web site can be found at **http://www.cyberplex.com/cgi-bin/ctc/ctchome.pl**.

CYBER TIP There are many Canadian companies with job postings on their Web sites. Check the list of companies you targeted back in Chapter 6. Then visit the Web site for each of your top prospects. You can get there by typing in the company's name in the AltaVista search engine (at **http://www.altavista.digital.com**). Or find links to a variety of Canadian companies, organized by industry at **http://www.yahoo.ca/Regional/Countries/Canada/Business_and_Economy/Companies**.

2. Job Sites

If you don't feel like surfing from one company to the next, you can always try a centralized job site. These are Web-based pages that advertise a variety of jobs or contract positions from all sorts of different companies.

The best thing about these sites is the convenience that they offer. You can often use a specialized search engine, on-site, to look for a position by province, city, industry, type of job or company (or some combination thereof).

Fragmentation Abounds While this sounds wonderful in theory, the practical aspects can be disappointing. Once again, most of the jobs that you will find are on the open market. My experience has also been that the number of jobs in any of the traditional fields is still quite limited.

I guess this should come as no surprise, since most services are pretty new. Moreover, many of them charge the employer for each job that they post. Hence, employers are wary of spending money until the site proves itself to be viable. At the same time, so many of these job sites have sprung up lately that market is highly fragmented.

CYBER TIP Many job posting sites on the Net also let you post your résumé online. This gives you a better chance of hooking up with an employer, since you're using a combined approach. (Note that I said a better chance, not a good chance). Be prepared to upload your résumé properly if you choose to use these dual-sites to their best advantage. A good example of this is the Career Mosaic Canada site at **http://canada.careermosaic.com**.

Government-Sponsored Job Sites With this in mind, one of the better examples of a job list Web site has been created by Human Resources Development Canada. Their HRDC National Job Bank® is located at **http://jb-ge.hrdc-dhrc.gc.ca**. What you'll find is lists of jobs across the country which you can search by occupational category, job title or National Occupational Classification (NOC) Code.

HRDC has also put together a different site which lets you search by province and category of work. It's at **http://ccn.cs.dal.ca/Government/HRD-NS/orders/jobbanke.html**. And if you want to search locally, not just province-wide, HRDC has assembled a list of its regional job sites across the country. Sorted by city, it's available at **http://ein.ccia.st-thomas.on.ca/agencies/cec/jobs/jobbank.html**.

Private Sector Job Sites The private sector has also jumped in big time when it comes to job sites. You can find all sorts of postings, for example, at the JobSat site. Here's what this service is claiming in their advertising: "Free. Search thousands of employment opportunities. Listings are from multiple sources, across Canada and select U.S. locations."

My visit to the site confirmed that there are many jobs to choose from. According to them, more than 85 percent of the vacancies are Canadian (the remainder being mostly American). Plus, the database is searchable in a number of ways. The postings, however, tend to come from previously published sources (e.g. the open market). Also, check to make sure that the listings are recent. It's at **http://www.jobsat.com**.

Some other Canadian job listing spots to look at are listed below:

- Atlantic Canada Careers (**http://atl-can-careers.com**). Search for job vacancies in the Atlantic provinces for free, and post your résumé.
- Emploi@ (**http://www.login.net/emploi-a/public_html**). Quebec jobs and links to employment resources.
- Federal Government Jobs (**http://www.psc-cfp.gc.ca/recruit/hshorte.htm**). Public Service Commission of Canada vacancy postings.
- NetJobs (**http://www.netjobs.com:8000**). National database of job openings. Can also update your résumé (for a fee).
- Net-Work (**http://www.onsetmag.com/jobmarket**). Onset Magazine's database of job openings (register for free).
- Résumé Canada (**http://www.bconnex.net/~resume/index.html**). View job openings by category across Canada.
- WORKaccess (**http://www.workaccess.com**). Some Canadian jobs, but still in the building phase of operation.

- Worknet (**http://www.worknet.ca/**). National job database brought to you by Electronic Access Systems Inc.

There Is Life North of the 49th Parallel In addition to sites born and bred in Canada, the large U.S. web-based career centres have discovered that Canadians do exist, and indeed may have money to spend (as devalued as it is compared to the almighty American dollar).

To take advantage of this, more than a few are now offering Canadianized versions of their job search engines. The Monster Board is a case in point. Although its owners reside in Montreal, it caters primarily to U.S. clients because that's where it started out. Even so, they have a Canadian job list at **http://www.monster.com/jobseek/csearch/search_sb_front.mb.html**.

Other American-based Internet career services with Canadian jobs online include:

- CareerMosaic Canada: **http://canada.careermosaic.com/cm/canada/canada2.html**
- CareerMagazine: **http://www.careermag.com/cgi-bin/search banner.cgi**

CYBER TIP When surfing one of the big American career centres on the Web, search their homepage for links to Canadian or International material. That's where they've put the job sites that apply to us in the Great White North.

3. Associations and Professional Group Web sites

I'd mentioned in Chapter 6 that the association representing your profession can be an excellent source for networking. Some professional groups have also started to act as online job intermediaries. They list positions from member companies as a service to their clients. If you'd like to see a good example, investigate Job Listings in Academia at **http://volvo.gslis.utexas.edu/~acadres/canada.html**. This site is typical of those that list positions for a particular field.

From what I've seen to date, not many Canadian associations are providing this type of service. One thing you can do is search for your particular industry group, using the Associations Canada Online Web site (**http://www.clo.com/~canadainfo/assocon.html**). There's no guarantee that you'll find job listings. On the other hand, you might just run into some other information that will assist you in your search for work.

4. Recruiters and Search Firms

Employment agencies and recruiting firms are just discovering the power of the Internet. The hi-tech recruiters were the first to market positions online and accept e-mailed résumés. Now this is filtering through to some of the more generalized search companies.

Recruiters who are online still tend to focus on advertising their services, rather than posting jobs. And the jobs that they do post online are likely to be the ones you've seen in the newspapers. In spite of this, there are some good examples of Canadian recruiter sites to view.

One is from The Caldwell Partners. It has some job listings and some immediate contract positions too. Note that this particular firm specializes in high-end placement (e.g. senior managers, presidents and CEOs). It's an interesting place to visit even if you're not looking in this stratosphere. (**http://www.caldwellpartners.com/adintro.htm**).

For lists of some other Canadian employment agencies online, you can visit the following:

- A searchable list of recruiters in Canada, by city. Look under Agency at **http://www.worknet.ca**.
- A list of Canadian employment agencies (unsorted, but fairly thorough). Check under Employment Agencies at **http://www.yahoo.ca**.
- The Canadian Job Source site. Look under Recruiters at **http://www.irus.rri.uwo.ca/~jlaw/job_can.html**.

REAL LIFE *Employment agencies, recruiters and search firms operate in different ways. Some charge the employer a fee only if they find a suitable candidate. These are called contingency firms. Others are paid a flat fee whether they find someone or not. This is the retainer firm. It is important to know that many firms specialize in placing people within specific industries or levels of jobs.*

5. Classified Ads Online

Has this ever happened to you? You're anxiously awaiting the arrival of your morning newspaper, eager to check out the latest career ads, when you notice something at the bottom of your birdcage. Turns out the Employment section has already been used by your significant other—as a liner for your little budgie.

Fret no more, fellow Web meisters. You can now find most of the help wanted and employment ads from your city's paper online. Better yet, most of these sites provide a search engine, so you can locate recent job ads by criteria such as job category and location. Remember, though, that this service is a convenience only. Your competition may be pulling the pages from their birdcages (or cat-litter pans) and responding to the same ads at the same time as you.

Here are some of the newspaper Web sites that carry their employment advertisements in a searchable format:

- *Globe and Mail,* CareerConnect Ads **http://web.theglobeandmail.com**
- *Ottawa Citizen,* Worknet **http://www.worknet.ca/**
- Planet SUN, Classified Search **http://www.canoe.ca/classified/JOBsearch.html**
- *The Toronto Star,* Careers **http://www.thestar.com/thestar/classified/plmonster.html**

CYBER TIP Don't forget the Commercial Online Providers as a source for job postings. America Online Canada has several areas where jobs for Canadians are posted. At their search area, type in "jobs canada" and see what comes up.

III. JOB SEARCHING ON USENET NEWSGROUPS, FREENETS AND LISTSERVES

The Usenet, you'll recall, is the part of the Internet where messages are exchanged in Newsgroups via e-mail. There are a number of Canadian Newsgroups dedicated to jobs. These are places where people have e-mailed in positions for you to review. And it's also where some people post their résumés.

Such Nice Technology, So Primitively Deployed

I was stunned when I first ventured into a job-oriented Newsgroup. Maybe I'd been spoiled by the attractiveness and graphics of the Web. Or perhaps I was just expecting...well, something better. After all, this is leading edge technology we're dealing with here. At any rate, I was quite disappointed.

In my opinion, the setup of these Newsgroups leaves a lot to be desired. Yes, there are jobs, hundreds of them. Jobs that are posted in an absolutely random order. Jobs for people who can program in C^{++} and speak other alien computer languages. Plus, and this is where I just shake my head, hundreds of opportunities to involve yourself in multi-level sales schemes and other such questionable practices.

Not Well Maintained Either To top it off, the vacancies can remain online for an eternity. It's not like some official body monitors the content. Whatever goes on can stay on without being removed. So even if you do finally see something (a glimpse of that needle, perhaps), once you call it up it could be six months or even a year old.

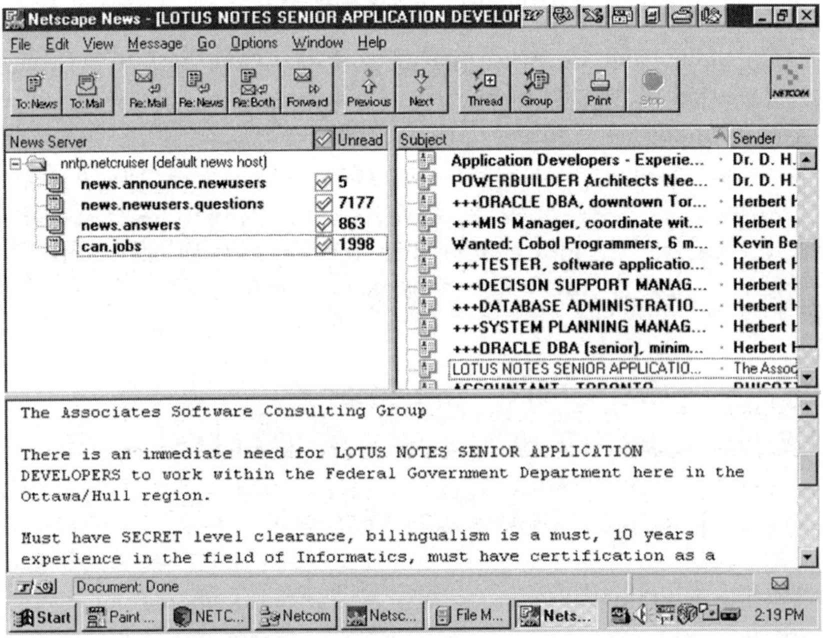

Have I made it sound attractive? It's not that bad, I guess. I mean, some people in the hi-tech industry swear by Newsgroups. As for me, most job hunters I've spoken to about Newsgroups swear *at* them. Take a look for yourself at one the Newsgroups listed below:

- ab.jobs (Alberta Jobs)
- bc.jobs (British Columbia Jobs)
- can.jobs (Canadian Jobs—National)
- nb.jobs (New Brunswick Jobs)
- ns.jobs (Nova Scotia Jobs)
- ont.jobs (Ontario Jobs)
- qc.jobs (Quebec Jobs)
- sk.jobs (Saskatchewan Jobs)

Where to Find More This is just a sampling of the Canadian Newsgroups focused on jobs and employment. There are many for specific cities as well, as cited later in this chapter. To find a complete list of related Newsgroups, try the CACEE WorkWeb at **http://www.cacee.com/usenet_jobs.html**. Another excellent list is in the Usenet section of The Canadian Job Source: **http://www.irus.rri.uwo.ca/~jlaw/job_can.html**.

With all these Newsgroups kicking around, you can imagine what a chore it would be to surf them all individually. Thank goodness someone else (who knows what they're doing) was thinking the same thing. Some search engines have been created to dig into several Newsgroups at once. So you can input your criteria (e.g. city and type of work required) and get results from multiple sources. Two of the best of these search engines are located at **http://www.worknet.ca/filter_nf.html** and **http://www.careermosaic.com/cm/cm36.html**.

CYBER TIP To access the Newsgroups, you'll need an Internet Service Provider that provides a Usenet reader (almost all of them do). However, not every Provider carries each one of the many thousands of Newsgroups. Check with your ISP if you're having trouble locating a Newsgroup listed in this book. They can sometimes arrange to import it for you.

Freenets

A close cousin of the Usenet groups are Freenets. These tend to be local in nature and they often contain employment or job listing sections. Like their Usenet brethren, jobs listed on Freenets tend to be randomly arranged. One advantage though is that the positions listed are typically local in nature. There is one thing you have to watch for here. Some Freenets are located on the Web, while others can only be accessed through Telnet (one of the older Internet applications). If you want to know which is which, check under Freenet at the Canadian Job Source site (**http://www.irus.rri.uwo.ca/~jlaw/job_can.html**). Moreover, a good list of Web-based Freenets can be found at **http://www.InfoNET.st-johns.nf.ca/OtherFreenets.html**.

Listserves

Getting blisters yet from scrolling through all these sites? You're probably wondering if there's an easier way to see job postings on the Net. The answer, happily, is yes. How would you like to have new job postings sent directly to your computer? It can be done using Listserve technology.

The principle here is that you subscribe to a mailing list (Listserve) that specializes in Canadian jobs. You specify the type of job you want (e.g. industry, level, location etc.). If a job of that type gets posted, it will automatically be sent to your e-mail. All you have to do is check your in-basket on a regular basis and view any relevant files.

> **REAL LIFE** *My advice is to use Listserves solely as a complement to all your other work-search efforts. There's no doubt that being notified of postings automatically is convenient. From what I've seen though, there do not seem to be very many positions coming through this avenue as of yet. The message: don't give up your active approach for passive techniques.*

Try a Few Out One of the better mailing list services is provided by the *Globe and Mail,* through its CareerConnect site. Just go to **http://careerconnect.theglobeandmail.com** and click on Career Alert! You can fill in the details right there and then. They'll automatically send appropriate job listings to your e-mail address.

Other Listserves that you may want to investigate include:

- Job Alert! from The Employment News at **http://www.employmentnews.com/Employment_News/en_docs/jobalert.html**
- Net-Work Smart Match at **http://www.onsetmag.com/jobline/html/register.html**
- NetJobs mailing list form at **http://www.netjobs.com:8000/NJmail.html**
- The JobBoard at **info@pax.com**

Or try the search engine specifically for Listserves. It's called Liszt (cute, eh?) and it can be found at: **http://www.liszt.com/resources.html**.

SPECIAL SECTION: JOBS FOR HI-TECH WORKERS

Unlike people in traditional fields, those of you in hi-tech positions will significantly increase your odds of finding work by looking at job postings on the Net. The reason is simple: more and more employers who are looking for technical people are using the Internet as their primary recruitment tool.

In fact, a growing number of hi-tech employers are posting technical jobs *exclusively* on the Internet. Here's what they're really saying: "If you're not knowledgeable enough to use the Net and find our job openings, we don't want to deal with you."

This goes a step further when it's time to send in your application. You're often expected to know how to submit your résumé and cover letter via e-mail or Web form. So now what they're saying is: "Good, at least you found us. If you can figure out how to get your résumé to us electronically, in the exact format that we need, *then* maybe we'll contact you."

This phenomenon applies to those of you in the computer field (information systems, information technology, programmers, administrators etc.), as well as engineers and other hi-tech professionals. There are numerous job sites and resources set up online specifically for you.

If you are a hi-tech worker, you'll want to look at all the sites described earlier in this chapter. In addition, there are sites devoted to bringing hi-tech workers together with companies. A great example of this is the HiTechCareer Centre. Sponsored by the CEO Group, it's designed for people in information technology, information services, computers and engineering. Here you'll find direct links to employers who are hiring, as well as places to post your résumé online. You'll also see something called a virtual job fair. These are online gatherings of companies looking to hire hi-tech workers. Moreover, there are listings of actual job fairs that take place in cities across Canada, where you go to actually meet with company hiring departments. This is a must see at **http://www.hitechcareer.com**.

Some other high-tech recruitment sites worthy of note are Fleethouse (IT and Engineering) at **http://www.cnc.ca** and the Lendman Group at **http://www.lendman.com**.

One quick reminder here. Don't stop networking or sending out mailings just because there may be jobs for you on the Net. On the other hand, make sure that you look for jobs online as well. A useful place to start, strangely enough, is your local newspaper. Watch for ads in the career section that are targeted to hi-tech workers. They often include a Web site address (URL). Surf these sites, and you're on your way to getting matched up with your next position.

IV. POSTING YOUR RÉSUMÉ ONLINE

The previous section looked at the many ways to find job postings online. Now we move into the flipside of this coin: displaying your résumé for employers to see. The goal here is to snare the eye of potential employers as they troll cyberspace at hiring time.

I'll say straight out that I'm unconvinced of the effectiveness of this particular approach. It may sound cool at first, but the results have been less than spectacular to date.

More Options, But Nothing to Hang Your Hat on Yet

If you do decide to follow this route, be aware that there are two basic ways to go: passive and semi-active. The passive road is when you simply throw your résumé online and hope that someone who is looking to hire people finds it. This includes the following tactics:

- résumé banks,
- usenet job newsgroups, and
- your personal homepage.

I will discuss these options in the next few sections.

The semi-active side is where you upload your résumé to sites where open jobs exist. This has two distinct subsets. In one, you upload your résumé to special matching services. The service tries to match you up automatically to specific jobs. For the other, you wait until you spot a job listing and then respond to it by sending in your résumé electronically. Both of these tactics are thoroughly reviewed later in the chapter.

Step Right Up and Play the Game of Chance

Posting your résumé on line today can be summed up in the following way: "You pays your money, and you takes your chances." What you're basically doing is uploading your résumé to the places you think are most likely to be surfed by the type of employers you'd like to work for. This could be a Web-based résumé bank, job-related Newsgroup, matching service or even responding to a an advertised position electronically.

Then...you wait.

If your résumé happens to get spotted by the appropriate person, it's possible that they'll put you into their pile of potential candidates. Of course, that's not the end of it. The employer has probably seen a number of competing résumés by this time. Some will be on the Net, just like yours; others will have come from the employer's ad which is being advertised in traditional media.

At this point, things proceed in a normal fashion. The employer screens all the applications. If they choose to, they may invite you in for an interview. You could then prepare and follow-up in the manner described back in Chapter 7.

To Display or Not to Display

This one approach alone is very unlikely to find you a job (unless you're a hi-tech worker). So why bother investigating it? Well, you could use it as yet another arrow in your job hunt quiver. If that's the case, there are a couple of reasons to consider putting your résumé online. Here are a few:

- You can market your credentials 24 hours a day, 7 days a week.
- If you're looking for inexpensive national and international exposure, here it is.
- Not everyone's doing it yet, so it gives you a chance to stand out from your competitors.

- You may just impress a potential employer with your ability to post online.

Tread Carefully Once again there are some downsides that you should keep in mind. The biggest concern is the risk factor. Posting your résumé on the Internet can put you in a potentially vulnerable position, unless you take certain precautions (outlined later). You are basically tossing your private, personal information into the air, where anyone can get hold of it.

Ponder these potential scenarios:

- A recruiter or employment firm could find your résumé, duplicate it, and start sending it out to all sorts of companies without your knowledge or consent.
- If a troubled individual happens to be lurking on the Net, and they get hold of your résumé, they could make undesirable changes to it and re-post it widely.
- That same troubled person now has your phone number, address and other private information about you. Need I say more?

I'm not trying to alarm you. It is, however, my duty to make you aware of all the possibilities. These encompass both the good and the bad.

No Focus, No Results Other negatives include the relatively low success rate of online résumé postings for non-techies. The situation today is that if you're in a traditional field, don't bet on this option. Remember that the most effective job seekers take a targeted approach. Moreover, employers in Canada don't really expect people from every walk to be online yet. They're in the experimental phase, as are the job-seekers.

Putting your résumé online can be considered the modern-day equivalent of the broadcast letter. You can't really have a cover page attached, since you have no idea who's going to be viewing your file. Remember that the cover letter lets you customize your message to a specific employer. Without it, you're just shooting for whoever stops by.

And don't believe for a minute that employers will go out of their way to find you. They'll be looking only where they expect to find other candidates in your field. This assumes, however, that they are bothering to look online at all. A recent study indicated that relatively few Canadian employers actively search the Net for résumés.

Starts Free, Then Adds Up Fast Let's not ignore the potential costs. To increase the odds of being seen, you'll probably want to upload your résumé to more than just one site. This won't be a problem if you stick to all the free sites. But many employers prefer to surf the sites that charge a fee to clients, assuming that this will attract higher quality, more serious workers.

What could end up happening is that you put out $25 here, $35 there...and suddenly you've just spent a couple hundred dollars. Since most services charge you again every three to six months if you're still using their space, things can add up.

V. PASSIVE APPROACH ONE: THE WORLD WIDE WEB

If you haven't been put off yet, there are several ways to post your résumé online. We'll look at the World Wide Web first, particularly résumé banks, which are collections of online résumés. The Web is also where you can post your résumé on your own personal homepage (though it's not recommended for traditional job seekers). After that we will explore other parts of the Net where you can post your résumé, such as employment Newsgroups on Usenet.

How a Résumé Bank Works

The original concept here was not at all that complicated. It's based on the same simple principle that many of us use when we do our shopping. We often have so many other things to do during the week that we rush to one favourite store and hope to find everything we need there. We may not get exactly what we want, but it's close enough. And it saves us from running around all day, wasting our precious time.

That's how résumé banks were supposed to be structured. They wanted you, and as many other job-seekers as they could get, to sign up for their service. Then they'd go out to employers and offer them one-stop shopping for applicants in every shape and size. "Better variety, more convenience." (Is it me, or does this sound strangely like an ad for A&P?)

Which Came First? Things have evolved a little less smoothly than planned. Largely, this is a result of the fragmentation that's taking place. If you tour the Web today, it seems that anyone with some time and a few dollars to spare has created a new résumé bank. Many are free, others charge a fee. Some are private sector, while others are operated by the government. A few cater to specific professions, while most will accept applications from just about anybody.

This proliferation of sites has left employers and work searchers in a quandry. Which ones do you use? Most résumé repositories now suffer from a chicken and egg syndrome. Here's what I mean. Qualified job seekers, afraid of wasting time and money, avoid posting their résumés to a site unless they believe that relevant employers will see them. Employers, wary of wasting time and money, don't bother to visit a résumé bank unless they're confident of finding qualified candidates. If both sides hold off, not a heck of a lot gets done.

Does Paying For It Get You Further Ahead?

On top of all this, there is also the fee versus free issue. You can find many job banks which allow you to post your résumé at no charge. Sometimes they charge the employers a fee to view or download the résumés, or they could just be doing the whole thing as a public service.

There are also services that cost you money to use. They may then let employers search the profiles for free, or they may also charge them to access the résumés.

Which ones are better? The jury's still out. It's too soon to tell how many job-seekers are actually connecting to employers through any of these services. Furthermore, the résumé banks themselves haven't exactly been bragging about their success ratios. This leads me to believe that the whole concept has yet to establish itself in these early stages. Only time will tell if it will succeed or not long-term.

1. Résumé Banks That Won't Cost You a Dime

The debate over the usefulness of these résumé banks won't resolve itself overnight. Meanwhile you can check a few out for yourself. There are several worthwhile destinations to choose from. CareerMosaic Canada is a fine example. You'll discover a veritable career centre online. You can post your résumé on their RésuméCM database. It will stay active for 90 days. After this you can re-post it, again at no charge. Check it out at **http://canada.careermosaic.com/cm/canada/canada11.html**.

CYBER TIP Some résumé banks ask you to upload your résumé electronically, while others will take your paper version and input it manually or through scanning. Make sure you find out which format they want (e.g. scannable paper, e-mail or Web form, full-format or ASCII). Full details on uploading your résumé electronically are in Chapter 5.

The Privacy Issue Notice that on many of these sites, you are allowed to look at all the other résumés that are posted. This brings up an interesting question: Just who exactly has the right to look at your résumé once it's on one of these databases? The answer varies by site. In many cases, virtually anyone on the Internet can view your résumé. So, if you're worried about protecting your identity, look carefully at how each service operates.

For comparison purposes, here are how some other free résumé-posting services work:

- The Monster Board (Résumé City) **http://www.monster.com/jobseek/csearch/search_sb_front.mb.html**. You'll want to know that "after submitting your résumé to Résumé City, your personal contact information is separated into a private database. The employer must purchase your résumé before your personal information is revealed." In reality, anyone who wants to shell out a few bucks can get your information.
- World Wide Jobseekers **http://cban.worldgate.edmonton.ab.ca/résumé**. Anyone can see your résumé, but you don't have to provide your name (you can put just your e-mail or phone number down instead). Also, you fill in a standardized Web form, instead of uploading your full résumé.
- The Job Tree (JobLink Canada) **http://www.netnation.com/joblink**. You input your information into a detailed, easy-to-use Web form. Then everyone can see it—it's not disguised in any way. Although they claim that the "information is confidential between you and any employers you apply to," they make it plain for all to see.
- ABC Mall (located on Canada's west coast) **http://www.islandnet.com/~cvcprod/abcmall/empcentr.html**. This is a place to put up an employment wanted ad for free. In five lines or less, you tell the

world what kind of work you're looking for (and why you should get it). You can use your e-mail address only if you choose. The posting will stay up for one week, and can be renewed as many times as you like.

REAL LIFE *To determine if a résumé bank will attract the employers you're looking for, do a simple test. Surf the site. Go into the résumé area (if you're allowed to) and see if any other people have put résumés in the categories that apply to you. Contrary to popular thinking, the more here, the better. That's because employers are drawn to pools of candidates, not just single candidate postings.*

2. Résumé Banks That Will Cost You More than a Dime

Once you've exhausted the freebie databases, you may want to explore the ones that are fee-based. You'll discover that the going rate to post your résumé at one of these services is fairly consistent. Right now it costs between $20 and $50 to get your résumé listed on one of these services for anywhere from three months to a year. What's not predictable, however, are the results that you'll get.

Be a Smart Consumer Now that we're talking about investing some of your money, your caution level should perk up. So many fee-based résumé banks are cropping up that it's difficult to know what you're committing to. You can increase your chances of signing up with a legitimate, effective service by asking a few basic questions. The inquiries, and the responses to look for, are detailed in Table 9.2.

Fee-based Canadian résumé banks are everywhere. I've selected several here to demonstrate the range in pricing and services offered across the country. The site descriptions are quoted from the service providers themselves, to show you how they are promoting their products.

- Atlantic Canada Careers (Maritimes-based) **http://atl-can-careers.com/resreg.html**. "The Résumé Bank Registry is a discrete career management tool. Membership is $50.00 (GST included) for the initial year and $35/year afterwards. Members benefit by being contacted from time to time by leading employers about new 'hidden' career opportunities. Discretion is assured because Résumé Bank members

Table 9.2 Questions to Ask a Résumé Bank Before Signing Up

QUESTIONS TO ASK	HOW THEY SHOULD ANSWER
What is the going rate to post my résumé?	Between $20 and $50 for three to twelve months of online exposure is the average.
What is your success rate in finding jobs for candidates?	"There's no accurate way to track this data yet" (if they do give you a figure, ask for documentation).
Are there any hidden costs?	"No." (Make sure you read the fine print.)
What about additional options that you might charge me for?	"You may be charged extra to have the service design your résumé for you, or to input it online (instead of you e-mailing it), or for a privacy option." (See the next Real Life.)
Can I make periodic changes to update my résumé?	"Yes," (once every month or two—for free).
Do you automatically match my credentials to jobs that are posted on your system?	"No. Employers can view your résumé and select it if they like." (See the Job Matching section for more details.)
Are recruiters or search agencies allowed to view and possibly download my résumé with my name on it?	"No. We do not release your name and number unless you agree to it first."
If you post the résumés by job category, can I put mine into more than one category (e.g. marketing and sales as well as management)?	"Yes." (You should be able to put your résumé in at least two or three categories at no extra charge.)

identify those organizations they do not wish to see their résumé (i.e. current employer). Members may revise their résumé twice a year."

- NetJobs (national, based in Ontario) **http://www.netjobs.com:8000/index.html.** "NetJobs Information Services is an Internet publishing service division of Sea Change, that provides a convenient and central location for employment seekers to facilitate their job search on the Internet. NetJobs creates an interactive forum for the exchange of information related to employment information and acts as an arena for recruitment. The cost for placing your résumé on NetJobs is $30 (plus GST). Your résumé will be online for a six month period."

- Résumé Canada (locations across Canada) **http://www.bconnex.net/~resume/canmall.** "Résumé Canada offers you the choice of posting your résumé on our Résumé Canada Web site or on any one of our Canada Super Malls city sites. There is a nominal posting fee of $18.00 plus G.S.T. for a two page résumé for six months. If you wish your résumé to be posted in multiple résumé categories, there is an additional charge of $5.00 per additional selection."
- JOBACCESS (Ontario-based) **http://web.globalserve.net/~jobs/**. "JobAccess was developed so that individuals needing a job don't have to spend a considerable amount of money advertising their résumé. JobAccess allows employers to search our résumé database at no charge. We also offer an on-line jobs listing updated weekly. This great offer costs only $19.99 for the 6 months period."
- Canadian Résumé Centre **http://netaccess.on.ca/~résumé/index1.html**. Bills itself as "the place to put your résumé when confidentiality counts." The design of a résumé costs $25.00 for 10 laser printed copies. E-mailed résumés: $25.00 for 6 months on the Internet database. Faxed or mailed résumés: $40.00 for 6 months on the Internet database. Confidential profile and subsequent contacts: $50.00 for 6 months of service. You can identify your résumé by a serial number (no name or phone number required). People who want to contact you must first e-mail the company and explain who they are.
- WorkAccess **http://www.workaccess.com/**. "The cost of posting

REAL LIFE *The truth about privacy on the Web is that it is almost nonexistent. Practically anyone can search résumé banks and view what you've posted. Try for at least some protection. Use code numbers or box numbers instead of your real name and address, and insist on finding out who the company is before releasing your identity. It may cost a little extra, but it could save you some hassles. Also, make sure you can restrict access to your résumé by employers you're avoiding, like your current company, if you're still employed, and don't want them to know you're looking.*

your résumé (entered on our Post Résumé page) is $25 for 6 months. The cost of Faxed or Mailed or E-mailed Résumé is $45 for 6 month. WORKaccess does not provide any security of the résumé contents." (I like their honest approach.)

Putting Your Résumé on Your Personal Homepage

One area we really haven't discussed yet is how to use your own Web site as a career marketing tool. There's a good reason for this. Unless you're going for a specific type of high-tech job, it's considered to be a waste of time.

Most recruiters and human resources managers are besieged by unsolicited résumés as it is. Why would they spend their precious time surfing aimlessly? This is understandable, especially when you take into account the staggering number of Web sites available today. What do you think the odds are that they'll happen upon yours?

If you have put together a Web site, do not hesitate to cite it on your résumé (right next to your e-mail address). Once again, it doesn't matter if the employer ever browses your site. It's the impression that you make of being wired and oh-so-current.

Multi-Media Résumés for Hi-Tech Folks There are some notable exceptions to this piece of advice. For those of you who are looking for employment in the Internet field itself, this could be a perfect way to advertise your skills. This includes technical positions such as Web design, to creative positions like layout and multi-media development.

For example, if you're looking for work as a Web site designer, you can put together a multi-media résumé with hyperlinks, pictures, soundbytes and even full-motion video. A wide variety of examples are acces-

CYBER TIP If you have a homepage on the Web, you may still want to post your résumé to other sites (e.g. résumé banks and newsgroups). Then you can mention your Web site on the résumé that's posted in these other sites. The employer can then visit your Web site and learn even more about you. Voilà, instant double-hit.

sible by going to the Alta Vista search engine at **http://www.altavista.digital.com/cgi-bin/query?pg=q&what=web**. Go to "Advanced" search, and type in "multimedia and résumé" (without the quotation marks).

VI. PASSIVE APPROACH TWO: USENET AND LISTSERVES

Another popular place to post résumés on the Net is career-related discussion groups. In particular, Usenet Newsgroups and Web-based forums are rife with résumés (and job postings too, as noted above). There is also a new breed of automated e-mail service (Listserve) that sends new job openings directly to you.

But my goodness, could you get any less proactive? I don't mean to offend the folks who use these tactics (and there are many that do). It's just that, unless you're in the hi-tech field, there are so many more effective methods of securing employment than tossing your résumé into cyberspace to see if anyone bites, or waiting around to get notified of new openings.

What I've noticed too is that the vast majority of the résumés in these areas are from techie types. You'll see lots of systems analysts and computer programmers advertising themselves online. But why would a real-estate manager or mutual fund salesperson go anywhere near here?

Usenet Newsgroups

You should also be aware that this approach is probably the *least* secure way to have your résumé on the Net. Absolutely anyone can download it, if they have access to Newsgroups. It's like putting your personal data on a bulletin board for the world to see (or for someone to take for themselves).

The other reason that I'm critical of this method is the onus that it puts on the people who do the hiring. You are asking a potential employer to sift through dozens of discussion groups to find you. How many employers will spend the time to seek you out from the hundreds of applicants buried here?

If this hasn't dissuaded you, here's a partial list of newsgroups to keep in mind. (This list includes newsgroups by city only—see Section III for provincial and national lists.

- island.jobs (Vancouver Island, British Columbia, Jobs)

- kingston.jobs (Kingston, Ontario, Jobs)
- Kw.jobs (Kitchener-waterloo, Ontario, Jobs)
- ott.jobs (Ottawa, Ontario, Jobs)
- sudbury.jobs (Sudbury, Ontario, Jobs)
- tor.jobs (Toronto, Ontario, Jobs)
- uwo.slis.job (London, Ontario, Library Jobs)
- vic.jobs (Victoria, British Columbia, Jobs)
- van.jobs (Vancouver, British Columbia, Jobs)

VII. SEMI-PASSIVE APPROACH ONE: EMPLOYMENT MATCHING SERVICES

Interested in a somewhat more interactive job search technique? If so, you'll like the following story that I read in one of the Canadian career discussion groups online. A fellow named Jack was looking for work as a sales representative in Prince Edward Island. A friend told him about a service that would take his résumé and match it electronically against actual job vacancies. Before I tell you the rest of Jack's story, I should explain what employment matching is.

Employment Matching Versus Job Sites and Résumé Banks

It might be a bit confusing trying to distinguish between all these options. At job sites you can locate posted vacancies online. In résumé banks you can upload your résumé and display it to potential employers. And at many of these locations, you can do both.

Employment matching is different in one very significant way. The previous strategies do not automatically make connections between the employer and the employee. When you surf a job site, you have to search job listings individually (although the better services provide a search engine). Still, you have to read each ad, decide if there's a fit, then send in your application.

These connections are made for you with employment matching. Once you send in your material (in the format requested by the matching service), it goes on to the database, gets compared to existing openings, and you are notified if an employer wants to contact you.

REAL LIFE *Employment matching is considered to be semi-passive because you're still relying primarily on widely-posted or partially-hidden jobs. Thus, it's one more tool to consider as a support mechanism in your overall search strategy. Your best chance is to keep on with an integrated search.*

It Can Work, But There Are No Guarantees

So, let me get back to Jack's employment matching story. As I mentioned, Jack was looking for a job as a sales representative in Prince Edward Island. He'd been pounding the pavement for several months. On two or three occasions he'd come close to finding work, but nothing had clicked.

If at First You Don't Succeed... A friend told him about the new job matching services on the Web. Jack figured that for $25 he couldn't lose. So he registered with a service. He e-mailed in his résumé (and a cheque) to one of the growing number of computerized job matching services. They electronically scanned his application and entered it into their private database. Then they compared it to the job orders that employers had placed with the company. There wasn't a single match.

In the meantime, Jack continued his networking, research and targeting, along with a mailing campaign. Plus he signed up with two more employment matching services (at $20 and $45 respectively), just to keep his name online.

It May Not Happen Quickly Lo and behold, Jack received a call a month and a half later from the service he'd signed up with initially. An employer had seen his résumé and wanted to talk to him directly. When Jack heard who the employer was, he nearly flipped. It was a sales director with whom he had networked just the month before.

Turns out that the sales director was looking for someone who could communicate with clients across the country via computer. He'd forgotten to ask Jack about his computer skills during their networking session. When he found out that Jack was still looking for work, and that he'd sent in his résumé electronically, he immediately invited Jack in for a formal interview.

Disappointingly, Jack didn't get offered the job. But a month later the same sales director called him back and said that he'd just joined a new company and wanted Jack to come work for him.

Another Part of the Equation

Job matching sounds like a dream come true. All you need to do is send in your résumé and the rest is done for you. In some cases, you don't even have to know how to use the Net (you can mail in your material by regular post). Theoretically, you then get automatically matched to every job on that database for which you qualify.

Here's the catch: *every* job means, in reality, only those vacancies that companies have posted on that particular database. Unfortunately, that doesn't currently translate into very many. As for what *qualify* means, well, employers can run a keyword search. They can ask for specific experience, educational requirements and any skills that they want. If the computer doesn't find these on your résumé, you don't make the cut. This still doesn't mean that you need a keyword résumé, as described in Chapter 11, just one that's scannable.

To Pay Or Not to Pay Matching services, like the résumé banks described earlier in this chapter, come in two types: free and fee-based. In either case, you should pose questions similar to those shown in Table 9.2 (Section V) to the services you are thinking about using. Some additional questions to ask fee-based services (where you're spending your hard-earned money) are as follows:

- How many employers in your field are listing jobs here?
- What types of jobs are there (e.g. level, occupation, location)?
- Are any recruiters allowed to view the résumés? If so, what guarantees are there that your résumé won't be downloaded and widely distributed without your knowledge?
- In what format do they want your résumé (mailed or electronic, ASCII or regular)?

Job Matching for Free

To get an idea of what's out there, you can again begin with the free services. There are two in particular that are trying to build nationwide services. Both happen to be government-sponsored initiatives:

- Electronic Labour Exchange (ELE) **http://ele.ingenia.com.** "The Electronic Labour Exchange is a new computer-based service developed by Human Resources Development Canada to help job seekers identify employment opportunities suited to their qualifications and employers find appropriate candidates. The ELE automatically matches jobs to people and people to jobs." At the time of writing, the ELE was still focused on the Ottawa area; however, it is beginning to build a national representation.
- National Graduate Register (NGR) **http://ngr.schoolnet.ca/ngr/home/.** "An Internet searchable database funded by the Canadian Federal Government (Industry Canada)...designed to match recruiting employers with qualified graduates. The NGR provides anonymous résumés to enquirers, based on matches between the job skill requirements of employers and the skills of students and graduates as presented in the résumés registered in the system." Employers must go through NGR, who then contact you to ask if you want to release your name and number. Also, you can electronically link with guidance, career and labour market information to assist in your job-search efforts.

Job Matching for a Fee

On the private sector side, there are only a few genuine Canadian job matching systems. Most of the résumé banks and job sites still rely on manual processing. Two of the better known national employment matching services are JCI JobMatch and CareerConnect:

- JCI JobMatch™ **http://www.jcitech.com/jobmatch.** For $25, you can have your résumé posted to JCI's private database for six months. According to the promoters, "résumés are input into the database and classified according to some 4,000 job and industry categories. Employers can specify job criteria and download résumés via the Internet or by calling a 1-800 number."

JCI Technologies Inc. has formed alliances with newspapers in the Southam chain (e.g. *The Toronto Star*). They are also doing a trial with select Canada Employment Centres, where job-seekers can submit their résumés to the JobMatch™ database free of charge. The database claims to have approximately 50,000 résumés and 4,300 registered corporations.

- CareerConnect (*Globe and Mail*) **http://web.theglobeandmail.com/.** Leave it to the *Globe and Mail* to come up with a wide-ranging career resource on the Web. Their CareerConnect site is more than just a matching system. It's also a place to find loads of information on job hunting, résumé preparation—even discussion groups with fellow career-seekers. The cost of the job matching service is $24.95 for six months. You can send them your material by e-mail, Web form or regular mail.

VIII. SEMI-PASSIVE APPROACH TWO: RESPONDING TO ADS ELECTRONICALLY

There is a slightly less passive way to post your résumé online. This involves responding to job ads by submitting your résumé and cover letter electronically. I say that this approach is only slightly proactive because you still have to sit and wait for relevant jobs to be published and come to your attention. As such, you'll be wasting valuable time, and may only be exposed to ten percent of all available jobs.

What It Can Do for You

At least you can show some degree of technical proficiency here. Uploading your résumé properly means that you have to know which method is best. This will be determined, of course, by the needs of the employer. See Chapter 5 for detailed instructions on the options that you have.

The other nice thing about responding to ads electronically is that it may get you noticed immediately. Rather than going through the typical screening process, your application gets processed a little differently. It comes through faster and is often seen directly by the human resources department or hiring manager. Traditional applications can lay around unopened in their mailing packages for quite some time.

A Few Rules

- If you find a job ad in the newspaper, and it gives you an e-mail address as well as a regular address, you can send your résumé and cover letter by e-mail if you want to stand out.
- If that same ad only gives you an e-mail address, you'd do best to respond accordingly. Remember to contact the company first to check on the exact format they require.
- If you see a job ad on the Internet, check to see if the company has a

Web site. They may provide you with a Web form to fill out in a standardized fashion. Also, just because the job is posted on the Net doesn't mean the company wants an e-mailed application. Check first to make sure.

REAL LIFE *When submitting an application electronically, consider sending a hard copy as a back-up (by mail, courier or, if pressed, fax). Mention on the electronic version that you've also sent a hard copy. Note on the hard copy that you've also sent an electronic version. That way you can be sure that it gets noticed and processed properly.*

IX. WIRED WRAP UP

There is no doubt that the thought of searching for jobs in cyberspace is appealing. What better way could there be to look for work? From the comfort of your chair, you seek out every posted job in the world, and sit back in comfort while employers actively look for your résumé on the Net. Soon the job offers come pouring in. Right?

Unfortunately, the system doesn't quite work that way (yet, anyway). At best, it's a faint hope. *Maybe* someone will see your résumé. *Possibly* they'll contact you (along with many others), if they have a vacancy that your qualifications seem to match. And *perhaps* you'll stumble upon a job that seems right for you somewhere on a job site or Newsgroup. The fact that it's likely—though not always—the same posting that everyone is seeing at the same time in their newspaper means you don't necessarily get an edge.

At it's worst, you could spend money unnecessarily, and lose control of your most cherished personal marketing tool—your résumé—to a demented Net surfer. Moreover, you could squander valuable time thinking that the online resources are doing your hard work for you, when you should also be out conducting a traditional work search campaign.

The best advice I can give you here is to use the approaches outlined in this chapter sparingly. *If* you can find relevant sites to post your résumé on, if the right employers are looking at these sites, if your privacy can be guaranteed and if it doesn't cost too much, then go ahead and use electronic job, résumé and matching sites.

Remember, though, that you need to balance this passiveness (waiting for jobs to come to you) with an active strategy (networking in the hidden job market). Only then will you be maximizing all of your resources.

CHAPTER 10

The Self-Employment Option

Virtual Definition: **client** ('klī-ənt) *noun*

A software program that is used to contact and obtain data from a server software program on another computer, often across a great distance.

I. THE TREND TOWARDS GOING YOUR OWN WAY

Ever wondered what it would be like to give up your job and work for yourself? For a growing number of us, this is the new reality. More and more individuals are turning to self-employment instead of traditional jobs. In fact, the number of self-employed Canadians has risen steadily in the last decade to nearly 2.5 million people!

It's Not Always by Choice, But It's Happening More Often Although some of us are deliberately choosing self-employment, many of us are doing so because we simply cannot find a steady, traditional job. This has led to a substantial increase in the number of consultants, contract and part-time employees, franchise owners and small business people.

The trend away from traditional jobs does not appear to be slowing. In 1996, over 16 percent of all working Canadians were self-employed. This is up from 12 percent in 1981, and 14 percent in 1991. As it turns out, self-employment represents more than 75 percent of the net gain in employment between 1990 and 1995, according to the Canadian Labour Congress. Colin Campbell, author of *Where the Jobs Are in Canada,* states that fully 1/3 of Canadians expect to be self-employed within five years.

Some Underlying Reasons for This Shift What's behind this significant adjustment in the way that Canadians work? One major cause is that corporate downsizings have taken their toll. Many people are being forced involuntarily into self-employment as traditional vacancies decline.

Author and career expert Janis Foord Kirk summed this up well in the following headline to one of her *Toronto Star* columns: "The Jobs Won't Come Back But There Still Will Be Work." In other words, there are fewer traditional jobs (e.g. full-time positions with established companies, including a steady paycheque and full benefits). Instead, companies are turning increasingly towards outsourcing, contractors and part-timers.

On a positive note, this trend has opened the door for many people who are willingly pursuing self-employment. Affordable technology has been a key factor in allowing people to leave the corporate, government or academic sectors, in order to work from home or a small office. This SOHO (small office/home office) movement is one of the greatest trends in the way that Canadians are working today.

REAL LIFE *Look before you leap. You may have to resist the temptation to chuck it all and live the good life of the self-employed. No more bosses, take off and play anytime you want, write off every last expense...seems mighty appealing. Try talking with an entrepreneur or two face-to-face to get the real lowdown. It may not be precisely as you picture it.*

II. SELF-EMPLOYMENT IN A NUTSHELL

The topic of self-employment is so large that it has filled many books. My purpose here is simply to give a quick overview of the subject, and then point out some of the relevant electronic resources.

Debunking Some Myths

Let's start by shattering some misconceptions that surround working for yourself. First of all, you never really work for yourself. You must have customers and clients who pay for your services. In essence, you have several bosses, instead of that single person you love to hate when working for a big company.

This ties in well with the misconception that self-employed people make their own hours. The hard truth is that you often work longer and harder then when you had a "real" job. Either you get your project finished on time—or you don't get paid!

It Doesn't Have to Consume Or Isolate You Forever

Happily, most successful self-employed situations evolve over time. They turn into a cycle of marketing, selling, servicing and administering that sustains the business. Like anything you do for the first time, there's a heavy learning curve. The key is to determine as quickly as possible what works best.

Also on a happier note, being self-employed doesn't necessarily mean that you work by yourself. It can actually take many forms. This can range from working alone in your home, to sharing an outside office with several colleagues or partners, to being part of a virtual network of freelance employees.

The Categories of Self-Employment

Kevin Hood, consultant and "Canada's self-employment guru" (according to the TV show *W5*), explains that there are four basic ways to embark on self-employment. They vary in terms of risk, capital required to get started and degree of structure. These formats are outlined in the Table 10.1.

Some Pros and Cons of Self-Employment

I've worked on a contract or consulting basis for over half my career. What I've learned is that every day brings with it new challenges, small successes and the normal dose of frustrations. This may not sound much different from people with permanent jobs; however, there are joys and sorrows of working for yourself that should be considered.

Table 10.1 Self-Employment Options

SELF-EMPLOYMENT OPTION	BRIEF DESCRIPTION
Consulting	• You provide your expertise and advice to clients • Start up costs can be relatively low • Need to do continual marketing to secure new contracts • Tends to be unstructured (you make your own rules)
Operating a Franchise	• You purchase an established business operation or concept (e.g. a Midas Muffler outlet or Mailboxes Etc. store) • Typically requires significant upfront financial investment • Tends to be highly structured (you must adhere to company policies and pay fees on a regular basis for marketing and administration)
Running a Small Business	• Can invest in an ongoing enterprise, or start your own business • May require financing and backers (e.g. partners) • Often has a substantial start-up period with low (or no) revenues • Degree of structure varies on your level of ownership. Full-owners have lots of latitude (and risk). Partners may have less of each
Acting as an Agent or Representative	• You would act as an agent or representative of an established organization to sell their products or services • Many of the benefits of a franchise but without the upfront financial investment

Acting as an Agent or Representative	• Primarily focused on selling established products or services into new markets • Usually has a full marketing, sales, servicing and administration support system

A Few Positives to Consider

- The potential for success is limited only by your energy, ability and number of hours in a day.
- You can (hopefully) use your true skills and talents to do work that you genuinely enjoy!
- Corporate politics affect your life much less drastically on a day-to-day basis.
- The tax benefits can be significant.
- Your creativity and personality can be expressed in the way you do business.

CYBER TIP To get a good idea of self-employment in general, try surfing the Web to The Entrepreneurship Centre. This site contains vast deposits of information and resources to broaden your understanding of being a proprietor. It's at **http://www.entrepreneurship.com.**

A Number of Negatives to Contemplate

- The world of self-employment can be harsh. There are no benefits plans, paid holidays or time off for sick leave. Employment insurance and subsidized pension plans are out of the question.
- You survive on the business that you bring in. Much of your time must therefore be devoted to marketing, in order to always have enough clients to pay your bills.
- Start-up periods can involve long, hard work with the possibility of little or no income.
- The customer is king. If you want them to pay you, you'll need to develop a service attitude.
- Just like traditional jobs these days—there are no guarantees!

Technology Can Assist You at Every Stage

To help make the shift to self-employment smoother, you can always turn to technology. Computers, software packages and office equipment for small businesses have revolutionized the marketplace. Now the Internet is taking this to a new level. Today's self-employed can learn how to start a business, network with other small business people, find financing, create a business plan and manage the enterprise—all with the help of online resources.

III. BEFORE YOU MAKE THE LEAP

Like any other major life transition, you should try to approach self-employment in an informed, planned way. Not that this is the way it always happens. I've known a number of people who went into their own businesses after losing their jobs. Some have succeeded well beyond their own expectations. Others have failed miserably, plunging them into despair and financial hardship.

Knowing What It Takes

It turns out that there are certain characteristics among people who succeed on their own. They tend to be optimistic, hard working and believe that their efforts lead directly to results. They are willing to take manageable risks, but take the time to put together sound business plans before getting started. It helps to have some expertise and experience in a specific area that is in demand (e.g computer programming or training and development). Then perseverance, patience and determination come in to play.

Online Tests to Determine What's Right for You

The qualities stated above are prerequisites for doing well as a small business person. Unfortunately, they won't ensure success. According to consultant Kevin Hood, there is at least one more factor that can make all difference in the world: matching your skills, personality and goals to the appropriate type of self-employment.

Different Strokes For Different Folks Simply stated, this means understanding what's involved in each category of self-employment (as outlined briefly in table 10.1). Then you can make a deliberate decision to go the route that fits you best.

As an example, someone who dislikes structure and reporting lines might want to avoid becoming a franchisee. You would likely be put off by too much routine and not enough room for your personal touch. If, on the other hand, you have a strong entrepreneurial flair and a taste for risk, starting a brand new business might be right up your alley.

Evaluating Your Self-Employment Potential Online Fortunately, there are some Web-based tests that can help you determine where your predispositions lie. Here are just two of them:

- Are you a virtual Entrepreneur? **http://www.dnai.com/~career/ccbus.htm**. If you think that starting an Internet-based business is easy, think again. This site, from Online Career and management Consulting, provides an enlightening test to see if you have what it takes.
- Could You Succeed in Your Own Business? **http://www.globalx.net/ocd/minding/mind-eng/succ.html.** This test is from HRDC's Mind Your Own Business site, which explores the world of self-employment. I like it because it states frankly that "your decision (to be on your own) must be based on more than simply a desire to change your situation. A new venture is risky. It may make heavy demands, financially and time-wise, on you and on those close to you. It might not provide you with security such as a regular pay cheque, medical and dental benefits, and a pension plan." The test that they provide allows you to determine if you have the right skills and temperament to be self-employed. The site also encourages you to be as "honest with yourself as possible."

REAL LIFE *You shouldn't rely on a single test (or even a series of tests) to tell you how to run your life. It's important to talk to career advisors as well as small business experts. Fortunately, much of this can be done online as well. For information on getting career advice, refer back to Chapter 3. To find online advice about starting and managing a small business, read on.*

IV. BEGINNING AT THE BEGINNING

If you've decided to investigate self-employment further, it's time to scope out the opportunities. Remember that your choices are not limited. You don't have to create a huge company from scratch to be considered an entrepreneur. There is also consulting, contract work, franchising and being an agent. In fact, the breadth of opportunity is so vast that the question I most often hear is, "Where do I even begin?"

Fortunately, help is but a mouse-click away. Because of the shift in Canada towards self-employment, a whole new sub-industry has sprung up: consulting on starting small businesses. No where is this more evident than when you go online. You can find software, Web-based booklets and courses, Net discussion groups and small business centres all dedicated to helping you develop and succeed with your enterprise.

Online Manuals: Instructions for Your Start-Up

There are all sorts of "how-to" guides online that focus on self-employment. They tend to cover everything from how to set yourself up and where to register your business to finding funding and developing a business plan. Some of the best of these have been produced by government sources. They are free, and easily accessible.

Government Guides Are Great As an example, Human Resources Development Canada has an excellent Web-based booklet called *Minding Your Own Business*. It describes itself as being "designed to help you decide if running a business is a realistic career choice for you. Information on the right qualities and skills needed to run a business, advice on different approaches to starting a business and writing a business plan are included." The full text is available at **http://www.globalx.net/ocd/minding/mind-eng/index.html**.

Another comprehensive resource for those just beginning is the *On-Line Small Business Workshop*. It is, essentially, a business start-up manual. Brought to you by the Canada/British Columbia Business Service Centre, the manual is "designed to provide you with techniques for developing your idea, starting a new venture and improving your existing small business." Workshop components are described in sections like Starting With a Good Idea (e.g. 40 Ideas For Small Businesses), Marketing, Financing and Planning Fundamentals (including Sales Forecasting and

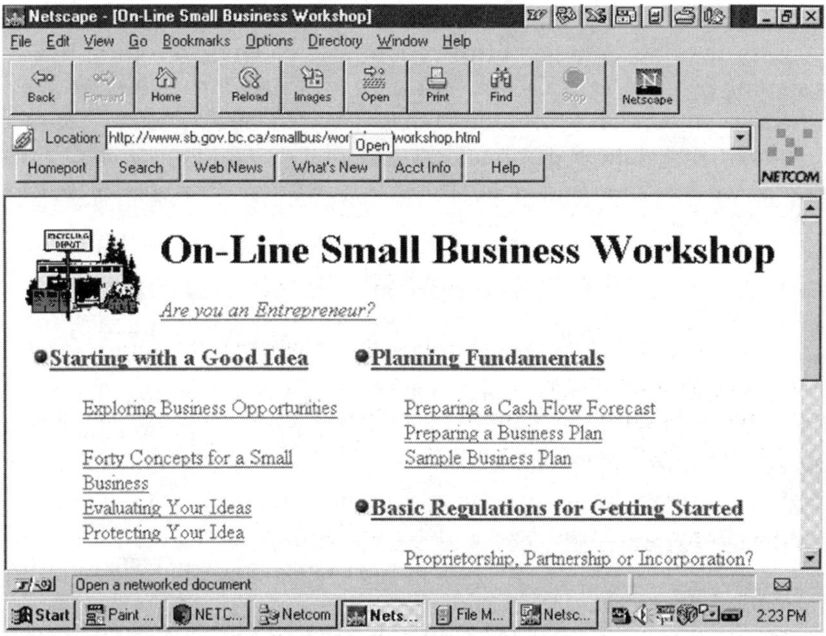

Promotion) and Basic Regulations for Getting Started. For full details, go to **http://www.sb.gov.bc.ca/smallbus/workshop/workshop.html**.

Small Business Centres on the Net

The resources for getting started in self-employment are in no way confined to books and manuals. Our government is committed to fostering small business through a number of local, provincial and federal initiatives. Many of these are now accessible on the Net. I've listed a few to select from.

Canada Business Service Centres (CBSCs) The CBSCs are designed to "improve business access to a wide range of information on government services, programs and regulations." The centres are a collaborative effort between federal, provincial and private sector organizations. Industry Canada is the main player. There are more than 20 federal business departments taking part.

An actual CBSC has been established in a major urban centre in every province. Here you can pick up a collection of leading-edge business products which include interactive videos, publications, business directories, how-to manuals, CD-ROM products and external database access.

Use the CBSC Web site (**http://reliant.ic.gc.ca/english/index.html**)as a starting point. It has links to a wide variety of support services for those who are contemplating self-employment. The site also offers visitors access to a large database of business-oriented federal government programs, services and regulations. The search engine for this service is *Open Text* (a fine made-in-Canada search engine).

Self Employment Development Initiatives (SEDI) SEDI is a not-for-profit Ontario-based organization that was founded in 1986. Its goal is to promote small business and self-employment. You can find it at **http://www.sedi.org**. Some of the programs it offers are:

Youth Capital Link: A pilot program that provides young individuals ages 18 through 29 with the opportunity to receive business training and counselling. This project has a unique situation for tracking and monitoring youth businesses to determine solutions to one of the most cited barriers to starting a business, access to start-up capital. For more information e-mail ccosgrove@sedi.org.

Developing Enterprising Women's Initiatives (DEWI): DEWI is a comprehensive program for low income women. Its main goal is to assist individuals and resource-poor women's organizations to build their capacity to "develop and create successful micro-enterprises which will lead to economic independence for their clients." For more information e-mail ccayenne@sedi.org.

Self-Employment Assistance (SEA): The Self-Employment Assistance program provides training and income support for people receiving Employment Insurance benefits, who want to start their own business. It is funded by Human Resources Development Canada.

Each participant receives two months intensive self-employment training, resulting in the creation of a comprehensive business plan. They then receive ongoing business counselling in the start-up and development of their business over the remaining ten months. The program provides income support for up to one year.

SEAnet links Self-Employment Assistance delivery sites, clients and resources on the Internet. It brings together business experts in an interactive forum at **http://www.the-wire.com/sedi/seanet.html**.

Sites for All Seasons Small business centres are excellent places to begin your search for self-employment information. Once there, you can link to a huge variety of sites devoted to small business. Some are very specific, such as the Canadian Exporters and Manufacturers Alliance site at **http://www.palantir.ca/the_alliance**. Others are more general, including the Business Development Bank of Canada (BDC) at **http://www.bdc.ca**.

V. CHOOSING YOUR DIRECTION

Once you get a feel for the basics of starting a business, you'll want to select the path that's right for you. This involves a couple of steps. First, you need to know what's out there. Second, you have to create a viable action plan. Here are some of the ways to do this.

Finding Business Opportunities

If you're looking for ideas on what kind of venture to get involved with, the Net holds great promise. It has the potential to bring together people and opportunities all across the country. An example of this is The Monster Board's Be the Boss page. It focuses on franchising, and can be accessed at **http://www.monster.com/btb/welcome.html**.

A more comprehensive approach is available on a site called Inbusiness Canada, from The Business Press Group Inc. This is one of the new breed of searchable databases. It's designed to highlight regional business opportunities throughout the country, including:

- businesses for sale and businesses wanted,
- franchise opportunities,
- agencies and dealerships available and wanted,
- investments available and wanted,
- start-up and home business opportunities, and
- technology and new product opportunities.

Inbusiness and the Regional Business Opportunities (RBO) are at **http://www.rbo.com**. This site lets you "browse all listings for free for a general idea of what kind of opportunities are offered." Or you can search for a specific kind of business, price range and location, also at no charge. If you wish to see the name and contact number for a specific opportunity there is a subscription charge of $10 per month. You can also let the system work for you to find an appropriate business opportunity and send it to you automatically by e-Mail or fax.

Preparing a Business Plan

Having a good idea and selecting your direction for self-employment are just part of the battle. You must then create a strategy and steps of action to set things in motion. This is where a business plan becomes essential.

Virtually every self-employed person needs to plot their approach to finding customers and providing service. The business plan is the document that outlines the fundamentals of your enterprise. It looks at things like how you will promote yourself to what type of customers with what products or services and at which price. The plan also forecasts your revenues and expenses.

Why You Absolutely, Positively Need a Plan A plan is essential in determining the direction of your business. It also gives you a basis for tracking your success against predetermined objectives. And, oh yeah, ever tried to borrow money for your small business? If so, what are the first things your financial institution asks you for? If you answered, "Collateral," you'd be right. If you also said, "A business plan," you'd be on the money again (literally)!

Online Resources for Planning In terms of online business plan resources, they are many and varied. You can start on the Web by going to **http://www.entrepreneurship.com/busplan.html**. This site, hosted by The Entrepreneurship Centre in Ottawa, gives you much of what you need to prepare a solid business plan. At **http://www.sb.gov.bc.ca/smallbus/workshop/market/sample/sample.html** you'll find an actual sample of a full business plan. You can review it and use it as a bench mark.

On the software side, there is an abundance of business planning programs. A typical package shows you how to define your market, analyze your competitive strengths and weaknesses, forecast sales on a monthly basis, and plot out activities to help you achieve your goals.

Software ranges in price, quality and degree of sophistication, but can

> **CYBER TIP** For free software to help you write a business plan, go to your bank, trust company or credit union. The larger ones all have their own business planning programs on diskette (e.g. The Royal Bank's The Big Idea for Business). They're yours for the asking!

generally be picked up for between $20 and $60. One example is BizPlan Builder, from Jian Tools for Sales Inc. It's a template-driven program. This means you are guided step-by-step along the way, filling in the blanks with your customized information. The end product? A professional looking, fully-detailed plan that's ready to print out and be used. Download a demo version at **http://www.jianusa.com/prod/swbpbfrm.html**.

VI. GETTING SET UP

Once you've committed to going on your own, you need to do a few more things before opening for business. Don't be fooled. Just because you're not with a big company anymore, doesn't mean that your clients will settle for anything less than professional-looking results. This means that you need the proper office equipment and marketing materials.

Equipping Your Office

To start things off, you'll want to invest in some equipment to help you with your business. Fortunately, business machinery has come down in price, while going way up in quality. Consider the laser printer. Today it's an absolute necessity if you're sending out business correspondence (e.g. letters, proposals and reports). Five years ago, a decent piece of machinery would have set you back well over $1,000. For that you would get a printer that put out maybe three pages a minute, at 300 dpi (dots per square inch). Now you can pick up a laser printer for under $500, with six pages per minute speed and 600 dpi resolution.

A Shopping List of Business Equipment

You will undoubtedly spend some money when you first start your business to assemble a functional office. Whether you lease or purchase is a decision your accountant can help you with. In any event, there are some equipment needs that must be met.

The Essentials of a Wired Office

- **Computer**: Desktop PC or laptop, depending on the power and portability that you require.
- **Modem**: For sending and receiving e-mail messages, and hooking up to the Internet.

- **Printer**: Laser-quality preferred for professional looking documents.
- **Phone System**: Possibly a separate line or distinctive ring feature with a unique number for your business, depending on your volume of incoming and outgoing calls.
- **Fax Machine**: To send and receive business documents instantaneously.
- **Answering Service**: A telephone answering device or service to pick up your messages.
- **Internet Service Provider**: To provide access to the Internet, including e-mail and the Web.

Not Essential, But I'd Love to Have Them All There are some other items that appeal to those who are seriously into equipping their home offices. These include:

- **Scanner**: Enables you to take pages of information (from a magazine, brochure etc.) and load them into your computer as image files to use in any documents you produce.
- **Optical Character Recognition (OCR) software**: Works with a scanner. Allows you to convert scanned images into text that you can use in a word processing file without retyping.
- **Colour Printer**: For spicing up your presentations and proposal printouts.
- **Photcopier**: Useful if you plan to make many copies of documents.
- **Multi-Function Machine**: Combines five or six functions into one piece of equipment. Typically includes printer, scanner, fax machine, PC fax and photocopier (even voicemail and fax-back on some models).

Road-Warrior Gear If you're on the road a great deal to visit with clients, you may require additional equipment to stay constantly in touch. For those of you who travel regularly on business, here's the latest gear:

- **Cellular Telephone**: For making and receiving calls in your car, or just about anywhere.
- **Multimedia Laptop PC**: Comes with built-in CD-ROM and graphics accelerator. Great for giving presentations to potential clients. Also, hook it up to your cellphone with a cellular-capable modem

and you can send and receive faxes and e-mail, plus hook up to your company's internal network (if there is one).

- **Personal Digital Assistant (PDA)**: A kind of mini-PC to store client data, keep track of your schedule and even send or receive faxes and e-mail.
- **Pager**: Can alert you whenever you receive a phone call, fax or e-mail.

Specifications Vary, So Watch Out! I could obviously go into far more depth on each piece of business equipment. Things like minimum baud rate for your modem (28.8k, by the way) and PC storage capacity (2 gigabytes of memory recommended) are helpful to know. Potential costs are critical too.

Your needs will vary widely depending on the type of business you have, the services you provide and the bucks you have to spare. For a general guide to setting up a home office, try the Web site at **http://www.hometime.com/ps/95/ps2offce.htm** or pick up a copy of *The Idiot's Guide to Running a Successful Home Business for Canadians*.

Creating Marketing Materials

Remember the old adage that says, "If you build a better mousetrap, the world will beat a path to your door?" Well, it ain't true! No matter how wonderful your products or services are, you will have to promote them in order to drum up business. That's where your marketing materials come into play.

Everything You Produce Is a Marketing Piece It's a funny thing, though. When I talk to some small-business people, they

REAL LIFE *There are ways to minimize your initial costs and lower your risks of business interruption. First, consider leasing your computer and office equipment. If you plan it right, the monthly payments can be tax-deductible. Also, spend the extra money to get an on-site replacement warranty for your equipment. This will come in handy if your system ever fails. Finally, invest in some small business insurance. Rates are fairly low—and most home insurance policies don't cover business-related perils.*

think of marketing in terms of the big picture. Things like glossy, full-colour brochures or multi-media advertising campaigns come to mind. They are surprised when I tell them that the most common, effective promotional material is their stationery.

CYBER TIP If you use large quantities of letterhead and envelopes, consider getting them produced at a print shop. Then you can use your own printer for black and white text, and the occassional splash of colour. This saves wear and tear on your machine, cuts down on ink costs and gives you the professional look that your clients demand.

You heard me right. The simple things like your letterhead, envelopes and business cards can make the biggest impression on clients and potential customers. Yet these are the items that are most often taken for granted.

Not anymore. Inexpensive colour printers and stationery software mean that just about anyone can produce great-looking stuff. Remember back in Chapter 4, we looked at how to produce business cards at home. The same thing can be done with letterhead, envelopes and brochures with even better results.

Table 10.2 outlines some software packages to consider.

Table 10.2 Software to Help Create Marketing Materials

PRODUCT NAME	WHAT IT CAN PRODUCE	MANUFACTURER
Printshop Deluxe	Letterhead, envelopes, business cards, brochures and more	Broderbund Software Inc. **http://www.broder.com**
Stationery Shop	Brochures, letterhead, envelopes, business cards and more	Expert Software **http://www.expertsoftware.com**
Business Cards and Certificates	Business cards and stationery	CompuWorks (WizardWorks Co.) **http://www.wizworks.com**
Easy Business Cards	Business cards	Claris (Apple) **http://www.claris.com**

VII. LEARNING ABOUT HOW TO ENLARGE YOUR BUSINESS

Once your enterprise is up and running, there are all sorts of online resources available to help you. These range from simple tips to elaborate information gathering sites, all the way to networking with other entrepreneurs in dedicated discussion groups. The goal is to fill you with ideas to increase your competitiveness and expertise.

Tips on Running Your Business

There will be times when you want to see the latest advice from experts in small business. You could, of course, run out and buy a magazine. Or you can click on the Web and get up-to-the minute suggestions from E-zines (electronic magazines) and Web sites.

One place to head for is Inc. Magazine's Web site, at **http://www.inc.com**. Inc. is the afficionado's source for information on minding your small business. Here you'll find topics like Resources for Growing Your Small Business, among other useful features.

Business in Canada Has Its Own Qualities For the Canadian perspective, tune in to The Canadian Home Business Online Resource Centre at **http://www.discribe.ca/yourhbiz/howto/helphint.htm**. This site is hosted by DISCribe Ltd., out of Fredericton, New Brunswick. The part called Helpful Hints for Home Business is especially informative.

Also try Canadian Business @Home Network (**http://www.home-bus.com**). You'll find services such as The Home-Based Business Directory,

CYBER TIP To help you manage your business, there is plenty of **software** available for your small office or home office. If you have a PC with a 386 processor or higher, you can run programs for almost every aspect of your operation. Trying to balance the books? Use accounting software. Making a customer profile list for future marketing or sales efforts? Invest in a database program. And what about getting paid? Try forms software to generate your invoices, and a scheduling program to remind you when to send them out. A visit to your local software retailer is definitely in order.

which is designed to increase awareness and promote this industry. There is also a mini-magazine containing articles of benefit to both potential home-preneurs and those already established. Articles are mainly Canadian and are written by those working in this industry every day.

Resources for Small Businesses

If you're looking for experts to talk to, associations to join, places to get financing and lists of publications, you can surf the Net. There's some really useful stuff there, especially from government agencies in conjunction with the private sector.

For starters, pop on over to Industry Canada. Their *Strategis* site is full of resources for small businesses. In particular, take a good look at what they've done with Contact!, The Canadian Management Network. This is an unbelievable place for "Canadian small businesses and their support organisations to meet, learn from each other, develop business opportunities, and connect with people who are otherwise outside of their network."

Contact! is working with over 40 partners in the private sector and several federal and provincial government bodies. Do not miss this site. And check out the rest of Strategis while there at **http://strategis.ic.gc.ca/sc_mangb/contact/engdoc/homepage.html**.

Another Web site to check out is The Entrepreneurship Centre, which operates out of Ottawa. Its mission is "to assist entrepreneurs attain their goal of self employment through the development of a new or existing business in the region." The Entrepreneurship Centre is assisted by volunteers from the region's top businesses and professional firms. You can find it at **http://www.entrepreneurship.com**. You can also visit the YMCA Enterprise Program for a different perspective. It's at **http://www.the_wire.com/sedi/ymca.html**.

There's Much More If you can't find what you're looking for in the sites I've already described, don't fret. This is just the beginning. For a general search of small business resources on the Net, go to Yahoo Canada (**http://www.yahoo.ca**). Look under Self-employment. Or to see the mother of all small business databases, try out AT&T's Home Business Resources. It's at **http://www.att.com/hbr**.

Networking on the Net

For small business people, just like job seekers, networking can give you the edge you need to succeed. Imagine what it would be like to share ideas with—and get questions answered by—other self-employed people from across the country. You can do it today on the Web. Here are several sites that may be of use to you.

- DISCribe Online Canadian discussion groups for small business. **http://www.discribe.ca/yourhbiz/yourhbiz.htm**
- Strategis Contact! forums. **http://strategis.ic.gc.ca/sc_mangb/contact/engdoc/homepage.html**
- The Water Cooler Self-Employment forums (primarily U.S.). **http://www.hardatwork.com/HyperNews/get/forums/employment.html**

VIII. MARKETING ONLINE

You've all heard the hype about how the Internet will create a whole new world of commerce. Experts predict that Canadians will purchase several hundred million dollars of products and services over the Net by the year 2000. Today, however, selling online is in its infancy. Don't expect to make a fortune (or even a single sale) just by putting up a Web site.

On the other hand, using the Net can help you with your business in a number of ways. It can assist you in identifying your prospects. You can also keep up-to-date on news and changes in laws that affect you (see Chapter 6 for business research techniques). Perhaps most importantly, the Net is a place to promote your business and make connections with potential customers and existing clients.

Learning to Use the Net For Business

Knowing how to navigate the World Wide Web is one thing. Understanding the potential for online commerce is a whole other issue. That's why resources are springing up to enable you to use the Net for business. In book form, look for *The Canadian Internet Advantage* by Jim Carroll and Rick Broadhead. It covers everything from strategic planning to building a Web site (more about this at **http://www.handbook.com/advantage.htm**).

Another great initiative to get you going is the Student Connection. A partnership between Industry Canada, members of the Canadian information technology industry and post-secondary institutions, the Student Connection Program is intended to help Canadian small and medium size businesses learn to use online business services of the Information Highway.

Here's how it works. Over the three year program, an estimated 2,000 university and final year college students will be employed as student business advisors to train in the Internet and Canadian online services. Some 50,000 small and medium size business managers will be provided with introductory level training sessions aimed at showing them the benefits to be gained through the use of online information services in solving real day-to-day business issues. Information is available at **http://strategis.ic.gc.ca/sc_hures/student/engdoc/fctsht.html**.

As a complement to this program, you can access a comprehensive online manual. It's called *Making the Connection—Your Business and the Internet*. This Canadian guide shows you how the Internet is "bringing you information and the ability to participate in the global marketplace," and how to take advantage of "an affluent and growing market for your products and services." Find it at **http://strategis.ic.gc.ca/sc_mangb/engdoc/homepage.html**.

CYBER TIP You can do prospecting (getting information on potential customers) by using Web-based directories. InfoSpace is free, with directories for phone, fax and e-mail numbers. It's at **http://www.infospace.com**. For a fee, you can use pre-assembled databases that you can search by selected criteria. One such Canadian product is Eagle, presented by the Multi-Active group of companies. For more info, head to **http://www.maximizer.com**.

Promoting Your Business with a Web Site

An obvious attraction of the Internet is its widespread connectivity. It can put you in touch with potential clients seven days a week, 24 hours a day. The Net also transcends geographic boundaries. That means you can do business locally, nationally or all across the globe.

To take advantage of this, many businesses have created their own Web site on the World Wide Web. There are a number of benefits to doing this. Your clients can learn more about what you have to offer (assuming that they can find your site, which is an issue discussed in some of the online manuals I've mentioned). You may be able to offer free trials or special deals. Customers can communicate with you directly through e-mail. And you can provide customer support with Frequently

Asked Questions (FAQs) online. To top it off, it is relatively inexpensive to design, host and maintain a Web site.

All Engines Slow at First I'll bet you can't wait to rush out and create your presence on the Net, right? Not so fast, friend. According to authors Jim Carroll and Rick Broadhead, "Despite all the hoopla...it is obvious that no one has truly figured out the role of the Internet in a business context." They suggest that you ask yourself a series of questions before spending any time or money on your site:

- What are the business objectives of your Web site?
- Who is your target audience and what are their needs?
- How much of your marketing budget will you devote to creating and maintaining the site?
- Will you host it yourself or lease space on a third-party server?
- How often will you update your material?
- Who will design the site—you, or a Web company?
- Will your site be stand-alone or part of a cyber-mall?
- How and where do you plan to promote your site?

There Are Many Steps Involved In addition to the this, there are other considerations to deal with. You'll probably want to register your domain name to reflect your business (e.g. mine is **http://www.wiredhired.com**). Then you should plan to list your site on a variety of search engines, so that people can find you. Of course, there are costs and time considerations associated with all of this.

So many issues, and we haven't touched on design yet. Your site could be of the short and sweet or deep and delicious variety. In other words, you might have a few pages or many pages. It will depend on many of the factors discussed earlier. Then comes the issue of techno-complexity. No doubt it's cool to use Java, Shockwave and frames on your site. However, what if your audience is surfing with an older browser and a slow modem? Your site could be completely useless to them.

Where To Go For Answers I won't even bother getting into other questions, such as whether you should learn to code in HTML or just buy a Web development software package. Let's just say that it may be worth the one or two hundred dollars to buy software such as InContext Spider (**http://www.incontext.ca**) or HoTMetal (**http://www.softguard.**

com). They automatically encode your document into HTML.

My point is that there are strategic and tactical aspects to the Web site question. Do your homework before jumping into the fray.

One place to get some answers is the Website Development FAQs list. You can find it on the Web at **http://www.impactonline.org/internet/webfaq.html**.

Another site to try is Creating Your Own Homepage. It contains articles and links related to designing and hosting a Web site (**http://www.screen.com/understand/HTML.html**).

REAL LIFE *You may want to talk to your Internet Service Provider about developing your homepage. They will probably be able to give you some useful advice. Many ISPs will help you design your site on a consulting basis (read: they'll charge you). Remember too that most of them offer free (or reduced-rate) Web site hosting to their customers.*

IX. WIRED WRAP UP

It used to be that self-employment was a nice way of saying, "I don't really have a job." Not so anymore. In today's changing economy, more and more people are going it on their own. Almost one out of every four Canadian households now operates some sort of home-based business.

To service the needs of this growing market, electronic resources are being developed almost daily. The range is enormous. You can learn how to start a business by taking a course on the Internet. Afterwards, you can match your skills and aspirations to specific business opportunities posted on the Web. You can even use a CD-ROM to identify prospects and create targeted marketing letters.

With online resources, you're never alone. If you need some advice, click on one of the Web sites designed to help you with your small business. Or network on one of a growing number of e-mail based discussion groups. The point is that you're no longer isolated just because you're not part of a big company.

Technology has even changed the very nature of how we can manage a business. It used to be that administration meant doing the paperwork. Today it's more like inputting the spreadsheet or e-mailing the correspondence. Once you learn how to use these new tools, you can speed up the flow of information and increase your capacity to service your customers.

Keep in mind that your choice to be self-employed should be based on who you are and what you really want from life. No sense pretending to be a high-rolling entrepreneur when what you truly want is a consistent income and 9 to 5 hours. Similarly, don't bother going into a home-based business if you love to be surrounded by people all day (spouses and kids don't count here).

On the electronic side of things, use only the tools that will help you become more effective. Why shell out $8,000 for a top of the line multimedia laptop if you can do very nicely with a $2,000 desktop PC? The same thing goes for upgrading your software. Computer programs are updated every 6 to 12 months (you know, version 4.3 becomes version 4.8). There's no need to run out and get the latest program unless your previous version isn't satisfactory.

In conclusion, self-employment is a way of mind as much as it is a way of life. Even if you're working for a company today, you need to have entrepreneurial skills to stay on top of things. My suggestion for taking the plunge into self-employment is to try before you buy. If possible, start a small business by moonlighting. That is, do it part-time (e.g. evenings and weekends) before you immerse yourself fully. That way you'll gain some experience while keeping your other options open. Then, if you decide to pursue your own enterprise, it just might reward you—financially and otherwise!

PART 4

STAYING WIRED AND HIRED

CHAPTER 11 A Glimpse into the Future

Virtual Definition: **baud** (bôd) *noun*

In common usage the baud rate of a modem is how many bits it can send or receive per second. Technically, baud is the number of times per second that the carrier signal shifts value. For example a 1200 bit per second modem actually runs at 300 baud, but it moves 4 bits per baud (4 x 300 = 1200 bits per second).

I. DON'T BLINK—THE FUTURE'S HERE!

From the time that I began writing this book until the moment I finished, change was taking place all around us. That's why I've decided to dedicate this chapter to the future. I'd like you to appreciate that we must be forward looking, even while struggling to understand the present. That leaves us one way to prepare ourselves: anticipate what will happen next, then plan accordingly.

Employment and Work-searching in the Future

Centuries ago there lived a famed futurologist name Nostradamus. His predictions were, in many cases, uncannily accurate and are remembered by people today. What people don't remember are all of the forecasts that either never came true, or were wildly wrong.

In this same spirit, I would like to offer a speculative look at what lies ahead. Specifically, how work will evolve, and where work-searching techniques are heading.

What Are Today's Experts Saying?

After 10 chapters, you've probably heard enough of what *I* have to say. It seems only fitting that other professionals in career-related fields should have a turn at making the forecasts. With that in mind, I contacted a number of leading-edge authorities (by e-mail, appropriately enough) to solicit their views. The respondents represent a cross-section of career and human resource experts in Canada.

Profiles of the Authorities

Nuala Beck: Well-known Canadian economist and keynote speaker. Author of *Shifting Gears* and *Excelerate*. Coined the term The New Economy®.

Frank Feather: Futurist, speaker and career advisor. Author of *Canada's Best Career Guide.*

James Fehrenbach: Manager of recruitment, Canadian Tire Corporation. A leading advocate of technology in the field of recruitment.

Janis Foord-Kirk: Career consultant and author of *Surviving Upheaval in The Workplace* and *Survivability*. Writes weekly column for *The Toronto Star*.

Stephen Gibson: Publisher of *Online Sources for Human Resources*. Also a speaker and consultant in the area of online hiring.

Jeffery Lawrence: Graduate student extraordinaire and creator of "The Canadian Job Source," one of the first (and still one of the best) online indexes of Canadian career-related Internet resources.

Deborah McGrath: Vice president of The CEO Group, one of the top high-tech recruiting firms in Canada.

Margaret Riley: The U.S. superstar of Internet career resources. Compiled *The Riley Guide*, which predated almost every other online career manual.

Alan Schweyer: Manager of the National Graduate Register, Canada's premiere online résumé bank for students.

Four Simple Questions To keep things manageable, I posed the same four questions to each of the experts I described above. Here's what I asked:

1) Are people actually having success looking for work online?
2) What are some key trends in recruiting and work-searching?
3) How will work itself evolve?
4) Do you have any warnings for people seeking work online?

The responses to these inquiries are listed below. Hopefully they'll provide some insight with regard to what you can expect down the road.

1. Are People Actually Having Success Looking For Work Online?

Frank Feather: "As far as evidence goes, my own daughter had two job offers in health care from the U.S. within a week of posting her availability and qualifications online. That is, firm job offers without an interview."

James Fehrenbach: "We are definitely starting to see the Web offer real value to job seekers. Lately we have started to interview more people whose first contact with us was on the Web. When I talk to my peers in organizations with a broader assortment of jobs and/or locations to recruit for, they indicate that they are seeing a higher volume of people viewing their sites and ultimately being hired as a result of contact on the Web. Furthermore, there is reduced processing time and costs of receiving applications electronically."

Jeff Lawrence: "At present, the only true revolution in job searching is in positions related to computers and other technical fields. Here there have been lots of advances such as search robots and job-matching programs. This will most likely keep changing as more nontechnical people come online."

Debbie McGrath: "Definitely, especially in the high-tech market. In fact, our company hired our Internet project manager from a Usenet résumé over a year ago and we have sourced more people since then. One of our U.S. clients sourced and hired over 50 Canadians from our résumé tracking system for opportunities across the Midwest. We are also seeing a large influx of sales and marketing people coming across our sites."

Margaret Riley: "Is it making an impact? Absolutely. It's allowing people to scan large databases using keywords and to find more job listings in five minutes than they can in an entire day of reading newspaper classifieds. Also, it gives you access to information that can make a critical difference in your ability to target specific companies."

Allan Schweyer: "I have personally hired people for contract, full-time and part-time work using Internet Newsgroups and tools like the National Graduate Register."

2. What Are Some Key Trends in Recruiting and Work-Searching?

Frank Feather: "I'm sure the Internet (or whatever it becomes!) will replace most career advertising over the next decade. It has always been true, however, that the best jobs are never advertised: they are found through word of mouth, connections etc. To the extent that word-of-mouth becomes word-of-modem, the Web will become the key marketplace for employment."

James Fehrenbach: "Basically what I see is the growing expectation of job seekers that organizations will have their jobs posted on the Web and that information about the company will be available for them to make more educated decisions about the companies they choose to work for.

"The other thing I see is organizations accessing shared services over the Net. This includes databases of résumés and job posting services. At Canadian Tire we are promoting a program we have designed called SAFIRE (Strategic Alliance For Identification, Recruitment & Employment). It should make it more efficient and affordable for companies to recruit electronically."

Janis Foord-Kirk: "In some ways, the process of matching workers and employers electronically is in its infancy. But, as people become more comfortable with technology and as the technology itself becomes "friendlier" this method of work search will become widely used for all types of positions and opportunities. If you have the right equipment and know how to use it strategically, you can virtually search the world for opportunities that might suit you."

Stephen Gibson: "'Disintermediation' is the buzzword to watch for. Companies may begin to rely less and less on third party recruiters and search firms. Instead, they will do their own scouting for candidates online—through job sites, résumé banks, and the use of intelligent search agents."

Margaret Riley: "People will be able to search on skills instead of job titles and to combine their varied interests and expertises into a new job area they might not have considered."

Allan Schweyer: "I believe that new online recruiting sites will taper off as the field across North America is already somewhat flooded. Strategic partnerships to integrate and make systems compatible is already happening and will continue. This may help people look for work by having access to many employers at a single site.

There will also be a trend towards specialization. Most sites now are general in that anyone is eligible to use them. There are already specialized recruiting tools like MedHunters, NGR, HiTechCareers etc. In the next few years there will likely be tools specific for engineers, lawyers, marketing and sales people, etc."

3. How Will Work Itself Evolve?

Nuala Beck: "We're in the midst of a radical change in work. This could ultimately lead to a whole redefinition of employment. One concept I'd like to see explored is the move towards *double-shifting*. This is where the work week would be reduced from 40 to 30 hours, allowing for two separate shifts of traditional employees a day. I call this concept jobs^2 (jobs squared).

"It would be supported by government policies that encourage double-shifting. The main element would be a reduction or elimination of the payroll tax. The benefits would be an increase in productivity, more equitable distribution of employment opportunites, more disposable income injected into the economy, and greater tax revenues from all the new workers. There may be social advantages as well, such as the elimination of a generation of latch-key kids."

Frank Feather: "The key trends in the future of work in Canada are as outlined in my book. Two major general trends are (1) a continuing shift towards knowledge workers and (2) telecommuting. The electronic revolution totally changes the nature of work. Indeed, jobs will tend to disappear as people work piece-meal on a sub-contract basis, electronically."

Janis Foord-Kirk: "Increasingly, jobs come in a variety of sizes and shapes.

We're seeing more part-time and temporary work, contract and consulting; nonstandard work as it's called. I expect that we'll see even more variations like these.

"Our careers, instead of following a steady, progressive path, will evolve in a much less linear way. Many of us, at different times in our working lives, will find some form of nonstandard work best suits our goals and circumstances."

4. Do You Have Any Warnings for People Seeking Work Online?

Frank Feather: "Instead of fearing the technology and vastly overblown privacy issues, focus on being totally upfront and honest: any fabrication on a résumé will be tracked down in an instant on the Web. In other words, the Web will create greater truth amongst the majority."

James Fehrenbach: "The only warning I can think of is to not depend exclusively on technology. Not all jobs are found there yet, and some that do are hard to locate. Keep your eyes on traditional media as pointers to companies or industries that are growing and use the Web to dig deeper and wider."

Janis Foord-Kirk: "The cyber-world is still rather lawless, a bit like the wild west. So you have to be alert and well informed. To appear professional and technically competent, you need to understand the etiquette and the language used. In other words, you need to be quite knowledgeable and proficient before you can use this search vehicle effectively."

Jeffery Lawrence: "Remember that the Internet is NOT the solution to all your problems. Job hunters should not and cannot forsake the traditional job hunting techniques such as networking and pounding the pavement. And don't expect people or resources on the Internet to do all your work in finding a job.

"Moreover, be as cautious about what you say on the Internet, as how you would be in real life. Since there is no face to face contact, we are dependant wholly on what we type on the computer keyboard. The less you say, the less likelihood you can stick your foot in your mouth."

Debbie McGrath: "It seems like everywhere you turn there are companies offering online résumé services for a fee. I would only go with a brand name as the others have no way of getting clients to read their résumés. On the other hand, they can be easy to use and may offer incredible value at no large investment, so don't ignore them."

Allan Schweyer: "I would warn people against divulging their names, addresses and telephone numbers on recruiting sites that do not offer appropriate protection. It is well known that on the Internet in general, women are often harassed via e-mail and on discussion groups. Also, you want to make sure that employers who get hold of your application material are legitimate."

II. UPCOMING TECHNOLOGIES

In addition to potential changes in employment and work-searching, technology is continually evolving. In fact, careers and technology are now inextricably linked at every level.

Here's how the pattern is emerging. Computers and communication devices are becoming more powerful, less expensive and easier to use. Thus, companies, recruiters and job seekers are adopting them at an astounding pace.

Similarly, as companies face increased global and local competition, they are looking for ways to boost their competitiveness while adding to the bottom line. Thus, they are making increasing demands on employees and the technologies that facilitate productivity.

There are two areas of technology in particular that you may want to monitor: the Internet and recruiting methodologies. Both of these are moving ahead rapidly, and will have a growing effect on how you plan and manage your career, as well as how you secure and perform work.

The Internet

Nowhere are the shifts more evident than on the Net. It seems that every few months a major new advance is announced. Today it's high speed ADSL Connections (Asymmetric Digital Subscribed Line) and VRML (Virtual Reality Modelling Language). And tomorrow? Possibly JAVA-enabled Internet toasters that almost anyone can afford, making it more imperative than ever to be one of the early adopters of the new work-search approaches.

Here are some of the key developments to watch for. I suggest that you have at least a basic awareness of what these are, because they may very well have an impact on you sooner than you think.

Faster Connections One of the major complaints of Netizens is that the Internet is too slow. With the increased traffic, plus extended use of graphics and sound bytes, bandwidth and speed have become real issues. Several advances are available right now to accelerate the transfer of data.

- **Modems:** A number of manufacturers now produce modems that run at 56.6 kbps. Compare that to the current standard capability of 28.8 kbps.
- **Integrated Services Digital Network (ISDN):** Transmits data at 64 kbps. Estimated to increase as time goes on. Uses regular phone line and a special modem.
- **Asymmetric Digital Subscriber Line (ADSL):** Transmits data 50 times faster than a standard 28.8 kbps modem. Needs a special modem, but allows you to use your phone at the same time.
- **Satellite:** Direct transfer of data from satellite transmission to a modem. Expensive at present, but extremely fast.
- **Cable:** Bypasses the phone system completely. Cable companies set customers up with a dedicated Internet line that runs at 500 kbps (faster in the future).

Cheaper Rates and Equipment Another thing we're seeing is the falling cost of Internet access. That's because as more and more companies compete for your business, this service becomes a commodity. There are further developments expected in this area, including the equipment itself.

- **Flat Rate Plans:** More Internet providers (both ISPs and Commercial Online Providers) are lowering their monthly fees, and providing unlimited use of the Net for a flat fee ranging from $20 to $25 per month.
- **"Net Toasters":** You won't have to spend thousands of dollars on a fully-equipped computer to get full Internet capabilities. New stripped down network computers will sell for around $500, and will be Java-enabled.

Increasing Sophistication, But More User-Friendly It wasn't that long ago that all you needed was Netscape version 1.2 and a 14.4kbps modem to surf merrily (albeit slowly) across the Net. Now many sites won't even load up for you unless your browser can handle frames and HTML 3. Look what's going on.

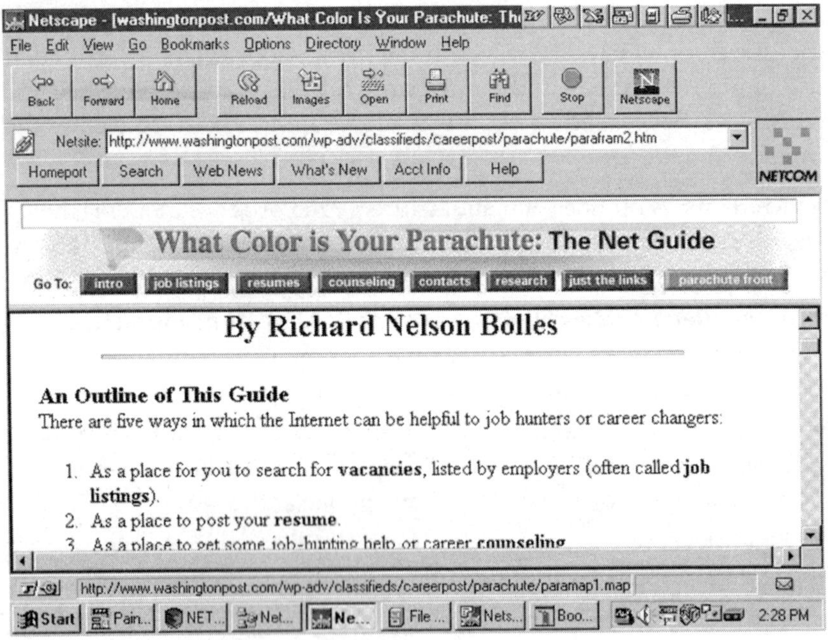

- **Frames:** Web sites can now be subdivided into separate areas on the same page. Each one has its own distinct URL. Your browser must support frames, although some sites are still providing a text-only version (for now).
- **JAVA:** The hot new programming language that just may revolutionize computing. Currently it lets you use animated graphics on your Web site. Tomorrow it just may become the biggest competitor to Microsoft's operating system.
- **Virtual Reality Modelling Language (VRML):** The ticket to 3-D Web sites.

Fee-Based Services Up until recently, most of the stuff out there in cyberland has been free. Get ready for a big change. Banks, credit card companies and other major players are gearing up to provide secure financial transactions online.

As the era of electronic commerce is ushered in, prepare to pull out your plastic. You can expect to start paying for everything from information downloads to résumé critiques. The positive side is that the quality and usefulness of information could increase, as should ease of retrieving what you really need. Will that be cash, or Digi-Charge?

Sending and Receiving Information E-mail is, in some ways, a wonderful improvement over traditional communication methods. You don't have to lick any stamps or envelopes, and you don't need a bulky machine. Mind you, there is that small issue of owning a computer and having an e-mail account. Plus you just don't get the immediacy and nuances of person-to-person contact.

Fret no more, for salvation is at hand. Here are two up and coming advances to keep your eyes (and ears) on.

- **Audio Conferencing:** Internet *telephony*, as it's called, has lots of potential. It enables you to hold real-time voice conversations with people around the world—without long distance charges. Both you and the person (or people) that you are talking to must have compatible telephony software, a PC, and an Internet connection.
- **Video Online:** Don't be shocked if you get interviewed for a position in your living room. While this may still be a few years away, video conferencing online is available today at a reasonable cost. You can get a QuickCam from Connectix Corporation (**http://www.connectix.com**) and CU-SeeMe software (**http://www.wpine.com/CU-SeeMe.html**) for under $200. Sure it's slow and jerky at this price range, and the person you're conferencing with must have a compatible setup. But this one could really take off when Net speeds increase and costs of advanced products come down.

Searching for Specific Data I know now why one of the most popular Web search engines is called YAHOO. After spending so much time trying to find precise information on the Net, when I finally get remotely close to what I'm looking for, I shout Yahoo!

Soon the process of searching will become far less onerous. Enter the intelligent search agents. These are little electronic robots that sift through the entire Net to find what you're looking for.

Right now you can get Pointcast for free (**http://www.pointcast.com**) to bring you news according to your personal preferences.

In the near future, you might program your agent to find every job posting or business opportunity that meets your description. Likewise, recruiters and employers could send their agents to sift out every online résumé that conforms to their requirements. This could dramatically speed up the matching process for people seeking employment or business opportunities.

Intranets Many companies are installing internal systems that allow employees to share information online. These so-called *Intranets* are the newest wave in data exchange. They work much like the Internet; however, people outside the company cannot access the information. Be prepared to use an Intranet for internal e-mail, company announcements, group scheduling and project management.

Recruiting Methodologies

Several times throughout this book I've used the terms *scanning, tracking* and *keyword résumés.* It turns out that these are the latest techniques in hiring. Companies and recruiters, particularly in the United States, have been quick to embrace these practices. The fact that they're now starting to filter over the border means that it's time to take notice.

I'm not about to go into great detail here. After all, there are entire books from the U.S. devoted to applicant tracking systems and keyword resumes (for instance, *The Electronic Résumé Revolution* by Joyce Lain Kennedy). It's sufficient for now to know what the terms mean, and how they may influence your future.

- **Scannable Résumés:** We first encountered scanning back in Chapter 5, Sending in Work Applications Electronically. It means that the résumé and cover letter you submit are put through a scanning machine. This turns the text into an electronic image, which is stored on the company or recruiter's computerized database.
- **Applicant Tracking:** Resumix and Restrac are but two versions of these programs. As your résumé gets scanned, the image is also converted back to text through Optical Character Recognition. Then your résumé is automatically sorted into an appropriate category for storage and retrieval on the database.
- **Keyword Résumés:** These are scannable, plain-text résumés that use precise nouns to highlight your skills, education and work experience. Employers and recruiters can then search their résumés for specific criteria (key words). If your application scores enough direct hits, it may get printed out for further consideration.

Applicant tracking, scanning and keyword résumés are already in use by the majority of Fortune 500 companies in the States. They can substantially reduce recruiting costs while enlarging the company's capacity to intake, process and screen applications. Mind you, it does tend to negate that thing we used to call the human factor.

Look at how it changes the wording on résumés that we've been using

CYBER TIP For examples and instructions on how to create a scannable keyword résumé, try the following Web sites: Resumix at **http://www.resumix.com/resume/resumeindex.html** and The Riley Guide at **http://www.jobtrak.com/jobguide/eresume.html**.

for many years. For example, your conventional résumé might say that you "led your team to increase productivity by 50 percent, using new computer programs." The keyword version of this same phrase might look something like the following: "supervisory skills productivity WordPerfect PowerPoint Excel Internet Intranet."

III. WIRED WRAP UP

Incredible, isn't it. Two years ago the idea of sending in an ASCII-formatted résumé to an employer's scanning system via e-mail was preposterous. Today it's the newest way to do things. Two years from now? It'll be standard operating procedure, if something else doesn't replace it.

That should tell you something about what you're up against. It not just you versus your competing work-searchers anymore. Now it's you against everyone else *and* the emerging recruitment systems. Talk about being overwhelmed.

Luckily it's possible to keep from getting swept away by these technological riptides. Basically, you need to behave like a well-tuned windsurfer. You monitor the water conditions so that you cruise along with the currents. If a big wave approaches, you decide in advance how to ride it. There's no getting around it. Either it will propel you to where you want to go, or dump you overboard without mercy.

So it is with these new recruiting systems and the latest technological developments. Your best bet is to spot them in advance. That way, *you* can select your course and move in the direction that you want to go. Otherwise you'll be left with your eyes and throat stinging from the salt, while you wonder why your career and work-search efforts have been overturned.

The choice, as I've said before, is yours.

CHAPTER 12 Closing Thoughts

Virtual Definition: **WAN** (wän) *noun*

WAN (Wide Area Network) is any internet or network that covers an area larger than a single building. This means that computers from a single company with branch offices across the country can be hooked up to a centralized main server. A vital element in corporate Intranets.

NOT THE END...JUST ANOTHER BEGINNING

And so we draw to a close. I thought long and hard about how to conclude this guide. After all, how do you reach an end-point when everything you're writing about is still in the midst of rapid change?

So I looked back to the notes I prepared when first putting my draft together. I was searching for key ideas or some overriding theme. My goal was simple enough: to leave you with a sense that you've taken the first steps in a very exciting journey. But also to remind you that this journey has, in some ways, just begun.

Built-in Obsolescence Then it hit me. This book is devoted to helping you move from the past, into the present—and on to the future. It focuses on some of the cutting-edge applications of technology with regard to career-management and the work-search. The irony of it all is this: now that you have the book in your hand, some of the material is already outdated.

Talk about revolutionary change. By the time you read these words, there'll be new Web sites, additional software programs, maybe even "the next big thing" about to make its debut. That's how quickly things are moving. It would be a shame for me to leave you hanging without a bridge to the future.

Possible Ways to Stay Current

With all of that in mind, I struggled to think of solutions. How could I keep the book from being out-of-date the moment you bought it?

Try to understand that I did this while finishing off my hundred thousandth word or so for this manual (at about 3:00 a.m. on a dark and blustery Thursday morning). You'll forgive me if some of my initial ideas seem a little bizarre. I've put them in table format so you can follow my thought process:

POTENTIAL UPDATE MECHANISM	REASON FOR REJECTION OF CONCEPT
• Calling each of you personally every day, to notify you of any changes.	• I need my phone line to surf the Web. I'd be left with just enough time to update you on one Web site per year.
• Sending you a floral arrangement monthly, with the URLs of new Web sites pasted to each petal.	• I can never remember when to send rhododendrons or gladiolus.
• Asking a different reader over for dinner each night of the week, for a one-on-one update.	• My wife and I aren't great entertainers and I have trouble folding napkins into those neat little triangles.

A Solution That Makes Sense for All

What better way to keep you apprised of online happenings than by doing it...online? Seems like a logical conclusion. That's why I'm inviting you to visit the new *Get Wired, Your Hired* Web site at **http://www.wiredhired.com**.

Here are some of the things that you'll find there.

Recent Internet Resources: This includes Web sites, Usenet Newsgroups and Listserves that can help you plan your career, locate work opportunities, promote yourself to potential employers and manage your small business.

Technology Updates: New career-related technologies will be featured on a regular basis.

Bonus Chapter: A full chapter devoted to concrete examples of people using the latest techniques. There's something for everyone here (but you can only get it online). Some of the people you meet include:

- Sharon: A recent graduate looking for her first full-time job.
- Harpreet: Mid-career, and time for a major switch.
- William: Unemployed...but not for long.
- Desiree: Looking for work internationally.
- Yong: Working from home, and staying connected.
- Carlos: "Don't call me 'disabled.'"
- Greta: A mature person looking for work.
- Louise: The Do-It-Yourselfer who just wants links to Canadian career resources.
- Arif: Modern day career consultant keeping on top of his field.

Career-Related Links: A wide assortment of hyper-links to other Web sites that could be of use to you at each stage in your work-search. Also, more places to communicate online with other Canadians going through the same process.

CONCLUSION

As we move towards the end of the 1990s, change has become the one thing that we can count on. The pace is speeding up, and competition is intensifying at every turn. Not a very comforting thought. But if you can accept this as the premise for planning your career, you've already won the toughest battle of all.

Every week I work with people who have just been thrust out into the new world of work. People who were loyal, hard-working team players in jobs where they were competent, established and comfortable. Suddenly they've been jettisoned into the maelstrom.

Flexibility and Adaptability Are Vital The ones who end up truly succeeding are those who can grasp the current realities. It's not a quick or painless process, believe me. The most common initial reaction is as follows: "I just want to replace what I had with exactly the same thing, only better." Unfortunately, that "same thing" often no longer exists. Moreover, the work-search methods that these people learned a while back may not be giving them the advantage they now require.

It's when these same men and women, ranging in age from mid-20s to their early 60s, seek me out for advice on the new ways of working and the latest ways to find employment, that I know they are poised on the brink of success. This has far less to do with my magical abilities to conjure up jobs than it does with their attitude. They have started to concede that things just ain't what they used to be, and that it's time to move on.

Go at Your Own Pace, and Follow Your Own Path

There is one piece of general advice that I can give people when they've reached this critical stage: treat your career and life as an ongoing journey, enjoying and learning at every stage.

The suggestion that life is a journey is what I'd like to leave you with as I sign off for now. Difficult as it may be, you've got to hold on to who you are—and what you're truly striving for—even while frenziedly looking for employment. I've found the following quote to be an excellent reminder to myself and my clients:

> As a general rule, you have to accept that no matter where you work, you are not an employee; you are in a business with one employee—yourself. (Intel's CEO, Andrew Grove, on "Managing Your Own Career" in *Fortune* Magazine.)

You Must Make Your Own Choices The crux of this quote is that today you work only for Me Inc. You alone are responsible for ensuring that the type of employment you select, seek out and secure is meaningful to you. Your friends, family, colleagues and career consultants can be a great source of feedback and comfort during this process. But they can't make decisions for you.

Recognize too that you don't just go through this process once. It's something that continues throughout each cycle of your career—and your life.

Helping One Another to Move Forward If this book has enabled you to move even a little bit closer to this, then I've achieved my central purpose. Remember what I told you at the outset. It was not my intention to turn you into some sort of high-tech, lean and mean, job-finding machine. Instead, I've provided you with choices. It's up to you now to use the appropriate tools and techniques in ways that will suit you.

My hope is that you utilize technology, along with the tips I have given you and advice from people you trust, to assist you in reaching your genuine career and life goals. If you do, you'll be more than just wired and hired, you will also be truly inspired!

Over 100 of the Best Work-Search Sites for Canadians

The most powerful way to surf the Web is by knowing exactly where to go. The CanWorkNet, an initiative sponsored by Human Resources Development Canada, has done much of the legwork for you. They've located career sites of interest to Canadians and have put them online for all to see—free of charge.

What follows is a sampling of sites found on CanWorkNet, which itself is a sampling of what's on the Net. Note that sites change periodically. All URLs listed below were accurate and active at the time of writing. Please log into CanWorkNet at **http://www.canworknet.com** for new sites and updates of existing sites.

I. CAREER INFORMATION

Sector Specific

B.C. Labour Market & Career Information Resources Database **http://workinfonet.bc.ca/lmcidb/default.htm** Information on more than 300 career and labour market related resources.

British Columbia Horticultural Coalition **http://hortcan.com/bc/index.html** Find out the latest in this industry's news, training programs and job bank listings.

Certified General Accountants **http://www.cga-canada.org** This site includes information on continuing education, employment referrals and student scholarships. Find out more about the organization, professional development seminars and courses you need.

Fisheries and Marine Institute **http://inseine.ifmt.nf.ca** Offering comprehensive education and training to over 1,200 students, the Institute also works with government and business to focus on research and development, technology transfers and public policy advocacy initiatives.

HiTech Career Centre **http://www.hitechcareer.com** The site provides show guides for career fairs around North America, as well as information about different hi-tech companies and their recruiting needs.

Institute of Chartered Accountants of Ontario **http://www.icao.on.ca** Students and professionals can become members of this organization. Benefits include job listings, seminars and networking possibilities.

Professional Engineers Ontario **http://www.peo.on.ca** PEO provides job postings and free information on engineering careers to Ontario students and schools.

Royal Canadian Mounted Police—Recruiting **http://www.rcmp-grc.gc.ca/html/recruit** Do you have what it takes to be a civilian or peace officer for the RCMP? Find out how to apply to the Cadet Training Program. The site includes information on qualifications, the program itself and salary and benefits for cadets.

SCWIST Work Pathfinder **http://www.harbour.sfu.ca/scwist/pathfinder/index** Guiding women in science and technology on their journey into the new workplace economy.

SkillNet—Career Education and Training Services **http://giant.mindlink.net/skillnet** Database search for course-sourcing, training products and resources in the technology industry.

Special Needs

Adult Vocational Rehabilitation Services via the Society for Manitobans with Disabilities **http://www.cyberspc.mb.ca/~smdlib/adult.html** Counsellors offer a variety of programs and services including employment training. Find out if you qualify.

CNet Learning Network—New Brunswick Student and Learning Assistance **http://cnet.unb.ca/clrn/nb/k** Learn how provincial government advocacy programs may help you, or link to the employment development programs to find job listings and referral services. The site also includes resources for students with disabilities.

DECSA **gopher://freenet.edmonton.ab.ca/11/i/decsa** If traditional job-search methods have not worked for you, this Canadian Employment Centre outreach program, based in Edmonton, Alberta, may be able to help. Offering employment preparation, vocational counselling and placement services.

Edmonton YMCA Enterprise Centre **gopher://freenet.edmonton.ab.ca:70/11/i/enterprs** Aimed at helping aspiring entrepreneurs, immigrants, the mentally disabled and troubled youth, the Y provides self-employment training, employment counselling, on-the-job training, career counselling, lifestyle management training and literacy skills upgrading.

Human Resource Centres of Canada **http://www.hrdc-drhc.gc.ca/hrdc/other/other_e.html** The HRDC in your area may provide additional or more detailed information on this subject.

Indie—Integrated Network of Disability Information and Education **http://indie.ca** Products and services for the Canadian and world-wide disability communities: employment, education, transportation, recreation, advocacy.

Job Accommodation Network **http://janweb.icdi.wvu.edu** Established by the Canadian Council on Rehabilitation and Work, it is an international, toll-free consulting service that provides information about job accommodations and the employability of people with functional limitations.

Links for the Blind **http://www.seidata.com/~marriage/rblind.html** You'll find a wealth of information on topics such as adaptive technologies, advocacy groups, training and assistance, books and magazines, commercial sites and employment resources.

Manitoba Senior Citizens Handbook: Employment Opportunities **http://www.mbnet.mb.ca/crm/other/genmb/msch/msch10.html** Find out about the latest job opportunities or enroll for counselling services geared for employees and job seekers, small business owners and the needs of immigrant women.

New Brunswick Job Corps —For Older Workers **http://www.gov.nb.ca/ael/empprog/english/jcorps.htm** Unemployed older workers, 50 to 65 years of age who participate in this pilot project, are guaranteed work placements of 26 weeks per year for a three year period.

New Careers Corporation **http://www.sasked.gov.sk.ca/progserv/corporat.html** New Careers Corporation (NCC) provides Saskatchewan people receiving social assistance with opportunities for increased independence through preparation for employment.

Ontario March of Dimes **http://www.omod.org** A range of employment programs focus on placement through vocational assessment, work hardening, computer skill training, supportive employment and job placement services.

Self Employment Assistance Program via the Ontario Social Development Council **http://www.sedi.org/sedi/programs.html**

Employment Insurance recipients who want to start their own business may qualify for training and income support through this program.

Spirit of Aboriginal Enterprise **http://www.vli.ca/spirit** Dedicated to exploring and assisting business development and entrepreneurship development among Canada's aboriginal peoples, this site includes resources and information for and about aboriginal enterprises.

Student Career Services

A wide variety of career-related resources are available through college and university homepages. To check out a post-secondary institution in your area go to **http://watserv1.uwaterloo.ca/ ~credmond/univ.html** for institutions that are members of the Association of Universities and Colleges of Canada, as well as a few other degree-granting institutions. For technical and vocational schools and community colleges, sorted by province, try **http://www.sp.utoledo.edu/canctcol.html#ontario**.

CACEE WorkWeb **http://www.cacee.com/workweb** Are you a student or recent graduate? Are you an employer looking for qualified employees? The Canadian Association of Career Educators and Employers is a charitable, non-profit partnership between education and business, established to find students and graduates relevant work.

Canadian Tire Corporation **http://www.cyberplex.com/CyberPlex/CanadianTire/CTHome.html** Find out more about the company, their campus recruitment schedule and career opportunities. You can also upload your résumé.

National Graduate Register **http://schoolnet2.carleton.ca/NGR** If you're a recent Canadian university graduate looking for work, this site offers free online services to help your career take off! It's a national database containing the profiles of recent post-secondary graduates which can be matched with employers instantly.

NB First Start for Post-secondary Graduates—New Brunswick **http://www.gov.nb.ca/ael/empprog/english/firsts** If you are a recent graduate or if you are an employer in need of hiring a fulltime employee, this training and wage reimbursement program may help.

Northern Training Opportunities —Ontario**http://govonca3.gov.on.ca/MBS/english/programs/NDM0481.html** Employers may be eligible for wage subsidies when they hire recent graduates and / or students.

Saskatchewan Partnerships Program for Students **http://www.sasked.**

gov.sk.ca/progserv/partners Businesses, farms, local governments and non-profit groups may be eligible for a grant subsidy when they can provide fulltime summer jobs for post-secondary students. Job seekers can get information here.

Summer Student Employment Program **http://www.psc-cfp.gc.ca/recruit/fssep1e** If you are a full-time high school, CEGEP, college, technical institute or university student, you can apply for summer jobs with the federal government.

Vancouver CommunityNet **http://www.vcn.bc.ca/community/employment** A Vancouver doorway to local information provided by government and non-profit groups including organizations which deal with employment related information.

II. WORK OPPORTUNITIES ONLINE

Canadian Work Opportunities

Aboriginal Youth Network—Job Opportunities **http://ayn-0.ayn.ca/PAGES/jobopps** This area of the Aboriginal Youth Network site links directly to job opportunities.

Atlantic Canada Careers **http://business.atcon.com/vhomes/careers/index** A career networking service for use by both job seekers and employers in the Maritimes.

CACEE WorkWeb **http://www.cacee.com/workweb** Are you a student or recent graduate? Are you an employer looking for qualified employees? The Canadian Association of Career Educators and Employers is a charitable, non-profit partnership between education and business established to find students and graduates relevant work.

Canada Employment Weekly **http://www.mediacorp2.com** A privately owned Canadian online magazine that brings you hundreds of new jobs every week from every province and territory. Check out the pages of job listings and career advice.

Career Internetworking **http://www.careerkey.com** Servicing and supporting Canadian business and industry, this privately managed site offers free listings for job seekers and job postings from across Canada.

CareerMosaic Canada **http://canada.careermosaic.com** Career Mosaic Canada will take you to some of the best jobs with some of the world's hottest employers.

Careers Midlyn **http://www.careersmidlyn.com** Looking for employment in Vancouver and British Columbia? Check out this site for career opportunities with employers in the province.

Chebucto Community Net Employment Page **http://www.cfn.cs.dal.ca/HumanResources/jobs** Job seekers can list their skills and local employers can list open positions.

Classified Job Ads in the SUN newspapers **http://canoe1.canoe.ca/Classified/JOBsearch** Search by city and job sector.

Croden, Waters Consultants **http://www.visions.com/clients/** If you are searching for jobs in accounting, administration or telecommunications, this links you with employers with temporary and permanent positions.

Electronic Labour Exchange —HRDC **http://ele.ingenia.com** This Canadian job matching service matches jobs to people and people to jobs right on the Internet. Free to employers and job seekers in Canada.

Employment Opportunities via the Newfoundland Provincial Information and Libraries Board **http://www.stemnet.nf.ca/Community/PublicLibrary/#jobs** Now job seekers can search for a job through the library! Check out the links to government job postings, student jobs through Memorial University and the great links to national and international job matching sites.

Engineering Central **http://www.interchange.ubc.ca/wtdenham** Your centre point for engineering information on the Internet! This Web site features employment resources for both employers and engineers.

Globe and Mail Career Services **http://www.theglobeandmail.com** Check Canada's national newspaper via the Web for recent career listings. A high-profile site for Canadian employers.

Heritage Employment Search **http://www.management.mcgill.ca/homepages/BRENT.D/veq-2e.** Employers in the Quebec City region who need bilingual employees are invited to access this non-profit service for free.

Inter-Job Services Inc. **http://www.interjob.com** Inter-Job offers a service designed to introduce employers looking to fill managerial and professional positions to qualified job candidates. As well, job seekers have an opportunity to get exposure to employers world-wide.

Jobs Canada **http://www.jcitech.com/jobmatch** Online job matching services for job seekers and employers.

Jobs via BC WorkInfoNet **http://workinfonet.bc.ca** Free to job seekers! This site is based in the province, but it also offers links to national and international job matching services.

JobSAT **http://www.jobsat.com** Free to job seekers! Offering hundreds of new job postings every day across Canada and in select U.S. markets, this is an employment database you'll want to check out.

Kelly Services **http://www.kellyservices.com** Provides temporary employees in the areas of office services, light industrial, marketing, technical, accounting and other professional services.

La Presse Careers Database **http://www.monster.com/lapresse/lapresse3** Explore this exclusive database of professional opportunities in Quebec. Search through job listings by discipline, company, or job title, or post your résumé for prospective employers to view.

Listing by field of World-Wide Job Seekers **http://www.cban.com/resume** Access this Canadian résumé database by profession.

Manpower Temporary Services **http://www.vaxxine.com/infomall/manpower/mtsjobs.htm** Offering temporary employment services throughout Canada and internationally.

Net-Work **http://www.onsetmag.com/jobmarket** An online job matching service linking jobs seekers and employers. Users must register to gain access.

Ottawa Citizen Job Ads **http://ottawa.astranet.com** Access information about full-time, part-time, temporary or domestic jobs or check the training and employment services.

Résumé Hut—PenLan Career Group **http://www.islandnet.com/~penlan** Search for a job match by region, across Canada and internationally. The site also offers career couselling and related services.

Riley Guide—Jobs in Canada **http://www.jobtrak.com/jobguide/canada** Find local resources, freenets, local BBS, and government links.

Saskatchewan Jobs via the Star Phoenix **http://www.wbm.ca/users/sphoenix** Job seekers can scan the latest job listings by profession.

The Employment News **http://www.employmentnews.com** This Toronto-based service offers you the chance to search for jobs, training listings or volunteer opportunities for free. Use their job search resources to prepare your résumé or your job interview techniques.

The Haas Group **http://www.bplus.com/~chaas** This placement agency specializes in career placement for permanent, unilingual English jobs. Check out available jobs.

The People Bank **http://www.herzing.edu/peoplebank/home** Owned and managed by the Herzing Group, this job matching service posts temporary and permanent job openings for administrative/support and technical/professional positions.

Today's Newspaper Job Ad **http://www.icom.ca/~willow/jobform** Links to online classified job ads across Canada.

Toronto Star Career Ads **http://www.thestar.com/thestar/classified/plmonster** Use the search engine to find available job listings.

WebJobs NS Home Page **http://magi.ns.ca** For employers and job seekers in Nova Scotia. Employers are given free access to client résumés in the Résumé Bank, and may also post their jobs. Job seekers will find links to various job search areas, job listings, and a place to highlight their skills in the Résumé Bank. There is a fee for certain services.

Worknet **http://www.entrenet.com/easi/worknet** Worknet is free to job seekers. It is a current list of Canadian Jobs posted on the Web, in a one-stop shopping format.

International Work Opportunities

Career Connections **http://www.career.com/ heart** Offering job listings across the U.S. and some international markets, including Canada. Chosen as one of the top 25 Web site by recruiters, this site offers free listings for job seekers who wish to post résumés.

Career Net **http://www.best.com/~cnet** Career Net provides matchmaking services for job seekers and employers/search firms throughout the U.S., UK, Germany, Japan, and New Zealand including both mailing campaigns and online exposure of jobseeker credentials.

CareerExchange **http://www.careerexchange.com** CareerExchange is an international career search database. Free for job applicants.

CareerMosaic **http://www.careermosaic.com** This site offers U.S. based employment services with international (and Canadian) links. Job seekers can post their résumés, check current job listings and read employer profiles.

CareerNet **http://www.careers.org** CareerNet provides matching services for job seekers and employers or search firms throughout the U.S. and Canada, including both mailing campaigns and online exposure.

CareerWEB **http://www.cweb.com** Matches U.S. employers with job seekers. There is some useful online information to help you improve your résumé, earn a promotion or find a better job.

Get A Job —International Job Matching Service **http://www.getajob.com** Searchable database of job openings, with links to other employment resources.

IntelliMatch **http://www.intellimatch.com** Free to job seekers! Build your résumé and find out background information on potential employers.

International Programmers Guild **http://www.ipgnet.com** IPG offers an international job matching service for programmers, as well as training programs and certification.

International University Job Listings via NISS **http://www.niss.ac.uk/noticeboard/index** The National Information Services and Systems is a UK based information source, with international links, for the academic community. It includes job vacancies, research opportunities, events (training and conferences), press releases, and classified ads.

JobCenter Employment Services **http://www.jobcenter.com** This American based service offers job matching services for graduates, the public and recruiting professionals. Check their corporate profiles, scholarship fund information and articles or request their information package.

JobWeb **http://www.jobweb.com** A large, U.S. based resource that posts jobs, offers job search and industry information, career planning information, and information for human resource professionals.

Mainstream Worklife Center **http://www.worklife.com** Join a community of your peers in the workplace by networking, sharing job leads, support and assistance. Free to job seekers, this site offers job listings, a résumé database, articles and employment services. There are also links for entrepreneurs, career professionals and sponsors.

National Home Workers Association **http://www.homeworkers.com/homeworkers** Interested in working from home? This North American broker has openings for teleworkers. Members can receive updated job postings daily, via e-mail.

Online Career Center **http://www.occ.com/occ** Job seekers—submit your résumé and access the searchable database. Employers—submit advertisements for jobs. Search for information on cultural diversity programs, career fairs and events. U.S. based site.

The Monster Board **http://www2.monster.com:80/home** Free access to 55,000 international job listings. This site also includes information for recruiters, human resource professionals and hiring managers.

TKO Personnel **http://www.tkointl.com/csites** Looking for work in Japan, the U.S. or Asia Pacific? This is a valuable recruitment and job listing resource.

Virtual Press—International Job Opportunities **http://tvp.com/jintl** Job listings for North America, Europe, Asia, Australia, and Africa.

Self-employment and Small Business Sites

Aboriginal Business Canada **http://www.vli.ca/abc** Business services and support to Indians, Inuit and Metis including individuals, partnerships and associations.

Assistance for Entreprenuers via Canadian Technology Network- Manitoba **http://mb.ctn.nrc.ca/english** If you run a small or medium-sized business in Canada, the CTN can give you access to a wide range of technical and business assistance through a cross-country network of advisors.

Atlantic Canada Opportunities Agency (ACOA) Homepage **http://www.acoa.ca** Established to improve the economy of Atlantic Canada, this federal government agency works to develop job opportunities and businesses. Find out about programs created to help new and established businesses or read some success stories.

BizWomen **http://www.bizwomen.com** Online interactive community for successful women in business to communicate, network, exchange ideas, and provide support for each other. Free membership.

Business and Economics Info via Schoolnet **http://www.schoolnet.ca/biz** Young, enterprising students can learn about career choices. This site also includes a link to the Junior Achievement of Canada.

Business and Industry Information via the Enterprise Network **http://www.entnet.nf.ca/eni/bus/home** Provides information on business start-up as well as information on specific sectors of the economy in Newfoundland and Labrador.

Canada—Ontario Business Call Centre (COBCC) **http://info.ic.gc.ca/CBSC/english/ontario/startup** Business Start-up FaxBack Catalogue and free FaxBack service for business information, and links to other sources of business start-up information for Ontario and Canada.

DISCscribe Home Business Resource Centre **http://www.discribe.ca/yourhbiz/yourhbiz** A privately run Canadian site that offers personal replies to questions, helpful hints, software reviews, online discussions and a business planning group to entrepreneurs.

Entrepreneur—New Brunswick Assistance Program **http://www.gov.nb.ca/ael/empprog/english** Get help getting started or maintaining your business. Find out if you qualify for provincial government programs and services.

Entrepreneurship Centre **http://www.entrepreneurship.com** Aiming to help small businesses succeed, this Ottawa-based service offers workshops, seminars, resources and mentorship programs to entrepreneurs.

Heartland Community Futures Development Corp. **http://www.portage.net/heartland/index** Supporting economic development in Manitoba's heartland, this organization offers business counselling, training, resource referral and financial assistance services to heartland communities, businesses, organizations and individuals.

Investment Opportunities in Newfoundland **http://www.compusult.nf.ca/ditt/invest** For labour market information, investment, or to find the career you want to pursue, check this Department of Industry, Trade and Technology site. It includes background information on a variety of industries, including marine, manufacturing, information, environmental, engineering and health services.

Literature and Publications for Manitoba **http://www.cpnet.net/cp/lit** Entreprenuers via Central Plains, Inc. These publications may help you start your own business. Publications include the entrepreneur's handbook series, do-it-yourself business planning package and information on small business management.

Manitoba Agri-Ventures Initiatives Program **http://www.cpnet.net/cp/programs/man.agriven** If you have an idea or business venture that could add value to the agriculture and food industries, this organization may support or fund the venture. Find out if you qualify for help in developing a business plan, evaluation of your business concept or marketing advice.

Mauldin Inc. Business Planning Primer **http://WWW.CAM.ORG/~jmauld/English** Use this free primer to develop your own business plan or find out more about the research, planning and communications services offered by this company. Great for entrepreneurs.

Minding Your Own Business **http://www.globalx.net/ocd/minding** Are you the kind of person who can run their own business? This publication could help you determine a career as an entrepreneur.

New Brunswick Business and Economy Network **http://cnet.unb.ca/cbus/nb** Find out about the latest training and resources information for business including links to arts and culture, construction, food and beverage, government, labour, manufacturing organizations and associations, products, services, technology, transportation, and regional information.

Newfoundland Business and Economy Network **http://cnet.unb.ca/cbus/nf** Find out the latest training and development information on business issues and markets through this site. It links business, government and learning resources to create a local picture.

B.C. Online Small Business Workshop **http://www.sb.gov.bc.ca/smallbus/workshop/workshop** Hosted by the provincial government this site is full of practical advice, exploring tips on small business opportunities, patents, marketing basics, sales forecasting, business plan development, taxes and how to become an employer.

Self Employment Assistance Program via the Ontario Social Development Council **http://www.sedi.org/sedi/programs** Employment Insurance recipients who want to start their own business may qualify for training and income support through this program.

Self Employment via the Women's Enterprise Bureau **http://nf.ctn.nrc.ca/web** Want to start your own home based or micro business but don't know where to start? Access the training and counselling services, get help with a business plan or network with other entrepreneurs.

Starting a Business via Communication-Quebec **http://www.comm-qc.gouv.qc.ca/start** A helpful guide for entrepreneurs that outlines procedures and requirements as well as technical, financial, employment development and training assistance in the province.

Strategis —Industry Canada Online **http://strategis.ic.gc.ca/engdoc/main** An information-packed site with all you'll need to know about markets, trade and investment, industrial perspectives, micro-economic research and analysis, managing your business, marketplace services.

INDEX

CanWorkNet: Canada's New Coast to Coast Internet Partnership to Connect Canadians to Their Futures

CanWorkNet is about helping Canadians take charge of their work futures through easy access to a database of information and services. It is a directory on the World Wide Web for people who have lost their jobs, or worry that they might. It's for those seeking employment and entrepreneurial advice ... for students and trainees planning their futures ... for employers looking for workers ... for people moving from home to work, or work to retirement ... for researchers, counsellors, teachers, community agency staff and human resource practitioners seeking to improve the services they provide.

http://www.canworknet.ca

CanWorkNet: Le nouveau partenariat national que lie les Canadiens à leur avenir grâce à l'Internet

L'objet de CanWorkNet est d'aider les Canadiens à prendre en main leur avenir sur le marché du travail en leur permettant d'accéder facilement à une base de données sur des source d'information et des services. Il s'agit d'un répertoire sur le World Wide Web à l'intention des personnes qui ont perdu leur emploi ou qui craignent de le perdre. CanWorkNet s'adresse à ceux et celles qui veulent obtenir des conseils en matière d'emploi et d'entreprenariat ... aux stagiaires et aux étudiants qui désirent planifier leur avenir ... aux employeurs à la recherche de travailleurs ... aux personnes qui font la transition du foyer au monde du travail ou qui se préparent à prendre leur retraite .. Aux chercheurs, conseillers, enseignants et employés d'organismes communautaires de même qu'aux spécialistes des ressources humaines qui cherchent à parfaire leurs services.

SYMPATICO SERVICE AGREEMENT

Read Carefully. This Agreement Imposes Obligations Upon You.

Sympatico provides access to the Internet (the "Service"). This Agreement between Your Service Provider ("Your Service Provider") and you sets out duties and responsibilities associated with providing you with the Service through a designated account (the "Account"). By accessing the Service, you agree to the terms and conditions below. If you do not wish to be bound by these terms and conditions, you may not access or use the Service.

1. **Service Provider.** For the purposes of this Agreement, Your Service Provider is determined by the location of the telephone line for which you are seeking Internet access (your "designated billing address"). When you register for the Service, Your Service Provider will be identified to you on the screen of your computer. To confirm the identity of Your Service Provider before registering, please call 1-800-773-2121.

   Only Your Service Provider is responsible for providing the Service to you within its operating territory.

2. **Use Subject to Service Provider's Policies.** You are solely responsible for all access to the Service through your Account. You agree to comply with Your Service Provider's policies respecting the Service as provided from time to time, including those attached to this Agreement or to which you are directed when using the Service. You agree to hold Your Service Provider and its affiliates harmless from all liabilities and expenses related to any violation of this Agreement by you or any user of your Account, or in connection with your or their use of the Service.

   While using the Service, you may not post, transmit or otherwise distribute information constituting or encouraging conduct that would constitute a criminal offense or give rise to civil liability, or otherwise use the Service in a manner which is contrary to law or to Your Service Provider's policies or would serve to restrict or inhibit any other user from using or enjoying the Service or the Internet.

3. **Fees and Charges.** You agree to pay such fees and charges, including applicable taxes, incurred in connection with the provision of and/or use of the Service through your Account in accordance with the rates and terms established by Your Service Provider for the Service and as such rates and terms may be amended by Your Service Provider upon reasonable notice to you or which you are directed to review when using the Service.

4. **User Information.** Your messages may be the subject of unauthorized third party interception and review. An individual with Internet access can cause damage, incur expenses and enter into contractual obligations while on the Internet. All such matters are your responsibility.

   Your Service Provider has no obligation to monitor the Service. However, you agree that your Service Provider reserves the right to monitor the Service electronically from time to time and to disclose any information necessary to satisfy any laws, regulations or other governmental request, to operate the Service or to protect itself or others.

5. **No Liability for Content.** Be aware that some content, products or services ("Content") available with or through the Service may be offensive to you or may not comply with applicable laws. You understand that neither Your Service Provider nor any of its affiliates attempt to censor or monitor any such Content. You assume total responsibility and risk for access to or use of such Content and for use of the Internet. Your Service Provider and its affiliates assume no liability whatsoever for any claims or losses arising out of or otherwise relating to access to or use of such Content.

6. **Software and Documentation Supplied.** Any software or documentation supplied by Your Service Provider or its agents to you to access the Internet shall remain the property of Your Service Provider or its agents, as applicable. You shall take appropriate steps to protect same against loss or damage. The use by you of any such software and documentation shall be subject to such terms set out in the License Agreement included with the software and documentation.

7. **Your Equipment.** It is your responsibility to ensure that your computer system meets the current minimum requirements stated by Your Service Provider as being necessary to use the Service. From time to time, the computer equipment required to access and use the Service may change. Accordingly, your computer equipment may cease to be adequate to access the Service. In such event, your sole remedy will be to terminate this Agreement.

8. **You Can Best Control the Risk and Therefore Are Responsible.** The fees charged by Your Service Provider reflect the allocation of risk herein and the limited recourse to Your Service Provider provided for in this Agreement. Your Service Provider will not assume any responsibility for your acts or omissions or of any individual who uses your Account. As between Your Service Provider and you, you are better able to put in place physical and procedural impediments to the inappropriate use of and to supervise your Account. Account and password protection shall be your responsibility.

9. **Limited Warranty.** The Service and any deliverables provided by Your Service Provider and/or its agents are provided "as is" and "as available" without warranties or conditions of any kind. Neither Your Service Provider nor its affiliates warrant the uninterrupted use or operation of the Service or any deliverable provided under this Agreement. The entire risk as to the quality and performance of the Service is with you. Further, neither Your Service Provider nor its affiliates warrant that any data or files sent by or to you will be transmitted in uncorrupted form or within a reasonable period of time, that such data or files will not be intercepted or that other users will not gain access to any of your computer equipment nor that any Content, or other material accessible on the Service is free of viruses or other harmful components.

   THERE ARE NO EXPRESS OR IMPLIED REPRESENTATIONS, WARRANTIES OR CONDITIONS WHATSOEVER (INCLUDING WARRANTIES OF TITLE OR NON-INFRINGEMENT, OR IMPLIED WARRANTIES OF MERCHANTABILITY OR FITNESS FOR A PARTICULAR PURPOSE) WITH REGARD TO THE SERVICE OR ANY MERCHANDISE, INFORMATION OR SERVICE PROVIDED ON THE INTERNET AND ALL REPRESENTATIONS, WARRANTIES, OR CONDITIONS OF ANY KIND, EXPRESS OR IMPLIED ARE, TO THE EXTENT PERMITTED BY APPLICABLE LAW, HEREBY EXCLUDED.

10. **Limitation of Liability.**

   (a) In the event of any breach by Your Service Provider, its affiliates or its agents including any breach of a fundamental term or any negligence, your exclusive remedy shall be to receive from Your Service Provider payment for actual and direct damages to a maximum amount equal to the fees paid hereunder by you to Your Service Provider in the last three months.

   (b) Other than as set out in paragraph (a) above, under no circumstances shall Your Service Provider, its affiliates or its agents be liable to you or any third party for:

      (i) any direct, indirect, special, or consequential damages, including loss of profits and loss of business opportunities, that result in any way from this Agreement including your use of the Service or to access the Internet or any part thereof, or your reliance on or use of information, services or merchandise provided on or through the Service, or that result from mistakes, omissions, interruptions, deletion or corruption of files, errors, defects, delays in preparations, or transmission, or failure of performance.

      (ii) any losses or expenses (including legal fees) arising out of or in connection with any allegation, claim, suit or other proceeding based upon a contention that the use of the Service by you or a third party through your Account infringes the intellectual property rights or contractual rights of any third party.

11. **Termination.** This Agreement may be terminated by you upon notice to Your Service Provider. Your Service Provider may suspend or restrict the Service or terminate this Agreement and the Service at any time if:

   (i) the operations or efficiency of the Service is impaired by the use of the Account; or

   (ii) any amount is past due from you to Your Service Provider; or

   (iii) there has been or is any breach of any term or condition of this Agreement.

Your Service Provider shall have no responsibility to notify any third party providers of services, merchandise or information of such termination or suspension. Any termination of this Agreement shall not relieve you from any amounts owing or other liability accruing hereunder prior to the time that such termination becomes effective.

12. **Amendment.** Your Service Provider may modify this Agreement from time to time by reasonable notice to you, and your continued use of the Service following notice of such modification shall be deemed to be your acceptance of such modification. If you do not agree to any modification of this Agreement, you must immediately stop using the Service.

13. **Information.** You hereby acknowledge that Your Service Provider and its affiliates may retain and use any information, comments or ideas conveyed by you relating to the Service (including any products and services made available on the Service). This information may be used to provide you with better service. Your Service Provider will open and maintain a customer file which will be kept at its office as indicated to you at the time of registration for the Service. You may access your customer file free of charge upon 24 hours' prior written request to the Sympatico Member Services Office. You can submit your request in writing by selecting Contact Us on the Sympatico home page (www.sympatico.ca on the Internet). If any information contained in your customer file is inaccurate, you may make a written request for rectification, specifying the information to be rectified and explaining the inaccuracy to our Member Services Office.

14. **Miscellaneous.** This Agreement, including any and all documents and the Service Provider's policies referenced herein constitute the entire agreement between Your Service Provider and you pertaining to the subject matter hereof. Your Service Provider's failure to insist upon or enforce strict performance of any provision of this Agreement shall not be construed as a waiver of any provision or right. If any of the provisions contained in this Agreement be determined to be void, invalid or otherwise unenforceable by a court of competent jurisdiction, such determination shall not affect the remaining provisions contained herein. Where any provision of this Agreement conflicts with an applicable tariff, the tariff shall supercede this Agreement only in respect of the conflicting provision. This Agreement shall be governed by and construed in accordance with the laws of the province or territory in which your designated billing address is located and the federal laws of Canada applicable therein. Your Service Provider may assign its rights and obligations under this Agreement to any affiliated entity without your prior written consent. The parties have required that this Agreement and all documents relating thereto be drawn up in English. Les parties ont demandé que cette convention ainsi que tous les documents qui s'y rattachent soient rédigés en anglais.

LICENSE AGREEMENT

THIS IS A LEGAL AGREEMENT BETWEEN YOU AND YOUR SERVICE PROVIDER ("YOUR SERVICE PROVIDER"). BY OPENING THE PACKAGE, YOU ARE CONSENTING TO BE BOUND BY AND ARE BECOMING A PARTY TO THIS AGREEMENT. IF YOU DO NOT AGREE TO ALL OF THE TERMS OF THIS AGREEMENT, DO NOT OPEN THE PACKAGE.

Service Provider. For the purposes of this Agreement, Your Service Provider is determined by the location of the telephone line for which you are seeking Internet access (your "designated billing address"). When you register for the Service, Your Service Provider will be identified to you on the screen of your computer. To confirm the identity of Your Service Provider before registering, please call 1-800-773-2121.

Only Your Service Provider is responsible for providing the Service to you within its operating territory.

GRANT. Your Service Provider hereby grants to you a non-exclusive license (the "License") to use the accompanying Netscape Navigator software product and documentation (collectively the "Software") on the following terms:

You may:

- use the Software on any single computer for the purpose of using the Sympatico' Service provided to you by Your Service Provider (the "Service");

- use the Software on additional computers so long as the first and subsequent computers are not used simultaneously and each is used solely for the purposes of using the Service; or
- copy the Software solely for archival or back-up purposes, provided any copy must contain all of the original Software's proprietary notices.

You may not:
- permit other individuals to use the Software except under the terms listed above;
- modify, translate, reverse engineer, decompile, disassemble, or create derivative works based on the Software;
- copy the Software or Documentation (except for back-up purposes);
- rent, lease, transfer or otherwise transfer rights to the Software; or
- remove any proprietary notices or labels on the Software.

SOFTWARE. This license does not grant you any right to any enhancement or update.

TITLE. Title, ownership rights, and intellectual property rights in and to the Software shall remain in Your Service Provider and/or its suppliers. The Software is protected by copyright law and international copyright treaties. Title, ownership rights, and intellectual property rights in and to the content accessed through the Software are the property of the applicable content owner and may be protected by applicable copyright or other law. This License gives you no rights to such content.

LIMITED WARRANTY. Your Service Provider warrants that for a period of ninety (90) days from the date of acquisition, the Software, if operated as directed, will substantially achieve the functionality described in the documentation accompanying same. Your Service Provider does not warrant, however, that your use of the Software will be uninterrupted or that the operation of the Software will be uninterrupted or that the operation of the Software will be error-free or secure. In addition, the security mechanism implemented by the Software has inherent limitations, and you must determine that the Software sufficiently meets your requirements.

Your Service Provider also warrants that the media containing the Software is free from defects in material and workmanship and will so remain for ninety (90) days from the date you acquired the Software. Your Service Provider's sole liability for any breach of this warranty shall be, in Your Service Provider's sole discretion: (i) to replace your defective media; or (ii) to advise you how to achieve substantially the same functionality with the Software as described in the documentation through a procedure different from that set forth in the documentation; or (iii) if the above remedies are impracticable, to refund the license fee you paid for the Software. Repaired, corrected, or replaced Software shall be covered by this limited warranty for the period remaining under the warranty that covered the original Software, or if longer, for thirty (30) days after the date: (a) of shipment to you of the repaired, corrected or replaced Software, or (b) Your Service Provider advised you how to operate the Software so as to achieve the functionality described in the documentation. Only if you inform Your Service Provider of your problem with the Software during the applicable warranty period and provide evidence of the date you acquired the Software will Your Service Provider be obligated to honour this warranty. Your Service Provider will use reasonable commercial efforts to repair, replace, advise or refund pursuant to the foregoing warranty within 30 days of being so notified.

THIS IS A LIMITED WARRANTY AND IT IS THE ONLY WARRANTY MADE BY YOUR SERVICE PROVIDER. YOUR SERVICE PROVIDER MAKES NO OTHER EXPRESS WARRANTY AND NO WARRANTY OF NONINFRINGEMENT OF THIRD PARTIES' RIGHTS (SOME PROVINCES AND TERRITORIES DO NOT ALLOW EXCLUSIONS OR LIMITATIONS OF THIS NATURE, SO THIS EXCLUSION AND LIMITATION MAY NOT APPLY TO YOU IN WHOLE OR IN PART). THE DURATION OF IMPLIED WARRANTIES, INCLUDING WITHOUT LIMITATION, WARRANTIES OF MERCHANTABILITY AND OF FITNESS FOR A PARTICULAR PURPOSE, IS LIMITED TO THE ABOVE LIMITED WARRANTY PERIOD; SOME PROVINCES AND/OR TERRITORIES DO NOT ALLOW LIMITATIONS ON HOW LONG AN IMPLIED WARRANTY LASTS, SO LIMITATIONS MAY NOT APPLY TO YOU. NONE OF YOUR SERVICE PROVIDER'S DEALERS, AGENTS, OR EMPLOYEES ARE AUTHORIZED TO MAKE ANY MODIFICATIONS, EXTENSIONS, OR ADDITIONS TO THIS WARRANTY. If any modifications are made to the Software by you during the warranty period; if the media is subjected to accident, abuse, or improper use; or if you violate the terms of this Agreement then this warranty shall immediately be terminated. This warranty shall not apply if the Software is used on or in conjunction with hardware or software other than the unmodified version of hardware and software with which the Software was designed to be used as described in the Documentation.

THIS WARRANTY GIVES YOU SPECIFIC LEGAL RIGHTS, AND YOU MAY HAVE OTHER LEGAL RIGHTS THAT VARY BY PROVINCE, TERRITORY OR BY JURISDICTION.

LIMITATION OF LIABILITY. UNDER NO CIRCUMSTANCES AND UNDER NO LEGAL THEORY, TORT, CONTRACT, OR OTHERWISE, SHALL YOUR SERVICE PROVIDER OR ITS RESELLERS BE LIABLE TO YOU OR ANY OTHER PERSON FOR ANY INDIRECT, SPECIAL, INCIDENTAL, OR CONSEQUENTIAL DAMAGES OF ANY CHARACTER INCLUDING, WITHOUT LIMITATION, DAMAGES FOR LOSS OF GOODWILL, WORK STOPPAGE, COMPUTER FAILURE OR MALFUNCTION, OR ANY AND ALL OTHER COMMERCIAL DAMAGES OR LOSSES, OR FOR ANY DAMAGES IN EXCESS OF YOUR SERVICE PROVIDER LIST PRICE FOR A LICENSE TO THE SOFTWARE AND DOCUMENTATION, OR FOR ANY CLAIM BY ANY OTHER PARTY. THIS LIMITATION OF LIABILITY SHALL NOT APPLY TO LIABILITY FOR DEATH OR PERSONAL INJURY TO THE EXTENT APPLICABLE LAW PROHIBITS SUCH LIMITATION. FURTHERMORE, SOME PROVINCES AND TERRITORIES DO NOT ALLOW THE EXCLUSION OR LIMITATION OF INCIDENTAL OR CONSEQUENTIAL DAMAGES, SO THIS LIMITATION AND EXCLUSION MAY NOT APPLY TO YOU.

TERMINATION. This license will terminate automatically if you fail to comply with the terms and conditions described above. On termination, you must destroy all copies of the Software.

AUDIT. Your Service Provider reserves the right to have audits conducted to verify your compliance with this license.

EXPORT. In addition, if the licensed Software is identified as a not-for-export product (for example, on the box, media or in the installation process), then the following applies: EXCEPT FOR EXPORT TO CANADA FOR USE BY CANADIAN CITIZENS, THE SOFTWARE AND ANY UNDERLYING TECHNOLOGY MAY NOT BE EXPORTED OUTSIDE CANADA OR TO ANY FOREIGN ENTITY OR "FOREIGN PERSON" AS DEFINED BY U.S. GOVERNMENT REGULATIONS, INCLUDING WITHOUT LIMITATION, ANYONE WHO IS NOT A CITIZEN OR NATIONAL OR LAWFUL PERMANENT RESIDENT OF THE UNITED STATES OR CANADA.

EXPORT CONTROLS. None of the Software or underlying information or technology may be downloaded or otherwise exported or reexported (i) into (or to a national or resident of) Cuba, Iraq, Libya, North Korea, Yugoslavia, Iran, Syria or any other country to which the U.S. has embargoed goods; or (ii) to anyone on the U.S. Treasury Department's list of Specially Designated Nationals or the U.S. Commerce Department's Table of Denial Orders. By downloading or using the Software, you are agreeing to the foregoing and you are representing and warranting that you are not located in, under the control of, or a national or resident of any such country or on any such list.

MISCELLANEOUS. This Agreement represents the complete agreement concerning this License between the parties and supersedes all prior agreements and representations between them. You acknowledge that you have read this license, understand it and agree to be bound by its terms and conditions. It may be amended only by a written amendment executed by both parties. THE ACCEPTANCE OF ANY PURCHASE ORDER PLACED BY YOU IS EXPRESSLY MADE CONDITIONAL ON YOUR ASSENT TO THE TERMS SET FORTH HEREIN, AND NOT THOSE CONTAINED IN YOUR PURCHASE ORDER. If any provision of this Agreement is held to be unenforceable for any reason, such provision shall be reformed only to the extent necessary to make it enforceable. Your Service Provider may assign its rights and obligations under this Agreement to any affiliated entity without your prior written consent. The parties have required that this Agreement and all documents relating thereto be drawn up in English. Les parties ont demandé que cette convention ainsi que tous les documents qui s'y rattachent soient rédigés en anglais. This Agreement shall be governed by and construed under the laws of the province or territory in which your designated billing address is located and the federal laws of Canada applicable therein.

Minimum Requirements

- a 386 personal computer (or faster) and a mouse
- a 14.4 kbps modem (28.8 kbps recommended) and a phone line
- a double speed CD-ROM drive or higher
- 8 megabytes of memory (RAM)
- 6 megabytes free hard disk space (12 megabytes recommended)
- Microsoft Windows 3.1, 3.11, or Windows for Workgroups 3.11, or Windows 95.

Note: Billing for the Sympatico™ service will begin after your first month of use or after 10 hours of Internet access, whichever comes first. When registering, choose from two convenient packages: $9.95 per month for 5 hours or, $24.95 per month for 60 hours. Any additional hours will cost $1.50 per hour. Prices are subject to change. Offer only valid in Canada. Some restrictions may apply*.

*The Sympatico™ service may not be available in all parts of Canada. Please call 1-800-773-2121 to find out if local service is available in your region.